American Political Parties

Decline *or* Resurgence?

Edited by

Jeffrey E. Cohen

Richard Fleisher

Paul Kantor

all of Fordham University

LCCC LIBRARY

CQ PRESS

A Division of Congressional Quarterly Inc.
Washington, D.C.

To Robert Himmelberg,
for his support, encouragement, and leadership

CQ Press
A Division of Congressional Quarterly Inc.
1414 22nd Street, N.W.
Washington, D.C. 20037
(202) 822-1475; (800) 638-1710
www.cqpress.com

Copyright © 2001 by Congressional Quarterly Inc.

Printed and bound in the United States of America

05 04 03 02 01 5 4 3 2 1

All rights reserved. No part of this publication may be reproduced or transmitted in
any form or by any means, electronic or mechanical, including photocopy,
recording, or any information storage and retrieval system, without permission in
writing from the publisher.

♾ The paper used in this publication meets the minimum requirements of the
American National Standard for Information Sciences—Permanence of Paper
for Printed Library Materials, ANSI Z39.48-1992.

Library of Congress Cataloging-in-Publication Data
In process

Contents

10-29-01   54.95

PART THREE
The Parties as Governing Institutions

Conclusion

Tables and Figures

Tables

Figures

Acknowledgments

The seeds of this book were planted in conversations among the three coeditors, whose offices are just down the hall from each other's. In those conversations, we began to evaluate the conventional view that the American parties of the last quarter of the twentieth century were feeble. Our conversations led us to another conclusion, that the state of the parties was more complex and multifaceted than we had initially thought, showing signs of strength alongside signs of weakness.

We understood that it would be no easy task to explain the road the parties have taken over the past twenty-five years or so to reach their current state. To that end, we thought it would be useful to students of parties, and of American politics more generally, if we could gather some of the best research on the current state of the parties, analyses of patterns of change over the past quarter century, and projections concerning the future of the parties. To do so, we required the support of many individuals and institutions, and we were fortunate in securing that support.

In preparation of this manuscript, we held a conference at the Rose Hill Campus of Fordham University entitled "American Politics at the Millennium: Political Parties and the Future of American Democracy." We brought together a number of the leading scholars on the American parties to participate, present their ideas, and interact with each other and the larger community of those interested in American politics and its parties. That conference was part of a continuing series run by the graduate program of the Department of Political Science at Fordham, the Fordham University Forum on American Politics. The forum has been in operation since 1997, bringing scholars and commentators on American politics to campus to discuss important topics in their field. The forum, like our conference, is generously supported by the Graduate School of Arts and Sciences of Fordham University as well as by the graduate program of the Department of Political Science.

Besides those who were asked to present papers, a large number of interested people and scholars from around the region attended our parties conference. We want to thank all those who attended and, by their attendance and participation, added to the conversation and provided stimulation for all involved. Special thanks go to Robert Erikson and Robert Shapiro, both of Columbia University, who graciously served as session chairs.

Our conference was the starting point for production of this book. A number of the chapters began as papers presented at that conference, although they have been substantially revised. These chapters include the contributions of James E. Campbell, Matthew Crenson and Benjamin Ginsberg, William Crotty, Roger H. Davidson, David G. Lawrence, Theodore J. Lowi, L. Sandy Maisel, and Gerald M. Pomper. Not every paper presented, however, found its way into this volume, and we have added a number of other papers not presented at the conference (those by Sarah A. Binder, Richard Fleisher and Jon R. Bond, and Victoria A. Farrar-Myers and Diana Dwyre).

Many other debts were accumulated in preparing this manuscript. The staff at CQ Press was especially important in shaping the final look of this book and seeing it through to completion. Brenda Carter, director of college publishing at CQ Press, offered many useful suggestions about the book that improved it greatly; Gwenda Larsen, associate editor at CQ Press, ably steered us through the publication and production processes; and Amy Marks diligently copyedited the manuscript, a daunting task considering the number of authors and their varying writing styles.

Special thanks go to Patrick Bernardo, Erin Larocco, Alex Ott, and Flagg Taylor, all graduate students at Fordham University, who in one capacity or another ensured that our parties conference ran smoothly and that our manuscript got to CQ Press in one piece. Andria Bordenga, Maureen Hanratty, and Dawn Silvestri provided us with outstanding secretarial and administrative support. Without the help of all of these people, this project would not have been completed.

We also incurred special debts to Deans Michael Gillan, Robert Grimes, S.J., and Jeffrey Von Arx, S.J., of Fordham University, for their support of this project, financial and otherwise, including the conference, preparation of this manuscript, and release time for Cohen to see to the book's timely completion.

Although Fordham University has been especially generous to us, allowing us to fulfill our ambitious vision, our deepest thanks go to Robert Himmelberg, who served as dean of the Graduate School of Fordham University while this project was undertaken. Under Bob's stewardship we secured funding for both the conference and much of this book. Bob kept us in check but also provided large doses of encouragement. For all that he has done, we dedicate this book to him.

Contributors

Sarah A. Binder is assistant professor of political science at George Washington University and fellow in governmental studies at the Brookings Institution. She received her Ph.D. from the University of Minnesota in 1995. She is author of *Minority Rights, Majority Rule* (1997) and coauthor, with Steven S. Smith, of *Politics or Principle? Filibustering in the United States Senate* (1997). Her work on congressional development, legislative gridlock, and Senate politics has also appeared in the *American Political Science Review, Journal of Politics,* and *Legislative Studies Quarterly.*

Jon R. Bond is professor of political science at Texas A&M University. He received his Ph.D. from the University of Illinois at Urbana-Champaign. He has published articles on presidential-congressional relations, congressional elections, and public policy in the *American Political Science Review, Journal of Politics, American Journal of Political Science,* and other journals. He has published two books with Richard Fleisher, *The President in the Legislative Arena* and *Polarized Politics: Congress and the President in a Partisan Era.* Formerly an American Political Science Association congressional fellow, Bond has served as coeditor of the *Journal of Politics*. He is a member of the executive council of the Southern Political Science Association and the publications committee of the American Political Science Association.

James E. Campbell is professor of political science at the University at Buffalo, SUNY. He was an American Political Science Association congressional fellow and has served as political science program director at the National Science Foundation. He is author of *Cheap Seats: The Democratic Party's Advantage in U.S. House Elections* (1996), *The Presidential Pulse of Congressional Elections* (1993 and 1997), and *The American Campaign: U.S. Presidential Campaigns and the National Vote* (2000). He coedited *Before the Vote: Forecasting American National Elections* (2000). Campbell's research has also appeared in numerous scholarly journals.

Jeffrey E. Cohen is professor of political science at Fordham University. He received his Ph.D. from the University of Michigan in 1979. His major areas of interest are American politics and public policy, especially as they relate to the presidency. His book *Presidential Responsiveness and Public Policy Making* (1997) was awarded the 1998 Richard E. Neustadt Award of the Presidency Research Section of the American Political Science Association.

Matthew Crenson is professor of political science at Johns Hopkins University. He received his Ph.D. from the University of Chicago in 1969. His teaching and research interests are urban politics and American political development. His most recent book is *Building the Invisible Orphanage: A Prehistory of the American Welfare System* (1998).

William Crotty is Thomas P. O'Neill Chair in Public Life and director of the Center for Comparative Government at Northeastern University. He is author of a number of books and articles on political parties, campaigns, and elections and has received the Lifetime Achievement Award of the Political Organizations and Parties Section of the American Political Science Association.

Roger H. Davidson, emeritus professor of government and politics at the University of Maryland, is now visiting professor of political science at the University of California, Santa Barbara. Among his books is *Congress and Its Members,* 7th ed. (2000), with Walter J. Oleszek. He has served on House and Senate committee staffs, consulted for the White House, and lectured or led workshops in the United States, Europe, Africa, Asia, and South America.

Diana Dwyre is associate professor of political science at California State University, Chico. She received her Ph.D. from the Maxwell School of Citizenship and Public Affairs at Syracuse University in 1994. Her research on campaign finance, political parties, and interest groups has been published in several journals and in books such as *Financing the 1996 Elections* and *The State of the Parties.* Her book *Legislative Labyrinth: Congress and Campaign Finance Reform* (2001), written with Victoria A. Farrar-Myers, was published by CQ Press. Dwyre was the 1998 American Political Science Association Steiger Congressional Fellow.

Victoria A. Farrar-Myers is assistant professor of political science at the University of Texas, Arlington. She received her Ph.D. from the University at Albany, SUNY. Her research on Congress, the presidency, and campaign finance has been published in *Congress and the Presidency* and *American Re-*

view of Politics and will appear in the forthcoming book *The Presidency and the Law.* Farrar-Myers is coauthor with Diana Dwyre of *Legislative Labyrinth: Congress and Campaign Finance Reform* (2001). She has received such honors as the American Political Science Association Congressional Fellowship and a research grant from the Dirksen Congressional Center.

Richard Fleisher is professor and chair of the political science department at Fordham University. He received his Ph.D. from the University of Illinois at Urbana-Champaign. His articles on presidential-congressional relations, congressional elections, constituency influence in roll-call voting, and electoral realignments have appeared in the *American Political Science Review, Journal of Politics, American Journal of Political Science, Political Research Quarterly, Legislative Studies Quarterly, American Politics Quarterly,* and *Political Science Quarterly.* He is coeditor of *Polarized Politics,* published by CQ Press, and coauthor of *The President in the Legislative Arena.* Fleisher is continuing his research on party polarization in American politics.

Benjamin Ginsberg is David Bernstein Professor of Political Science and director of the Center for the Study of American Government at Johns Hopkins University. He received his Ph.D. from the University of Chicago in 1973. Ginsberg was professor of government at Cornell University before joining the Hopkins faculty in 1992. He is author or coauthor of a number of books, including *Politics by Other Means; American Government: Freedom and Power; The Captive Public; The Fatal Embrace: Jews and the State; We the People; The Consequences of Consent;* and the forthcoming *From Citizen to Customer: How America Downsized Citizenship and Privatized Its Public.* The Hopkins class of 2000 awarded Ginsberg the George E. Owen prize for outstanding teaching and devotion to undergraduates.

Paul Kantor is professor of political science at Fordham University and president of the Urban Politics Section of the American Political Science Association. He received his Ph.D. from the University of Chicago. Among his most recent works are *The Dependent City Revisited* (1995) and *The Politics of Urban America: A Reader* (1998), coedited with Dennis R. Judd.

David G. Lawrence is professor of political science at Fordham University. He received his Ph.D. from the University of Chicago in 1975. His major area of interest is political behavior, with specific attention to voting, party systems, public opinion, and empirical democratic theory. He is author of *The Collapse of the Democratic Presidential Majority* (1996).

Theodore J. Lowi has been John L. Senior Professor of American Institutions at Cornell University since 1972. He received his Ph.D. from Yale University in 1961. Lowi has contributed to the study of politics in a variety of areas, including political theory, public policy analysis, and American political institutions. Author of *The End of Liberalism* (1969, 1979) and *The End of the Republican Era* (1995), Lowi is coauthor of one of the leading American government texts, *American Government—Freedom and Power,* 6th ed. (2000). The 1991 president of the American Political Science Association, he served as first vice president of the International Political Science Association from 1994 to 1997 and president from 1997 to 2000.

L. Sandy Maisel is William R. Kenan Jr. Professor of Government at Colby College, where he has taught for three decades. A graduate of Harvard College, he received his Ph.D. from Columbia University in 1971. He is author of *Parties and Elections in America: The Electoral Process* (2001), editor of *The Parties Respond* (2001), and general editor of *Jews in American Politics* (2001). His current research involves an examination of why potential candidates do and do not decide to run for the House.

Gerald M. Pomper is Board of Governors Professor of Political Science at the Eagleton Institute of Politics at Rutgers University. Author or editor of sixteen books, his publications include *Passions and Interests, Elections in America,* and *Voters' Choice.* His next book will be *The Election of 2000,* the seventh volume in a twenty-four-year series on U.S. national elections. Educated at Columbia and Princeton Universities, Pomper also has been a Fulbright scholar and visiting professor at the University of Oxford, Tel-Aviv University, and Australian National University.

The Places of Parties in American Politics

Jeffrey E. Cohen and Paul Kantor

Looking back on American political parties at the dawn of the twenty-first century, it is apparent that they have undergone pronounced changes during the past several decades. The 1950s often serve as a benchmark for comparison because of several events. First, in 1950 the Committee on Political Parties of the American Political Science Association (APSA) laid out in a special report several major criticisms of the parties, focusing on the lack of party responsibility (American Political Science Association 1950). Instead of being programmatically oriented associations held together by a coherent policy orientation, the parties seemed a looser collection of disparate voices. The report's authors, a distinguished group of scholars, concluded that the parties failed to offer voters coherent choices and were unable to organize or coordinate their incumbents in office to produce public policy.

Second, near the end of the same decade, the landmark study *The American Voter* (Campbell et al. 1960) was published. Based on the then-budding science of survey sampling and public opinion polling, the study presented the first comprehensive look at the political opinions of average Americans. Contrary to much speculation, the study found that the parties were critically important to voters. For the average citizen, a strong identification with one or the other party led to increased levels of political participation and greater levels of political interest and information and generally produced a citizen more involved in public affairs, however defined.

These two reports offered two apparently opposing portraits of the American parties at mid-century—on the one hand, not up to the task of governing; on the other hand, central to the organization of politics, especially in the public's mind. Nearly fifty years later, these two conflicting perspectives still influence our understanding of the role of the political parties in American life. Much as was the case in the 1950s, the role of the parties is shrouded in ambiguity.

This ambiguity in our understanding of the parties is partly a function of the multifaceted and complex role that parties play in mass democracies. Yet ambiguity also derives from the tumultuous changes with which parties have

1

had to cope since the 1970s or earlier. The aim of this book is to assess the current state of the American parties, especially how they serve our democracy, and to consider the implications of the many changes affecting the parties since 1970.

Two themes recur in the chapters that follow. The first theme deals with party change, specifically realignment and dealignment; the second deals with party responsibility. Realignment is a theory that seeks to account for the alternation in political fortunes of the political parties across U.S. history. For example, realignment theory has aimed to explain why the Democrats replaced the Republicans as the majority party in and out of government in the early 1930s. Realignment theory has also been used to explain the emergence of the Republican Party in the middle of the nineteenth century and its transformation into the dominant political force at the close of that century.

With the decline of the parties in the 1960s and 1970s, however, realignment theory gave way to dealignment theory. Instead of trying to explain the shifting fortunes of the parties (realignment theory's aim), dealignment theory tries to explain why both parties have weakened and become less relevant to voters and candidates for office. This book questions the dealignment thesis. Many of the chapters document a revival of the parties, suggesting that perhaps the era of dealigned parties has ended. Although dealignment has altered the character of American partisanship, there are signs of the renewed importance of party politics. Powerful crosscurrents are remaking the party system, strengthening it in some ways but also weakening it. If such crosscurrents do exist, then we must ask what kind of a party system is now emerging, and how did the dealigned parties revitalize?

The second theme addresses the issue of party responsibility in democracy. Advocates of party responsibility maintain that the competing parties should offer voters distinct and coherent programs and policies. They also believe that the members of the parties in government should act as a coordinated team whose aim is to implement their parties' proposals as policies. The team approach allows voters to hold each party and its elected officials accountable for their actions, the policies they enact, and the impact of those policies. In effect, responsible parties are viewed as critical to the functioning of democracy.

The authors of the APSA report took this view. They lamented the inability of the parties to hold their elected officials in line in trying to enact the parties' proposed policies, and they were critical of the lack of distinctiveness in the policy positions of the two parties. The contributors to this book suggest that today's parties are quite responsible, however. The authors of several chapters find that the parties at all levels—mass, electoral organization, and governing group—are now quite distinct in policy positions, perhaps even more than they have been since the early 1900s.

Ironically, however, the contributors to this book also reveal that important countervailing changes may be limiting party responsibility. Some authors suggest that the ability of the public to hold the parties accountable is diminishing because of divided government. Since Richard Nixon's terms of office in the early 1970s the national government has frequently been characterized by divided party control of the presidency and Congress. Other authors contend that the voters may actually prefer divided government. They note that voters frequently distrust both parties, viewing the Republicans as too conservative, the Democrats as too liberal, and both as too unbending and unwilling to compromise. Surely the proponents of greater party responsibility did not expect ideologically distinctive parties to be viewed by the public as too extreme, too uncompromising, and not worthy of the trust to run government alone. These countercurrents in partisanship complicate the issue of responsible parties.

Structure of the Book

Political parties occupy a complex position in modern democracy. One important definition of parties recognizes that complexity by distinguishing among three important elements of political parties: the parties in the mass public, the parties as electoral and political organizations, and the parties as governing groups (Beck 1997; Key 1964). We use this tripartite categorization to organize the chapters in this book.

The first section looks at the parties in the mass public. Whereas candidate recruitment and election campaigning were once the mainstay activities of political parties, in recent decades these tasks have shifted to the candidates themselves, giving rise to what is often termed candidate-centered politics. As such, candidates for office tend to emphasize their own talents, backgrounds, and characteristics rather then their association with either major party when running for office. Some commentators have suggested that this trend has led to a more personalized and less partisan electoral environment.

In Chapter 1 (Presidential Election Campaigns and Partisanship), James E. Campbell asks whether presidential election contests have become candidate centered at the expense of partisanship, as so many analysts now contend. Contrary to the conventional wisdom on candidate-centered politics, Campbell finds that presidential election contests from the 1950s through the 1990s are indeed heavily partisan contests. In particular, Campbell looks at the voting behavior of those who have not made up their minds about which candidate to vote for early in the campaign. If elections are party reaffirming, rather than being candidate centered, we should find that these undecided voters will, in the end, vote for their parties' candidates. This is just what Campbell finds.

In Chapter 2 (On the Resurgence of Party Identification in the 1990s), David G. Lawrence also finds partisanship increasing during recent decades. Lawrence documents that in the late 1960s and early 1970s the parties in the mass public had weakened in two ways: Party identification and the impact of party on the vote declined markedly. By the early 1980s, however, both party identification and party impact on the vote began to recover. But Lawrence's point is subtler. He shows that although party impact on voting fully recovered, if not surpassed, levels recorded in the 1950s, often taken as a period of strong mass partisanship, party identification recovered only about half of the loss of the 1960s and 1970s.

In Chapter 3 (Evidence of Increasing Polarization Among Ordinary Citizens), Richard Fleisher and Jon R. Bond critique dealignment theory. Although evidence of dealignment in the mass public seems appropriate for the 1970s, contrary evidence began to mount after the 1980s. Fleisher and Bond find a growing gap in opinions about candidates, issues, and presidents among citizens who identify as either Democrats or Republicans. In contrast, dealignment theory argues that citizens will be either alienated or indifferent to the major parties, not that large segments of the public will have become increasingly partisan in their orientations and opinions about politics. Also important, Fleisher and Bond show that voter polarization is not restricted to strong partisans, regions, or age cohorts. Rather, it is a more general and national phenomenon, one that is mirrored in the behavior of political elites and decision makers.

The first three chapters in the section on mass partisanship emphasize the strength of parties in the mass public in the 1990s compared with the decline that marked the late 1960s and 1970s. However, none of these chapters comes to grips with the overriding fact that voting participation has declined and is still depressed in the early twenty-first century, compared with what it was in the 1950s and 1960s. Nor do these chapters address the issue of why the level of mistrust and cynicism in the mass public is so high in the 1990s. If the party system has revived, why has turnout not increased and why have people in general not become more positive about the operation of our political system?

Matthew Crenson and Benjamin Ginsberg, authors of Chapter 4 (Party Politics and Personal Democracy), offer a potential answer to the apparent contradiction of greater partisanship with low levels of turnout and high levels of political mistrust in the mass public. Their theory hinges on the idea that the meaning of citizenship has changed, with people now viewing themselves more as customers than as citizens. Customers seek from government personal benefits, not collective ones. As a result, collective activities such as voting are less relevant to the political experience of ordinary people. At the same time, partisan competition takes place in arenas other than election contests, such as through the appointment of judges and bureaucrats and in the halls of the bureaucracy, where regulatory and other policy decisions are made. The implication is that political leaders have fewer incentives to mobilize voters. They can win their battles without voter support and without the mobilization of new voters. Thus, as Crenson and Ginsberg suggest, we can have a context of extreme partisanship with low levels of turnout.

The second section of this book turns to the topic of parties as electoral and political organizations. In Chapter 5 (American Political Parties: Still Central to a Functioning Democracy?), L. Sandy Maisel reflects on the role of party organizations in the recruitment of candidates for office. He finds that few prospective candidates are contacted by party organizations, either national or local, and asked to run for office. Thus, according to Maisel, as talent scouts for modern government the parties appear lacking. This is a far cry from earlier days, when party leaders actively sought candidates for office, making parties perhaps the most important institution in helping to recruit potential political leaders.

In contrast to Maisel's pessimistic critique of parties as political organizations, in Chapter 6 (Policy Coherence in Political Parties: The Elections of 1984, 1988, and 1992), William Crotty looks at the people who attended the national nominating conventions in three elections. He assesses how distinctive the two sets of convention delegates are in terms of background and sociological characteristics and policy viewpoints. Crotty finds that although the delegates of the two parties are somewhat similar in terms of background and sociological characteristics, they are quite distinctive in terms of preferences on issues. In this regard the parties appear to hew to the tenets of responsible parties. They are relatively vibrant organizations, and they offer citizens clear choices in terms of policy visions.

In Chapter 7 (Parties and Campaign Finance), Victoria A. Farrar-Myers and Diana Dwyre discuss the impact of campaign finance reforms and candidate-centered campaigns on the national party organizations. Farrar-Myers and Dwyre argue that in order not to become obsolete in this new age, the parties exploited the campaign finance reform laws passed in the early 1970s. By collecting large sums of money, the parties not only strengthened their national and congressional committees but also became important "service bureaus" for candidates and local parties. In fact, the parties have become highly successful at raising money and dispensing it in various ways, especially through soft money operations and advocacy advertising. As a consequence of that success the parties themselves have become objects of attack by reformers, who claim that the parties and their money have now become a corrupting influence on American politics. This is a far cry from the 1970s, when many commentators worried about the future of the parties, whether they would cease as viable political organizations.

Gerald M. Pomper also discusses the parties from the perspective of the doctrine of responsible parties, in Chapter 8 (Party Responsibility and the Future of American Democracy). Pomper finds that in the years since the publication of the APSA report, the political parties have instituted many reforms that are in line with the thinking of advocates of responsible parties. However, Pomper notes an irony in the adoption of these reforms. Although the parties have become more internally democratic and responsible, a point also noted in Crotty's chapter, this does not necessarily serve American democracy, as supporters of responsible party reforms once predicted. In representing the views of their members, the parties do not necessarily offer choices the voters like. In fact, to average Americans, who hold moderate views about the policy directions of government, the parties look too extreme and uncompromising.

The third section of this book considers the parties as governing groups. Roger H. Davidson, in Chapter 9 (Congressional Parties, Leaders, and Committees: 1900, 2000, and Beyond), compares the congressional parties at turn of the twentieth century with those of today. In many ways the parties then and now resemble each other. Both were strong, they took distinctive positions on major issues, the leadership possessed institutional resources to keep their rank and file in line, and divided government was the norm. But striking differences also exist between the parties of the two eras. In particular, today's party system is more candidate centered and has more difficulty reconciling differences in order to produce policies. Increasingly frustrated with gridlock, modern parties seem less able to govern than they were a hundred years ago.

In Chapter 10 (Can the Parties Govern?), Sarah A. Binder extends some of the themes found in Davidson's chapter. In particular, she asks whether the modern, ideologically distinct parties can overcome the barriers that divided government presents when trying to enact legislation. She finds that the ideological distinctiveness of the parties increases the likelihood of gridlock but

Jeffrey E. Cohen and Paul Kantor

that as the parties become home to more moderates, the potential for producing policies increases. As the parties have moved further apart in terms of the issue positions they take, and as both parties attract fewer moderates, they may be less able to find grounds on which to forge compromises. The modern parties may now be too hardened in the positions they take to govern, especially when the opposition party controls the other branch of government.

Theodore J. Lowi rounds out the critique of the party system by arguing, in Chapter 11 (Political Parties and the Future State of the Union), that our two-party system ill serves the nation. According to Lowi, the two-party system depresses turnout and limits representation because only two voices, Democratic and Republican, are heard, despite the diversity of the nation. Rather than a full-fledged, participatory democracy, the American political system looks like a plutocracy to Lowi. It serves Democratic and Republican Party elites. Lowi is not the first to criticize the American political system this way. But unlike other critics, who argue that only major constitutional reform will change the system, Lowi suggests that by electing members of Congress state-wide and at-large (in which several members of Congress would represent a state), instead of in single-member districts, parties would be strengthened and democracy better served. He believes that such a system would encourage more than two parties, increasing the representation of diverse voices. Further, he thinks that multimember at-large constituencies in Congress would encourage members to work together, strengthening the parties.

Overall, readers will find much diversity of opinion among the contributors regarding whether the parties have rebounded from the declines of the 1960s and 1970s, or whether the parties are still in decline. Several authors (for example, Campbell, Lawrence, Fleisher and Bond, Crotty, and Farrar-Myers and Dwyre) suggest that at least in some ways the parties of today are vital, vibrant, and offer much to the political system. In contrast, others (for example, Crenson and Ginsberg, Maisel, Pomper, Davidson, Binder, and Lowi) are not so sanguine.

Finally, in the conclusion to this book, Chapter 12 (Decline and Resurgence in the American Party System), we put these various findings and viewpoints into perspective. Jeffrey E. Cohen and Paul Kantor speculate about why the parties have undergone the cycle from the decline of the 1960s and 1970s to the resurgence, or at best partial resurgence, of the 1980s and 1990s. Further, they try to explain why the parties seem to be following a dual path of development—revitalizing in some respects but showing signs of decay and decline in other ways. They suggest that several theories help account for this state of affairs. These theories include the changing structure of society and the economy, the reaction of government and politicians to the massive increase of demands put on them in the 1960s and 1970s, the role of money in politics, and the strategies of politicians in an environment of uncertainty. Cohen and Kantor conclude that it is necessary to understand these forces that are changing the party system in order to assess the future of American democracy.

Jeffrey E. Cohen and Paul Kantor

PART ONE

The Parties in the Mass Public

1

Presidential Election Campaigns and Partisanship

James E. Campbell

Presidential Election Campaigns and Partisanship

How do presidential general election campaigns affect the partisan behavior of the electorate? Do campaigns undercut partisanship in the electorate or activate it? From one standpoint, by centering attention on the candidates running in a particular election, campaigns would seem to undermine partisanship. Ever since *The American Voter* (Campbell et al. 1960) drew the distinction between long-term and short-term influences on the vote and found party identification to be the preeminent long-term political influence, some election analysts have supposed that short-term campaign influences on the vote are at the expense of partisanship. Presidential general election campaigns emphasize the particular policy issues and candidate qualifications for office that concern voters at the time of the election; they are not directly about partisanship. To the extent that voters' attentions are drawn to the political issues of the day and to the merits and personalities of the specific presidential candidates, the impact of partisanship would seem to be overshadowed by candidate-centered campaigns. Campaigns may encourage many people to vote independently-minded for the "person and not the party."

There are additional reasons to suppose that presidential campaigns in recent decades may have drawn voters away from their partisan moorings and contributed to what some analysts have seen as a decline in partisanship (Wattenberg 1991, 1996). Presidential campaigns are far more expensive than they once were, and the technology available to candidates is far more sophisticated than in the days of front-porch speeches, whistle-stop campaigning, and static-

I would like to thank Bill Jacoby, Franco Mattei, and John Kessel for their comments on earlier versions and parts of this project.

distorted radio addresses. From cable news to entertainment-interview programs to their own web sites, presidential candidates now have virtually instantaneous and production-rich access to millions of voters any time they want. With these greater resources for candidates to communicate their messages to the electorate, we might well expect that candidate-specific considerations would receive ever-greater attention from the public at the expense of considerations of party affiliations. Moreover, with the public's strong disdain for parties in recent times and the political necessity of appealing to the middle-ground of independent voters in a competitive political environment, candidates have been loath to make much of their partisan backgrounds (West 1993, 38). In short, the messages of modern presidential general election campaigns draw voters' attentions to the here and now—that is, to the candidates, their records, and their stands on the issues. Partisanship gets short shrift.

Although there are reasons why campaigns may pull voters away from their parties, there are also good reasons why they may promote partisanship. Campaigns may revitalize partisanship for voters rather than diminish its importance to them. The candidates' campaign messages that provide reasons to vote for one candidate over the other emphasize differences and polarize voters, commonly along party lines. Moreover, a crucial component of any campaign strategy is the shoring up of the candidate's base. Any hope of winning the election depends on candidates securing the loyalty of their own partisans. In doing so, campaigns remind Democrats why they are Democrats rather than Republicans and remind Republicans why they are Republicans rather than Democrats. This reminder is especially important after months of divisive internal party nomination contests emphasizing differences within the parties. By emphasizing differences between the parties, even candidate-centered campaigns, with all of their attention on the short-term aspects of particular elections, may restore the potency of long-term partisanship.[1]

Which view of the campaign's effect on partisanship is correct? Have campaigns pulled voters away from their parties and contributed to party decline or have they drawn straying partisans back to their parties and contributed to party resurgence? Campaigns probably have both sorts of effects. The information conveyed by campaigns about the election's particular candidates and

1. A third possibility is that campaigns have no effect on party loyalties in the electorate. Because of the competitive balance of the candidates' campaigns and the tendency of those voters most attentive to the campaigns to have well-established preferences not easily dislodged by the campaigns' attempts at persuasion, campaigns may have minimal effects on voters, including their loyalty to their parties (Campbell 2000a, 10–12; Holbrook 1996).

issues may pull some voters away from supporting their parties. At the same time, the candidates and issues are thoroughly imbued with partisanship. Candidates have partisan backgrounds and associations, and policy issues have partisan histories. To the extent that campaigns provide voters with the candidates' messages and qualifications, they may also provide voters with information that indirectly, but importantly, revitalizes partisanship. As such, although campaigns draw some voters away from their parties' candidates, they may draw other voters closer to support for their parties' candidates. The real question is which effect is most prevalent in most presidential campaigns? In general, do campaigns weaken or reinvigorate the partisanship of the typical voter?

Approaching the Question

This analysis attempts to answer the question of whether presidential election campaigns are more likely to (1) take party-identifying voters away from their "standing decision," or predisposition, to vote for their parties' presidential candidates or (2) guide them back to their long-standing partisan commitments. Using the National Election Study (NES) surveys, conducted in the twelve presidential elections from 1952 to 1996, I compare the choices of voters who decided how they would vote sometime during the campaign (late deciders) with the choices of those who decided before the campaign began (early deciders). Voters are classified as late deciders if they said in the postelection survey that they decided how they would vote after the national party conventions or if they changed their reported vote from the vote intention they indicated in the preelection wave of interviews. The preelection interviews generally take place in September and the first weeks of October of the election year. Do these late-deciding voters, as a group, tend to decide in favor of their parties' candidates; or, with their attentions focused on particular issues and candidates, do they set aside their partisanship in arriving at their votes? Do these voters exit campaigns and enter voting booths with their partisanship reinvigorated or with it in doubt? With ever-increasing resources being devoted to presidential campaigns, the partisan implications of campaigns may play a large role in affecting the future strength of political parties.

One thing to keep in mind in examining the behavior of the campaign-deciding, or late-deciding, voters is that they selected themselves into this group. Late deciders are late deciders by choice or, more accurately, by their failure to make a choice. By virtue of their inability or unwillingness to reach an early decision, as most other voters do, they stand apart from the electorate as a whole. For the most part, late deciders are not simply procrastinators but rather voters who for one reason or another have some difficulty deciding how they will vote. Given that most late deciders are to some degree partisan, their reluctance to endorse their parties' standard-bearers suggests that they have at least mixed feelings about their parties' candidates. Additionally, late-deciding partisans tend to be less strongly identified with their parties than are early deciders.[2] Typically about half of early-deciding partisans and only about a quarter of late-deciding partisans indicate a strong identification with their parties. This observation accounts in part for the greater difficulty that late deciders have in reaching an easy (and therefore earlier) vote decision and also suggests that they will probably be less loyal to their parties, even if the campaign is as reaffirming of partisanship as possible. In short, even if the campaign consists of two full-fledged partisan rallies, we would expect less than a solidly loyal vote from late-deciding partisans because they have serious doubts about their parties' candidates from the outset. Put differently, the behavior of late deciders can say as much about them as it does about the impact that the campaign has on them. With this reason for caution in mind, an examination of the voting behavior of late deciders may still provide some insight into the impact of campaigns on partisanship.

What should we expect to see if campaigns activate or deactivate partisanship? If campaigns successfully compete with long-standing partisan commitments, we should expect loyal party voting among late deciders to be low. In landslide election years, when the political winds of the campaign are blowing strongly in one direction, we might expect defection rates among late-deciding partisans in the losing party to rise dramatically. If campaigns successfully pull voters away from their parties, on these occasions we might not even be surprised if the loyalty rates of late deciders dipped below 50 percent. Four elections in the period of study can be categorized as near landslides (1956) or clear landslides (1964, 1972, and 1984). If candidate-centered cam-

---

2. The strength of partisanship is consistently and positively related to early decision making by voters. The relationship was statistically significant in each of the twelve NES surveys ($p < .01$). The strength of partisanship was coded as 1 for strong Democrats and strong Republicans and as 0 for weak and leaning Democrats and Republicans. Pure independents were excluded. The time of decision was coded as 1 for major-party candidate voters who said they reached their decisions at or before the conventions and did not change their votes from their preelection vote intentions. The time of decision was coded as 0 for major-party-candidate voters who said they reached their vote choices after the conventions or who changed their votes from their preelection vote intentions. The consistent positive relationship between the strength of partisanship and early decision making is indicated by the Kendall tau-b nonparametric correlations ranging from .14 to .31, with a mean value of .24.

James E. Campbell

paigns are at the expense of partisanship, we would also expect that voters who change their minds during the campaign (that is, changing their votes from their previously stated vote intentions) change them in a way that costs their parties' candidates votes. If campaigns undermine partisanship, voters changing from indecision or a loyal vote inclination to defection should outnumber voters changing from indecision or a disloyal vote inclination to party loyalty.

In contrast, if campaigns draw voters back to their parties, we should expect substantial party loyalty from late-deciding partisans. Given that they are self-selected doubters about their parties' candidates (otherwise they would have decided early), the party loyalty of late deciders is likely to fall short of that of early deciders. Nevertheless, if the campaign reasserts the importance of partisanship, even if only indirectly by raising the issues and leadership qualities that the party values, late-deciding partisans ought to be quite loyal in voting for their parties' presidential candidates. Moreover, we should expect a majority of those who change their minds during the campaign to change them in favor of their parties' candidates.

The analysis proceeds in three steps. The first step examines the party voting of early- and late-deciding Democrats and Republicans from 1952 to 1996. Following Bruce E. Keith et al. (1992), independents who lean toward a party are counted as partisans throughout the analysis. The focus in examining voters by their time of decision is on the behavior of the late deciders, voters who reached a decision during the campaign. As noted earlier in this chapter, even with a strongly partisan campaign, we would not expect late deciders to be as partisan in their voting as those who reached an early decision, but the loyalty of early deciders provides a benchmark of sorts in evaluating the partisanship of late deciders. Because we are interested in the overall impact of campaigns on partisan voting, rather than what aspects of campaigns detract from or add to partisan voting, the analysis is of simple partisan loyalty rates instead of a multivariate analysis of how the various components of the campaign affect partisan voting.

The second and third steps in the analysis examine the vote decisions of two groups of late-deciding voters: those who reported voting for the same candidate they said they favored in the preelection interview and those who changed their preferences between the preelection interview and election day. Campaign effects ought to be less evident among late-deciding partisans who have apparently stable preferences. The pro-party or anti-party tilt of campaign effects should be most evident among late-deciding partisans who changed their votes.

Throughout the analysis the party loyalty and defection rates of late deciders are computed exclusively for major-party voters. A parallel analysis that also includes as defectors all partisans voting for third-party candidates confirms the basic findings of the major-party vote analysis.[3] Because of differences between the actual vote distribution and the distribution of the reported vote in the NES surveys, the NES data have been reweighted to bring them into line with the actual national division of the popular vote.[4]

The Findings

Do Late Deciders Vote with Their Parties?

Table 1-1 presents the percentages of early-deciding and late-deciding Democratic and Republican Party identifiers who voted for their respective party's presidential candidate (rather than the other major party's candidate) in each election from 1952 to 1996. As the data demonstrate, late-deciding Democrats and Republicans are less loyal in their vote choice than their early-deciding compatriots. On average, late deciders are almost fifteen percentage points less loyal than early deciders. This loyalty difference, however, is significantly reduced when the tendency of early deciders to have stronger party identifica-

3. Loyalty rates computed for all votes rather than two-party votes are approximately the same for early deciders but are somewhat lower for late deciders. The basis for this difference is that few third-party voters commit to an early vote decision, perhaps because third-party candidacies have less of a history for voters to evaluate early in the election year and the viability of these candidacies must be established in the campaign. As such, voters who defect from their parties to vote for third-party candidates are nearly absent from the ranks of early deciders but boost the number of late deciders and thus increase their defection rates (by about seven percentage points among late-deciding Democrats and Republicans).

4. The mean absolute error in the NES reported vote percentage (1952–1996) is about 2.3 percentage points (Campbell 2000a, 62). Considering that the average winning vote over this period was a 5.4 percentage point margin over an even vote split, the NES errors are nontrivial. Votes for Republican presidential candidates appear to have been overreported by NES early in the series and underreported late in the series. With the exception of 1964, Republican presidential votes were overreported in elections from 1952 to 1980. Democratic presidential votes were overreported by NES from 1984 to 1996. Because the extent and direction of the unrepresentativeness of the NES data is known (we know the actual vote percentages), we can correct for it by reweighting the data. For example, Bill Clinton in 1996 actually received 49.24 percent of the total popular presidential vote, and Bob Dole received 40.72 percent, with the remainder being cast for minor-party candidates. However, in reported votes in the NES surveys (in a cross-tabulation with party identification), the Clinton vote is overreported at 52.89 percent and the Dole vote is underreported at 38.31 percent. To correct for this inaccuracy, the data are weighted by the ratio of the actual vote percentage to the NES reported vote percentage. In 1996, reported Clinton votes are weighted by a factor of 0.931 and reported Dole votes are weighted by a factor of 1.063. The weight values (rounded to hundredths) for 1952 through 1992 are reported in the notes to the tables in Appendix B of Campbell (2000a).

James E. Campbell

Table 1-1. Partisan Loyalty in Presidential Voting by Time of Vote Decision, 1952–1996

| | Percentage of Early- and Late-Deciding Partisan Voters Who Voted for Their Parties' Presidential Candidates | | | |
| | Democrats | | Republicans | |
Election Year	Early	Late	Early	Late
1952	80	64	99	84
1956	83	58	98	82
1960	82	78	97	76
1964	95	69	80	75
1968	89	71	98	82
1972	59	63	99	74
1976	85	78	94	76
1980	85	64	94	90
1984	84	68	98	86
1988	91	75	98	79
1992	93	84	97	80
1996	98	85	92	74
Mean	85	71	95	80
Elections in Which Partisan Loyalty Was > 50%	12	12	12	12

Note: The percentages are calculated from NES data reweighted to the actual national vote division. The party loyalty rates are the percentages of partisans in categories who voted for their parties' candidates rather than the other major party presidential candidate. Third-party voters and pure independents are excluded. The mean loyalty rates computed for all votes rather than major-party votes are 85 percent and 65 percent for early- and late-deciding Democrats, respectively, and 95 percent and 73 percent for early- and late-deciding Republicans, respectively.

tions is taken into account.[5] Moreover, comparisons to early deciders aside, the most important point is that late-deciding partisans are strongly and consistently supportive of their parties' standard-bearers. In the typical election year,

5. An individual-level pooled analysis among the twelve election studies indicates that the impact of the time of decision on loyalty rates is partly attributable to differences in the strength of party identification. When the strength of party identification is taken into account, the estimated effects of the time of decision variable on party loyalty drop by about 20 percent. The conclusion from this observation and from an aggregate analysis of the loyalty rates in Table 1-1 is that a portion of the observed lower loyalty rate of late deciders simply reflects the stronger party identifications of early deciders and the increased party loyalty among those with stronger party identifications whether or not subjected to the campaign.

more than seven out of ten Democrats who reached their vote decisions during the general election campaign ended up voting for their party's presidential candidate. Republican late deciders were even more loyal.[6] Nearly eight out of ten late-deciding Republicans cast their ballots for their party's candidate. The loyalty of partisans of either party who decided during the campaign never dropped below 50 percent, and only once (in twenty-four opportunities) did it dip below 60 percent (for Democrats in 1956).[7]

If campaigns were at the expense of partisanship, we would expect that their impact would be most evident in landslide election years when the information conveyed by the campaign would most clearly favor one candidate. If presidential landslides are defined as elections in which the winning candidate received about 58 percent or more of the two-party popular vote, the twelve elections under examination have included three Republican landslides (1956, 1972, and 1984) and one Democratic landslide (1964). In all four landslides the loyalty rates among partisans of the losing party were below average. However, before we make too much of this, aside from the Democrats in 1956, between nearly two-thirds and three-quarters of late-deciding partisans remained loyal to their parties despite the campaigns ostensibly pulling them toward the opposition. Moreover, loyalty rates of losing partisans who decided before each of these campaigns were also lower than normal. In the 1964 Johnson landslide over Goldwater, late-deciding Republicans were about five percentage points short of their usual loyalty rate (75 percent versus an average of nearly 80 percent), whereas early-deciding Republicans that year were about fifteen percentage points less loyal than usual (80 percent versus an average of about 95 percent). In fact, in the face of the Nixon landslide over McGovern in 1972, Democrats who decided how they would vote during the campaign were actually more likely to vote with their party for McGovern than were Democrats who had decided how they would vote before the campaign (63 percent versus 59 percent).

6. Loyalty rates differed by party and over time. In elections since 1952, loyalty rates have been on average about ten percentage points lower among Democrats than among Republicans. However, these rates have changed in recent years as Republicans have gained numbers and become more diverse while Democrats have lost numbers and become more cohesive. As a result of the realignment toward Republicans (or toward a more competitively balanced party system), Democratic loyalties increased and Republican loyalties declined. In the most recent elections there appears to be no consistent and significant loyalty difference between the parties.

7. Paired samples t-tests were performed on the differences between the loyalty rates of early deciders and late deciders in each party and between late deciders in each party and the null standard of 50-percent loyalty (the expected loyalty rate if partisanship were not a consideration). All four differences were statistically significant at $p < .01$.

James E. Campbell

This review of the voting history of late-deciding party identifiers offers little support to claims that candidate-centered campaigns significantly weaken partisanship. Under even the most adverse conditions (landslides against their parties), large majorities of late-deciding identifiers in both parties voted loyally for their parties' standard-bearers. Two conclusions from these findings seem plausible: Either campaigns in fact support rather than undermine partisanship in the electorate or the party identifications of late deciders are more than a match for whatever distracting impact that campaigns have. Either way, whether despite the impact of campaigns or because of that impact, partisan loyalty does not appear to be appreciably weakened as a result of the general election campaign. Even when buried in a landslide for the opposition, large majorities of late-deciding partisans "keep the faith."

Despite the seemingly strong showing of partisan voting among late-deciding partisans, some of these late-deciding partisans may have been quite close to reaching a decision before the campaign. These late-deciding partisans may be only nominally late deciders. They may have been fairly well prepared to support their parties' candidates before the campaign and simply confirmed their near-decision during the campaign. They may have been 95 percent set in a party vote, and the campaign added the final slight measure to this certainty. If many late deciders are on the brink of a decision before the campaign, it may still be the case that the campaign may have anti-party consequences for the decisions of other late deciders who enter the campaign truly in a quandary about their choices. To assess this possibility, and to shed more light on the degree to which partisanship survives or is encouraged by the campaign, I next examine the decisions of both late deciders whose vote intentions were stable and those whose stated vote intentions changed over the course of the campaign (the voters most open to campaign influence).

Stable Preferences and Party Voting

Table 1-2 presents the party loyalty and defection rates for late-deciding party identifiers who voted for the same candidates they declared they would vote for in the preelection interview. These late deciders stayed with their initial inclinations. As one would expect, late deciders who were stable in their vote preferences voted in overwhelming numbers for their parties' presidential candidates. Typically, more than four out of five late-deciding partisans who stayed with their precampaign intentions voted loyally for their parties' candidates. The party loyalty of these stable-preference, late-deciding partisans rivals that of partisans who said they had decided their votes at or before the conventions.

Table 1–2. Partisan Loyalty Among Late-Deciding Partisans Who Had Stable Preferences During the Campaign, 1952–1996

Election Year	Vote Choice Was Unchanged from Preelection Vote Intentions (Late-Deciding Partisans Voting for Major-Party Candidates)		Percentage of Late-Deciding, Major-Party Voting Partisans Whose Votes Were Unchanged from Their Preelection Vote Intentions
	Percent Who Voted Loyally for Their Party's Candidate	Percent Who Defected to Vote for the Other Party's Candidate	
1952	81	19	57
1956	84	16	42
1960	89	11	56
1964	79	21	59
1968	83	17	52
1972	74	26	55
1976	84	16	57
1980	82	18	45
1984	81	19	63
1988	85	15	63
1992	87	13	68
1996	84	16	70
Mean	83	17	57

Note: The percentages are calculated from NES data reweighted to the actual national vote division. All respondents examined in this table reported voting for a major-party candidate, indicated an identification with one of the major political parties, and indicated that they decided their vote choices after the nominating conventions. Reported voters who indicated a preelection intention vote for their parties' candidates and then reported actually voting for those candidates were counted as stable loyal party votes. Reported voters who indicated in the preelection wave that they would vote for the opposition party's candidate and then reported doing so in the postelection interview are counted as stable defectors. When third-party votes are included, the mean loyalty rate is 75 percent, the mean rate of defection to the other major party's candidate is 16 percent, and the mean rate of defection to the third-party candidate is 9 percent.

These stable-preference late deciders were probably fairly sure of how they would vote before the campaign began, were most probably not very open to influence by the campaign, but were reassured enough by the campaign to vote as they originally intended (for the overwhelming majority this meant a vote with their parties). The campaign made a difference to these voters, and the difference in most cases favored a party vote, but the difference may not have been of great magnitude.

If all late deciders were so stable in voting their early party intentions, we

James E. Campbell

might conclude that the impact of campaigns, while apparently reinforcing partisanship, does not amount to much. The last column of Table 1-2, however, indicates that although a substantial proportion of late-deciding partisans held vote intentions that were unchanged by the campaign (on average, 57 percent), many did not. Many late-deciding partisans (typically about 43 percent) voted differently than they indicated in the preelection interview. These partisans are the late deciders who would seem to be most susceptible to campaign influence. If the anti-party effect of campaigns were to be found anywhere, it would be in the vote decisions of these late deciders who changed their minds during the campaign. The question is whether these changers were pulled back to vote for their parties' presidential candidates or induced to stray from their parties by the campaign.

Changers During the Campaign and Party Voting

Table 1-3 presents the party loyalty and defection rates for late-deciding party identifiers who voted for a presidential candidate of one of the two major parties but had indicated that they intended to do otherwise in the preelection interview. These changers may have initially indicated that they intended to vote for a major-party candidate other than the one they eventually voted for, that they intended to vote for a third-party presidential candidate, or that they did not intend to vote at all.

As Table 1-3 demonstrates, party identifiers who changed their minds during the campaign tended to move toward supporting their parties' presidential candidates rather than to defection. To be sure, in every election a significant number of partisans drift away from a party vote during the campaign. However, with the exception of 1956, when pro-party and anti-party changes during the campaign were equal, partisan voters who changed their minds during the campaign were more likely to back their parties' candidates than oppose them. Campaign movements by voters in support of partisanship have typically been almost twice as likely as movements away from partisanship support. In 1996, for example, 68 percent of late-deciding partisans who changed their minds during the campaign changed in a pro-party direction, whereas only 32 percent of changers voted for the opposition party's candidate.

Another way of looking at the impact of campaigns on the party voting of these changers is to compare what their rates of party voting would have been based on their stated preelection intentions with how loyal these voters actually were to their parties at the end of the campaign. The party loyalty rates based on preelection intentions and the loyalty based on the postelection reported

Table 1–3. Partisan Loyalty Among Late-Deciding Partisans Who Changed Preferences During the Campaign, 1952–1996

| Election Year | Vote Choice Changed from Preelection Vote Intention (Late-Deciding Partisans Voting for Major Party Candidates) | | Percentage of Late-Deciding Major-Party Voting Partisans Whose Vote Choices Changed from Their Preelection Vote Intentions |
	Percent Who Voted Loyally for Their Party's Candidate	*Percent Who Defected to Vote for the Other Party's Candidate*	
1952	54	46	43
1956	50	50	58
1960	63	37	44
1964	61	39	41
1968	66	34	48
1972	57	43	45
1976	67	33	43
1980	66	34	55
1984	64	36	37
1988	63	37	37
1992	72	28	32
1996	68	32	30
Mean	63	37	43

Note: The percentages are calculated from NES data reweighted to the actual national vote division. All respondents examined in this table reported voting for a major-party candidate, indicated an identification with one of the major political parties, and either indicated that they decided their vote choices after the nominating conventions or changed their vote choices from their precampaign vote intentions. Those reported voters who indicated a preelection intention other than a loyal vote (favored another candidate, undecided, or indicated that they would not vote) and then reported voting for their party's presidential candidate were counted as changers toward a loyal party vote. Those who indicated a preelection intention other than a vote for the opposition's candidate and then reported voting for the opposition's candidate were counted as changers who defected to vote for the other major party's presidential candidate. When third-party votes are included, the mean loyalty rate is 56 percent, the mean rate of defection to the other major party's candidate is 35 percent, and the mean rate of defection to the third-party candidate is 9 percent.

vote were compared for the same voters: party identifiers who reported voting for a major-party presidential candidate and voted differently from their preelection intention. In the typical election year, about 170 respondents in the NES surveys meet these criteria.

In calculating, from the stated vote intentions, what the extent of party loyalty might have been without the effects of the campaign, party identifiers who indicated they intended to vote for the opposition party's candidate were

James E. Campbell

Table 1–4. Partisan Loyalty Rates Based on the Vote Intentions and Reported Votes of Party Identifiers Who Changed Their Votes from Their Preelection Vote Intentions, 1952–1996

| Election Year | Percentage of Partisans Changing Their Votes from Their Vote Intentions and Voting for Their Parties' Presidential Candidates | | Difference Between Party Loyalty of Intentions and Votes |
	Party Loyalty of Vote Intentions	Party Loyalty of Reported Votes	
1952	54	54	0
1956	58	50	−8
1960	50	63	+13
1964	50	61	+11
1968	52	66	+14
1972	53	57	+ 4
1976	48	67	+19
1980	53	66	+13
1984	50	64	+14
1988	52	63	+11
1992	49	72	+23
1996	56	68	+12
Mean	52	63	+11

Note: The percentages are calculated from NES data reweighted to the actual national vote division. The unweighted number of changers ranged from 91 (1996) to 254 (1972) with a mean *N* of 172. See the text for a description of how party loyalty based on preelection vote intentions was calculated.

counted as would-be defectors and those who said they intended to vote for their own party's presidential candidate were counted as would-be loyal party voters. Those who said they would vote for a third-party candidate or would not vote at all were counted as half a defection and half a loyal vote for the purposes of determining aggregate two-party loyalty and defection rates. Because these intentions did not indicate whether the voter would contribute to the ranks of the loyalists or the defectors, they were assigned equal probabilities of falling either way.

Table 1-4 presents the rates of party voting by preference changers as they might have been without campaigns and as they actually were with campaigns. Although changers appeared to be less loyal to their parties after the 1956 campaign than they were at its start, and although the 1952 campaign had no discernible impact on the party voting of changers in that election, party voting increased as a result of the campaign in each of the other ten election years examined. In nine of the twelve elections, party voting increased by more than ten percentage points after the campaign. Based on the typical stated intentions of changers over these years, they entered the campaign season about as likely to oppose their parties as support them. After the campaign, however, almost two-thirds of these changers ended up voting for their parties' standard-bearers.[8] The conclusion is clear: Presidential general election campaigns reduce party defections and increase loyal party voting over what would otherwise be the case.

The Partisan Campaign

Partisanship in the electorate is robust, despite repeated claims that it has been in decline. Although some voters do not like to admit it, about nine out of ten voters identify (more or less) with either the Democratic or the Republican Party and most of these party identifiers usually vote for their parties' presidential candidates (Campbell 2000a; Keith et al. 1992). Contrary to the expectations of those who see parties in decline, presidential campaigns have played a positive role in sustaining and renewing this pervasive partisanship of the electorate.

Despite all of their attention to the candidates and the issues du jour and for all of their neglect of the political parties, presidential general election campaigns are, in the end, party-friendly events. They bring straying partisans back to their parties.[9] On their surface, presidential campaigns steer clear of the par-

8. Paired samples *t*-tests were performed on the difference between the precampaign and postcampaign loyalty rates of changers. The test indicated that the difference was statistically significant at $p<.01$.

9. Gelman and King (1993) mistakenly dismissed the "coming home of partisans" thesis based on a low and near constant percentage of undecideds in the preference polls, which suggested no gradual movement of partisans in the electorate. The percentage of undecideds in preference polls, however, greatly understates the extent of electoral indecision (Campbell 2000a). The percentage of late deciders is regularly several times the percentage of those who refuse to indicate a preference when pressed under the hypothetical conditions of the trial-heat polls ("If the election were held today. . ."). Nevertheless, the coming home of partisans thesis is consistent with Gelman and King's more general claim that presidential campaigns enlighten voter preferences, bringing their vote choices more in line with their underlying predispositions. The coming home of partisans to their parties finding is also consistent with Berelson, Lazarsfeld, and McPhee's (1954) notion that campaigns rally partisans by refocusing their attentions on partisan fundamentals; with Erikson and Wlezien's (1998) notion that campaigns polarize the distribution of voter preferences; and with Gopoian and Hadjiharalambous's (1994) findings that late-deciding voters (defined as those deciding their vote in the last two weeks of the campaign) were more likely to have supported a rival candidate for their parties' nomination and were ultimately influenced by partisan-

James E. Campbell

ties and emphasize the qualities and shortcomings of the candidates and their positions and records on matters of public policy. However, at their roots these campaigns are partisan affairs. The positive effect of campaigns on partisanship explains how so much emphasis can be placed on campaigns while the electorate can remain so overwhelmingly partisan.

The presidential candidates and the issues they address certainly have clear partisan pedigrees. In winning their parties' presidential nominations, the candidates have proven themselves to represent at least a large segment of their parties' faithful. In many cases the candidate is regarded as the leader of the party and virtually defines what it means to be a Democrat or a Republican. It is not too far off to say that, in their day, the terms "Roosevelt Democrat" or "Reagan Republican" were redundancies. Although candidates come and go and they lack the longevity of the parties, one should not underestimate how intertwined the candidates and the parties have become. In this regard, it is interesting to note that in the twelve elections from 1952 to 1996, in only one election (1964) did the Republican Party not have one of three candidates— Nixon, Bush, or Dole—on its presidential ticket.

The issues raised in campaigns usually also have a partisan history. Most issues that arise in a campaign, though taking twists that reflect the times, have been around for a while in one form or another—the economy, taxes, defense policy, crime, education, the environment, health care, an assortment of social issues, and so on. The positions that candidates take on these issues are usually the accepted positions of the party, or not far from them. The records that voters are reminded of during the campaign are also associated with the parties. The party of the incumbent president, for instance, is given the credit or the blame for the performance of the economy regardless of whether the incumbent is personally seeking reelection. Moreover, the evaluation of the candidates' supposed strengths and weaknesses and of their issue positions and records are colored by partisanship, as is the importance attached to any of these evaluations. In essence, the short-term forces of candidates and issues are

---

ship in their vote choices. Gopoian and Hadjiharalambous (1994, table 8, 64) found statistically significant "carryover effects" of the nomination (correlations between time of the vote decision and support for rival candidates for the party's nomination) in four of seven cases, and in each case the effect had the correct sign (indicating that supporters of rivals to the nominee were more likely to reach their general election vote decisions late). Although they found defection rates to be higher among late deciders (Gopoian and Hadjiharalambous 1994, table 11, 72), late deciders were consistently more likely to vote for their own parties' candidates than for the opposition's. Additionally, party identification significantly affected the vote choice of late deciders in four of the five elections they examined (1972 through 1988).

not so purely short term and not so easily separated from the long-term force of partisanship.[10]

The effect of campaigns in pulling partisans back to their parties is at least partly in keeping with the long-established finding that campaigns tend to reinforce preexisting dispositions (Berelson, Lazarsfeld, and McPhee 1954; Finkel 1993; Lazarsfeld, Berelson, and Gaudet 1944). For a variety of reasons, both psychological and rational, voters are unlikely to change their preferences dramatically during a campaign. Acknowledging this, the candidates' campaign messages and strategies work at the margins. The major candidates, for the most part, run cautious campaigns. They work with voters the way they are instead of trying to remake them politically. To a large extent, this means that campaigns generally work to reinforce or to increase the confidence that voters have in their preelection intentions (in most cases favoring their parties' candidates). However, as we have seen, the reinforcement effect of campaigns extends beyond reinforcing voters' initial vote intentions. Campaigns also reinforce voters' long-standing commitments to political parties and their candidates.[11]

From some perspectives, reinforcement would seem to be a campaign effect that is not much of an effect at all. Voters who are reinforced in their vote intentions do not vote any differently than those who are not. They may feel better about their votes, more certain that they are doing the right thing; but in the end they vote for the same candidates they would have voted for without

10. There are good reasons to suspect that the impact of partisanship on the vote is mostly, if not entirely, indirect in nature. In the examination of short-term influences on congressional elections, I found evidence that the long-term effects of partisanship are mediated nearly entirely by short-term political considerations (Campbell 1997). This view is also supported by theories of voting and empirical research (Campbell et al. 1960; see also Kelley and Mirer 1974). This claim also explains why partisanship can be so important to the vote and yet absent from virtually every forecasting model of presidential elections (Campbell 2000b).

11. A breakdown of the vote by the time of the decision and the consistency of the vote choice with the voter's original vote intention and the voter's party identification (for those identified with a major party who voted for a major-party candidate) indicates that more late-deciding votes are typically cast consistent with partisanship than with the voter's initial vote intention. On average, approximately 39 percent of party identifiers who voted for major-party candidates are late deciders (or changed their votes from their preelection intentions). Typically this 39 percent can be broken down further as follows: 18 percent voted as they said they were inclined to before the campaign and this was their party's candidate, 4 percent voted as they had intended to before the campaign but this was not their party's candidate, 11 percent voted for their party's candidate but did not originally intend to do so, and 6 percent voted for the other party's candidate but had not originally intended to defect. In summary, of the 39 percent of major-party-voting partisans who reached their vote decisions during the campaign, 74 percent (29 of the 39 percent) apparently were reinforced in their partisanship, and 56 percent (22 of the 39 percent) apparently were reinforced in their initial vote intentions.

James E. Campbell

reinforcement. The reinforcement effect of partisanship (as opposed to the reinforcement of the vote intentions), however, does change votes. As a result of reinforcing partisanship, party identifiers who intended to defect, who were flirting with not voting or with voting for a third-party candidate, or who were truly undecided about their vote choices are brought back into their party's column.

Why do general presidential election campaigns reinforce partisanship? Four reasons seem plausible. These are the four R's of campaign reinforcement. First, campaigns *remind* partisans why they are partisans. Second, they *refresh* partisanship by demonstrating that the parties differ in ways that are important to current politics. The campaigns update the substantive reasons for partisanship. Third, campaigns *reinvigorate* partisanship by building enthusiasm for the parties' candidates and issues. Finally, and perhaps most important, campaigns *restore* partisan unity after often fractious infighting for the parties' nominations.

The parties need not be explicitly mentioned by the candidates for voters to be reminded why they are Democrats or why they are Republicans.[12] The two major parties are virtually different subcultures, with different values, different views of history, and different heroes (and villains). These traditional differences carry over from one election to the next, and each election sets these differences in stark contrast to one another.[13] When the campaign is said

---

12. Wattenberg (1996, 172–173) and others have observed that presidential candidates seldom campaign using explicit appeals to party. West's (1993) examination of televised presidential advertising from 1952 to 1992 supports this observation. Party ranked seventh out of the seven content areas coded in West's study of 324 prominent ads (1993, 38). It may well be true, as Joel Silbey asserts, that "increasingly, presidential candidates [have] preferred to run as individuals, emphasizing their personal qualities rather than their adherence to party norms" (1998, 16), but this means that campaigns are less overtly partisan, not that they are any less partisan in their effect.

13. Party differences are so numerous and are on so many dimensions that one hesitates even to give examples. However, among the examples one might cite are the following: In manner, Democrats are more raucous and Republicans are more reserved and respectful. The greatest sin according to Democrats is hypocrisy; to Republicans it is relativism. When Democrats see a problem, they tend to look to the national government to solve it (even if it involves government providing benefits indirectly by placing mandates on private businesses). When Republicans see a problem, they tend to look first to the individual, then to the private sector, then to local and state governments, and only last and least to the national government. An example of the differences in the parties' views of history is in how they view the healthy economy of the 1990s. Democrats credit President Clinton and the tax increase early in his administration that supposedly set the government on track for a balanced budget and ultimately surpluses. Republicans credit the large tax cuts of the Reagan administration and the restraint placed on Democratic Party spending initiatives by Republicans in Congress (as well as the pressures not to add to already high budget deficits). They would view the slowdown in the early 1990s as the result of President Bush's ill-advised tax increase compromise with the congressional Democrats.

---

to polarize voters, it is seldom creating new divisions; it is reminding everyone of the long-standing old divisions.

The candidates and the issues they raise during the campaign represent what the political parties mean in the politics of the current election. In this way, the campaign refreshes or updates the parties' traditions and demonstrates their continued relevance. Although President Clinton had some differences with other leaders within the Democratic Party (most notably over free trade and welfare reform), his positions and approaches to issues during the 1992 and 1996 campaigns went a long way toward defining what the Democratic Party's positions were in the minds of most observers and what it meant to be a Democrat in the 1990s. Put more generally, parties are known by the candidates they nominate, and the success of the candidates and their parties are inextricably linked to one another (Campbell 1997; Farlie 1978).

The campaign also reinforces partisanship by reinvigorating partisans, giving them reasons to feel enthusiastic about voting for their parties' tickets. One of the functions of campaigns is to energize the party's base of support. If members of the party's base think that their candidate is far superior to the opponent, they will be sure to turn out to proudly cast their ballots for their party's ticket come election day. For most partisans, campaigns succeed in this function. When they do not, when a significant number of partisans in a party are unenthusiastic about their party's candidate or have doubts about which candidate is best, turnout declines, defection rates inch up, and elections are lost (Campbell 1997).

Perhaps the most important reason why campaigns reinforce partisanship is that they provide an opportunity to restore party unity. Following lengthy and often hotly contested nomination campaigns, parties are able to nominate their candidates—but not without a price. The nomination battle often exacts its toll on party unity and leaves embittered factions. The disappointed supporters of candidates defeated for the nomination may enter the general election campaign feeling they cannot possibly support the party's nominee, a candidate they had spent the previous months campaigning against. Besides the natural resentment and disappointment that may be felt toward the nominee, many disappointed partisans may also question how closely the nominee represents their views. The intraparty focus of nomination contests tends to exaggerate internal party differences (and ignore interparty differences). Small differences on the general political landscape are portrayed as vast chasms within the party.[14]

14. The 1996 Republican nomination contest provides a good example of how small differences among candidates of the same party are blown out of proportion in the heat of battle for a

After months of dwelling on differences within each party, the general election campaign turns voters' attentions to differences between the parties. When the general election campaign sets these differences in their proper general perspective, voters disgruntled about relatively minor disagreements with their parties' nominees seem to sober up. They realize that electing the opposition party's candidate is a far worse fate than electing their second or third choice within their own parties. In effect, even with all of their hoopla and histrionics, campaigns may encourage voters to vote with their heads or with their hearts rather than with their spleens.

―――――――

party's nomination. Among the many 1996 Republican hopefuls, Senate Majority Leader Bob Dole was portrayed as the moderate. Conservative Republicans looked upon his candidacy with considerable skepticism. Sen. Phil Gramm of Texas, in contrast, was widely viewed as a candidate seeking the mantel of the party's conservative wing. Prior to their 1996 nomination bids, both Dole and Gramm had established records in the Senate. Their tenure in the Senate overlapped from 1985 to 1996. During this period their voting records differed only at the margins. From 1985 to 1994, Dole's average ADA scores (an index of liberalism) were a very conservative 4.4 percent. Over the same period, Gramm's average ADA scores were only a smidgen more conservative (1.7 percent). Likewise, there was barely daylight between the two on their ACU scores (measuring conservatism). Dole voted for the conservative position in Senate roll calls about 89 percent of the time, and Gramm voted conservatively about 96 percent of the time. Was Gramm's record more conservative than Dole's? Yes, but the difference was slight. Contrary to the widespread perceptions created during the nomination campaign, both Dole and Gramm had exemplary conservative credentials.

2

On the Resurgence of Party Identification in the 1990s

David G. Lawrence

Almost all scholars who investigated the period of political instability that followed the collapse of the New Deal party system in the late 1960s concluded that a substantial source of the resulting chaos was a decline in the strength and impact of party identification in the mass public. Whether or not one accepted that the result was a full-blown era of electoral dealignment—complete with a new candidate-centered politics, volatility of election outcome, and split-ticket voting—in the mid-1970s the golden era of partisanship documented in *The American Voter* (Campbell et al. 1960) was indisputably at an end (Ladd 1982; Nie, Verba, and Petrocik 1979; Wattenberg 1991, 1998).

Two separate indicators pointed to the weakening of party identification. First, the *strength* of the partisanship that citizens reported to interviewers clearly declined in the decade after 1966: The proportion of the electorate claiming to be pure independents increased modestly, and, more important, respondents who were partisan increasingly reported that their partisanship was not very strong. Second, the *impact* of partisanship—the link between party identification and presidential vote choice—decreased substantially, as the importance of other considerations (such as issues or candidate orientation) rose and the percentage of identifiers who defected from their parties' nominees increased.

By the late 1990s, however, scholars began to see signs that mass partisanship might be making a comeback. Conclusions here were somewhat less clear-cut than was the case for the decline of party in the 1970s, largely because the two indicators had diverged somewhat. The overall strength of party identification had at least partially recovered its pre-1966 levels (Abramson, Aldrich, and Rohde 1999, 167). More impressively, Warren E. Miller and J. Merrill Shanks's *The New American Voter* (1996) claimed that the relationship between party identification and vote for president was as strong in the 1990s as it had been in the years originally documented in *The American Voter* (Campbell et al. 1960; see also Bartels 2000).

This all produces a bit of a puzzle. The weakening of mass partisanship was a central element in the claims of electoral dealignment that became so widespread in the 1980s and early 1990s, but it is not the only element. In particular, most of the system-level indicators of dealignment were securely in place in 2000. Lawrence (1996) has shown that changes in control of the White House from Carter to Reagan and Bush to Clinton are less indicative of electoral volatility than they initially seemed, given an historically high consistency in the pattern of the division in the popular vote for president. The continued significant role of third-party candidates, high levels of split-ticket voting, and persistently divided control of government remain clear indications of a world that looks very little like the stable party systems of the past. In this chapter, I investigate apparent divergence between individual and system trends through a careful examination of the extent and significance of the apparent resurgence of party in the 1990s.

Strength of Party Identification over Time

The concept of party identification originated in the earliest of the National Election Study (NES) surveys conducted by the Survey Research Center at the University of Michigan, published in landmark works such as *The Voter Decides* (Campbell, Gurin, and Miller 1954) and *The American Voter* (Campbell et al. 1960). The Michigan researchers discovered that ordinary citizens readily responded to a two-part survey question designed to determine if they identified with one of the two major American political parties. The first question simply asked, "Generally speaking, do you usually think of yourself as a Republican, a Democrat, an Independent, or what?" One follow-up question asked those who thought of themselves as Democrats (or Republicans) whether they thought of themselves as strong or not very strong Democrats (or Republicans). Another follow-up question asked those who initially did not think of themselves as Democrats or Republicans whether they thought of themselves as closer to one or the other party (*American National Election Studies* 1998). The result of combining the two responses from each respondent is a seven-point party identification scale (Figure 2-1).

The Michigan researchers saw party identification at the core of most citizens' political consciousness. An embryonic partisanship was visible in young

Figure 2-1. National Election Study Party Identification Scale

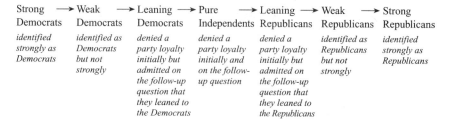

Strong → Democrats	Weak → Democrats	Leaning → Democrats	Pure → Independents	Leaning → Republicans	Weak → Republicans	Strong Republicans
identified strongly as Democrats	*identified as Democrats but not strongly*	*denied a party loyalty initially but admitted on the follow-up question that they leaned to the Democrats*	*denied a party loyalty initially and on the follow-up question*	*denied a party loyalty initially but admitted on the follow-up question that they leaned to the Republicans*	*identified as Republicans but not strongly*	*identified strongly as Republicans*

children, who inherited it from their parents. Young people used this party identification as a lens through which inherently ambiguous and confusing political reality was selectively perceived. Issues, candidates, and elected officials were all evaluated with the aid of party identification, producing an ever-increasing pool of partisan preferences that reinforced and strengthened the initial bias. So powerful and so fundamental were these party loyalties that even on those rare occasions on which a voter abandoned his or her own party's candidate in a given election, party identification survived, able to reassert itself as soon as the source of the aberrant defection passed. Party identification was the mechanism by which Americans connected psychologically with the political process: Identifiers were more interested in politics, paid more attention to campaigns, and were more knowledgeable about political issues than were independents.

Table 2-1 reports a mean partisanship score for the twelve NES surveys from 1952 to 1996. Pure independents are coded as 1, leaners as 2, weak partisans as 3, and strong partisans at the maximum value of 4. The mean score, crude though it is, shows clearly the decline in the psychological attribute of strength of partisanship, one of the indicators so important to dealignment theorists. After hovering around 3.03 to 3.07 from 1952 to 1964, with no clear pattern of rise or fall over the twelve years, the mean score begins a consistent fall in 1968 that reaches a low of 2.744 in 1980. This represents a decline of 9.6 percent from the 3.035 mean of 1956, the election year on which *The American Voter* was based, and a slightly greater fall of 10.7 percent from the high point of 1964. Although the low value is for 1980, the pattern of means makes clear that the decline in strength of partisanship that began after 1964 was essentially completed by 1976: The 1980 entry is barely lower than that for 1976.

What happens after 1980, however, is difficult to reconcile with a dealignment scenario: Mean partisanship rises in the four elections after 1980. The rise

David G. Lawrence

Table 2-1. Trends in Strength of Partisanship, 1952–1996

Year	Mean Strength of Partisanship
1952	3.057
1956	3.035
1960	3.034
1964	3.074
1968	2.900
1972	2.769
1976	2.746
1980	2.744
1984	2.839
1988	2.847
1992	2.790
1996	2.897

Note: Entries are mean partisanship scores based on a 1 (independent) to 4 (strong) scale.

is considerable in 1984, continues at a slower rate in 1988, and is considerable again in 1996. The upward movement is interrupted in 1992, but the 1992 fall-off is not large enough to erase the gains of 1984 and 1988 and is itself more than reversed in 1996. The increase from 1980 through 1996 makes up 46.4 percent of the maximum fall-off from 1964 to 1980.

Two substantive conclusions flow from this preliminary analysis. First, a weakening of partisanship indisputably occurred after 1964, but the decline lasted for only ten to twelve years, ended around 1976, and has to some considerable extent reversed itself. Second, the recovery in mean mass partisanship may be inconsistent with the expectations of dealignment theorists, but in no way can it be seen to re-create the pre-1968 era of *The American Voter.* On this first indicator of strength of partisanship, the recovery is real, but it is considerably smaller in magnitude than the decline it follows.

Vote Choice and Party Identification: The Bivariate Relationship

Vote choice would initially seem to be a particularly simple concept: The voter's selection of a candidate has a clear behavioral component that ordinary citizens should understand. Postelection assessment of vote choice should merely require recall of the vote cast; the preelection measure used here might require an intermediate category for those who intend to vote but have not yet determined their preferred candidates, but it also should refer to a real-world behavioral choice of some salience to ordinary citizens. Two potentially serious complications get in the way of any easy analysis of vote choice: turnout and third parties.

The existence of nonvoting has important implications for how we understand vote choice, particularly if the question at hand is party voting. The conventional treatment of nonvoters is simply to ignore them: Respondents who state that they will not be voting have no vote choice to explain. But the logic of party voting suggests that party identification is not merely a guide to how to choose between competing candidates. It is also a mobilization process, with party identification providing an incentive to cast a ballot in the first place precisely in order to support one's party's nominee.

Those who study turnout often see partisanship as a mobilizing factor. For example, Paul R. Abramson and John H. Aldrich (1982) consider a decrease in strength of partisanship as a major cause of the decline in turnout after 1960. But partisanship as mobilization has implications for vote choice as well: Partisans who do not get to the polls and who thereby fail to support their own parties' nominees clearly represent a failure of party voting, even if the failure is not quite as striking as supporting an opposing party's candidate might be. The simultaneous weakening of partisanship and decrease in turnout between 1968 and 1976 may reflect a deterioration in the ability of parties to act as mobilizing institutions that should be reflected in our measure of party voting.

Third parties are a second source of complexity in the analysis of vote choice, interfering with the clear ordering in the categories of vote choice (Democratic, undecided, Republican) in a way that complicates both substantive interpretation and statistical analysis. In the classic period of *The American Voter,* one could ignore the problem: There were no significant third parties to deal with, and analysis could therefore ignore the relatively few citizens who claimed to vote for one of them without losing large numbers of cases or complicating substantive findings. The few third-party voters who turned up were largely treated as missing data.

Emergence after 1968 of a persistent stream of third-party candidates who attracted widespread electoral support makes such an easy solution impossible. One cannot simply ignore supporters of candidates such as Wallace, Anderson, and Perot without losing large numbers of scarce and valuable respondents. More important, the variety of ways of including third-party candidates in a vote choice variable raises serious questions about how to compare elections that had significant third-party candidates (such as the election of 1968) with

David G. Lawrence

each other or with elections that did not (such as the election of 1956). For example, an analysis of the relationship between region and vote choice in 1968 that simply omits Wallace voters would produce the somewhat bizarre conclusion that the Democrats did only very slightly less badly in the white South than they did among whites elsewhere, a conclusion that clearly misses the significance of the concentration of Wallace voters among white southerners. Similarly, an analysis of social class and vote choice in 1968 that omits Wallace voters would suggest that class polarization was as great in 1968 as in any other post-1948 presidential election, a finding that is severely undermined if one looks at Wallace's strength among voters of relatively low socioeconomic status. Such analyses are particularly misleading given the potentially great significance of third parties as proto-realignment phenomena, that is, indicators of the inability of existing partisan coalitions to contain new and crosscutting issues that have the potential to realign an existing party system (Burnham 1970).

Multiple statistical techniques are available to analyze the impact of third-party voters (that is, without having to place them on a left-right or Democratic-Republican continuum). But such techniques are more complicated and harder to interpret than those used to analyze the more direct relationship provided by a two-party race (with undecideds occupying a position between the two major parties).

A first look at the relationship between party identification and vote choice is reported in the left column in Table 2-2. This column reports the association between party identification and a vote intention variable in which both nonvoters and third-party voters are excluded.[1]

The data in Table 2-2 on the link between party identification and vote choice are initially strikingly parallel to the data in Table 2-1 about strength of partisanship as a psychological attribute. Although some of the details and the precise timing differ, the overall patterns of change over time are quite similar. Table 2-2 shows a consistently high relationship of around 0.53 between party identification and vote choice in 1952–1960. This relationship corresponds to the stable high mean partisanship in those years (see Table 2-1) and reinforces the image of the late 1950s as a golden age in the strength of party identification. The two tables diverge somewhat in 1964. Strength of mass partisanship (see Table 2-1) remains at its previously high level in 1964; the decline that be-

---

1. The coefficient used is Somer's D, an asymmetric measure of ordinal association that in this case treats vote choice as a dependent variable and party identification as an independent variable.

Table 2-2. Party Identification and the Vote Choice, 1952–1996

Year	Two-Party Vote Choice*	All-Party Vote Choice**
1952	0.52	0.49
1956	0.54	0.53
1960	0.53	0.52
1964	0.41	0.40
1968	0.52	0.41
1972	0.38	0.37
1976	0.44	0.42
1980	0.47	0.38
1984	0.48	0.47
1988	0.50	0.49
1992	0.50	0.44
1996	0.51	0.48

* Nonvoters and third-party voters are excluded.

** Nonvoters counted as undecided and third-party voters counted as defectors.

Note: Entries are Somer's D (asymmetric) between vote choice and party identification. The seven-point party identification scale is used.

comes so obvious in the next decade does not begin until 1968. In Table 2-2, however, party has already begun to disintegrate as a source of vote choice in 1964, a development that would seem to be easily explicable by reference to the unprecedented pressures for defection among Republicans caused by the Goldwater nomination in that year. These defections, usually seen as indicative of the kind of ideological conflicts that divide partisan coalitions late in the life cycle of a party system and as indications of an approaching realignment, were the first signs of the forces that were to depress both the link between party identification and vote choice and the strength of party identification as a psychological force thereafter.

The 1968 election is the first in which handling of a third-party candidacy seriously affects the results in Table 2-2. The left column in the table suggests a considerable increase in the relationship between party identification and vote choice in 1968 from the level of four years earlier: The association rises from 0.41 in 1964 to 0.52, a value that is indistinguishable from the high levels of 1952–1960 and that indicates the considerable impact of party identification for those who chose between Humphrey and Nixon. Yet this value is

David G. Lawrence

misleading, being based on entirely ignoring the large number of partisans who planned to vote for Wallace. The year 1968 is therefore the appropriate place to introduce a way of thinking about third-party voters that is sensitive to the logic of defection that a simpler conceptualization of vote choice misses.

In a two-candidate race, defection consists of voting for the nominee of the opposing party. What is distinctive about the three-candidate race is the availability of more than one candidate not nominated by one's own party. For many purposes, the question of whether one votes for the other major party's nominee or for the nominee of a third party is important; but for the question of party voting that concerns us here, it is not. In elections with third-party candidates, there is simply more than one opposition candidate to whom one can defect. Whether a Democrat defects to vote for Nixon or for Wallace is irrelevant; in either case, a Democrat has voted for a candidate other than the nominee of his or her own party.

The operationalization of third-party voters as defectors that follows from this observation is straightforward. The new, defection-sensitive version of vote choice remains a three-value variable: All respondents who did not vote for a third-party candidate fall into the familiar categories of Democrat, undecided, or Republican. The treatment of third-party voters, however, is novel: Any partisan who plans to vote for a third-party candidate is put into the same category as a major-party defector. For example, Democrats who voted for Wallace in 1968 are put into the same category as Democrats who voted for Nixon, and Republicans who voted for Wallace are put into the same category as Republicans who voted for Humphrey.[2] The resulting variable is of no use in reporting vote choice per se, but it is useful in analyzing the impact of party on vote choice.

The right column in Table 2-2 reports the relationship for this defection-sensitive measure of vote choice and party identification, and it gives a clear indication of the dramatic decline in party voting in the twelve-year period between 1960 and 1972. The relationships for the party identification measure in 1952 to 1964 are essentially the same as for the vote choice variable that excludes nonvoters and third-party voters. None of the four elections had a major third-party candidate. Inclusion of the few citizens who nonetheless say they voted for a third-party candidate and the much larger number of nonvoters lowers the association in the right column only slightly. For 1968 the difference be-

2. Independents who vote for a third party are grouped with independents who are undecided. By definition, voting for a third-party candidate (or for anybody else) cannot be a defection for independents.

tween the two columns of the table is substantial: the 0.52 value on the left suggests that party identification is essentially as important for those who chose between major-party candidates in 1968 as it had been in 1956, the year on which *The American Voter* was based; the 0.41 on the right indicates the effect of treating Wallace-voting partisans as the defectors they in fact are. The way we handle nonvoters has rather modest impact on the relationship between party identification and vote choice, but the way we treat third-party voters turns out to be extremely important. The defection-sensitive version of vote choice is clearly the superior version.

Once we treat third-party voters the same way we treat major-party defectors, the pattern for the link between party identification and vote choice (see Table 2-2) shows a striking parallel to the data on strength of party identification (see Table 2-1). The 1968 data become part of a series of low associations between party identification and vote choice that begins in 1964 and extends through 1980. A modest rise in 1976 (a year without a major third-party challenger) is followed by a fall to 0.38 in 1980 that is essentially as low as any in the 1964–1980 period as a whole. The impact of party identification deteriorates in 1964, one election before the impact of the strength variable does; but the reason for its doing so makes considerable sense in terms of both the specifics of the 1964 election and the time lags expected in adjusting party loyalties to new circumstances. Dealignment theorists could scan the data to this point and see no reason to doubt their central thesis of party decline beginning in the mid-1960s.

The data after 1980 again pose a problem for those who support a simple dealignment hypothesis, and they are particularly troubling for those who think that Miller and Shanks's (1996) findings of a resurgent party identification is due solely to the way they handle nonvoters and third-party voters. The association rises from 0.38 in 1980 to 0.47 in 1984, a level higher than for any year since 1960, though slightly below the levels for 1952–1960. A further rise to 0.49 in 1988 makes clear that the recovery in the impact of party identification on vote choice is not an aberrant year-specific occurrence; and although the first Clinton election shows a modest fall-off to 0.44, his reelection year produces a resurgence to 0.48. The recovery in the apparent impact of partisanship is certainly greater when nonvoters and third-party voters are excluded: 81.3 percent of the loss suffered between 1956 and 1972 is recovered by 1996, compared with a recovery of only 68.8 percent if abstention and defection are properly recognized. Even when abstention and defection are properly recognized, however, the recovery in the impact is substantial in absolute terms and com-

David G. Lawrence

pared with the relatively modest recovery of 46.4 percent in the strength of partisanship.

Impact of Party Identification on Vote Choice: Confounding Factors

Two separate indicators point to an increase in the importance of mass partisanship that began by the early 1980s, following and to at least some extent reversing the dramatic decline of party in the decade beginning in the mid-1960s. The findings for the impact of party identification (that is, its link to vote choice) are more impressive than for strength of partisanship as a psychological factor. The recovery on the strength dimension is 46.4 percent; the recovery in impact is 68.8 percent. In neither case is all of the decline recovered, but the recovery for impact is considerable.

The difference in the extent to which the two indicators have strengthened themselves raises questions about the significance of the change. A recovery of about 45 percent indicates a reversal of the earlier weakening of party loyalties but leaves the current levels well below those of the golden age of party identification described in *The American Voter*; a recovery of nearly 70 percent suggests that the late 1990s look much more like the 1950s. The smaller recovery would suggest continuing dealignment of the electoral universe, albeit to a somewhat lesser extent than in the 1970s. The larger recovery would suggest the return of something much more like a return of the stable party system of classic realignment theory, however unlikely a new era of unified control of government might seem for the moment.

If one is concerned about the divergence in the two indicators of partisanship, it is surely impact rather than strength that seems questionable. On substantive grounds, an argument that dealignment continues in a somewhat weakened form conforms much better with system-level phenomena such as outcome volatility, split-ticket voting, and divided control of government than does an argument for an almost total reemergence of a strong party system. The relatively modest resurgence of party suggested by the strength dimension is also more plausible given the simplicity of the indicator: the familiar survey questions used to measure party identification in the first place. The impact dimension, which suggests larger resurgence of party, is conceptually and methodologically more complicated as well as substantively less plausible. It depends on the link between party identification and vote choice, a link that can be affected by several other factors that might play a role in explaining both the decline and the recovery in impact over time. Controlling for such factors is necessary to make the large increase in impact—and any resulting claims of the restoration of something that might resemble a stable party system—credible.

Issue Orientation

The divergence between the strength and impact of partisanship may result from other sources of vote choice that deflate the impact of party in the 1970s and exaggerate it thereafter. More specifically, the Democrats have been the larger of the two parties in numbers of identifiers since World War II, despite their fairly sorry pattern of presidential election outcomes in the years between Lyndon Johnson and Bill Clinton; the Republican surge in the mid-1980s narrowed the gap in number of identifiers, but it did not eliminate it.[3] The reason for the pattern of Republican presidential election victories lies in the Republicans' ability to dominate the Democrats on short-term considerations such as issue orientation and candidate orientation, producing sufficient numbers of cross-pressured Democrats and sufficient numbers of Democratic defectors to offset their initial party identification disadvantage.[4]

The interplay between Republican short-term forces and Democratic Party identification could explain variation in the impact of party identification on vote choice over time in three ways. First, in the 1970s this interplay produces cross-pressures that cause Democrats to defect in numbers sufficient both to defeat the majority party and to weaken the statistical relationship between party identification (which was still strongly Democratic) and vote choice (which clearly was not). Second, the tension between short- and long-term factors eases around 1984 as modest Republican gains in number of identifiers reduces the number of cross-pressured Democrats. Third, the Clinton years produce Democratic gains on short-term factors that reduce the number of cross-pressured Democrats and allow the majority party, however reduced its majority might be, to again win the White House.

---

3. Democrats outnumbered Republicans by 59 percent in 1980 (52.1 percent Democrats, 32.8 percent Republicans), a level slightly higher than in the two previous elections. These values fall to 21 percent in 1984 and 15 percent in 1988 before rebounding to 29 percent (49.8 percent Democrats, 38.6 percent Republicans) in 1992.

4. A cross-pressured voter is simply someone pushed in opposing directions by different causal forces, for example, a Democratic identifier who prefers the Republican candidate on the issues. A cross-pressured voter cannot act consistently with both forces simultaneously, as a Democratic identifier who prefers the Democratic candidate on issues can. In a sense, cross-pressured voters must choose between competing and opposing forces.

David G. Lawrence

Figure 2–2. Party and Issues: Cross-Pressures, 1952–1996

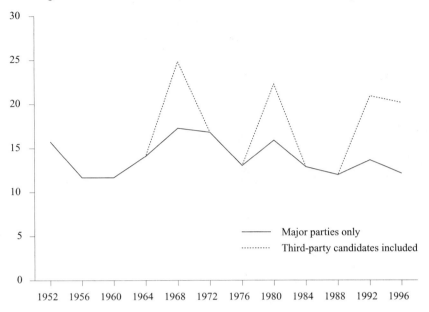

Percentage of Identifiers Whose Issue Orientation Conflicts with Their Party

Issue orientation is measured here as a simple combination of issue-related likes and dislikes of the parties and candidates expressed in open-ended questions that the NES surveys have used since 1952.[5] Figure 2-2 traces the percentage of cross-pressured respondents over the twelve election periods studied. The percentage of identifiers who prefer the opposition on issues falls from 15.8 percent in 1952 to a low level of 11.6 percent in both 1956 and 1960.[6] Cross-pressures increase thereafter, as the new issues of the 1960s and 1970s have their expected effect: The solid line indicates cross-pressures that involve the major parties alone (increasing to 17.3 percent in 1968). An uneven but

5. The great virtue of the measure is its open-endedness. It allows respondents to mention whatever kind of issue might be meaningful to them. It also maximizes exhaustiveness by freeing respondents from investigators' preconceived notions about what kinds of issues might be important, and it ensures at least minimal salience by forcing respondents to take the initiative in mentioning a subject. Weaknesses of the measure include that it weights all mentions equally, ignoring whatever differences in intensity the respondent might have, and that it is sensitive to articulateness, picking up more mentions from respondents who are more verbally self-confident or skilled. These are the same questions that, analyzed differently, produce the well-known measure of "levels of conceptualization" that has been widely reported since *The American Voter*.

6. The 1952 data indicate that the first Eisenhower-Stevenson election was somewhat different than the relatively placid 1956 rematch documented in *The American Voter*.

On the Resurgence of Party Identification in the 1990s **41** nonetheless clear decrease in the number of cross-pressures begins thereafter, reaching 12.0 percent in 1988 and 12.1 percent in 1996. The cross-pressure value for 1996 is all but identical to the 11.6 percent value in 1956 and 1960.[7]

The complicating effects of third parties are greater in dealing with issues than they are in dealing with party identification. Almost no respondents in any of the election years studied indicate that they identify with a third party, but the open-ended likes and dislikes questions produce a rather rich set of comments about Wallace, Anderson, and Perot.[8] Incorporating such comments produces a rather different picture of the extent to which citizens are cross-pressured (shown by the broken line in Figure 2-2). In 1968 the proportion of cross-pressured respondents rises from 17.3 percent when Wallace is ignored to 24.9 percent when perceptions of him are included. Some 56.7 percent of Democrats support Humphrey over Nixon on issues in a one-to-one comparison, a figure already somewhat smaller than the 66.5 percent to 72.7 percent levels Democratic nominees achieved in earlier years.[9] But a sizable number of Democrats prefer Wallace on issues: 12.9 percent of them prefer Wallace to either Humphrey or Nixon, and the proportion who prefer Humphrey in the three-candidate race falls to 49.4 percent.[10]

The years 1980, 1992, and 1996 show similar sharp increases in the number of cross-pressured respondents once third-party candidates are included in the analysis. The amount of cross-pressure falls slightly from one three-party race to the next, but all four years show a sharp increase in the number of

7. In 1964, Republicans are disproportionately cross-pressured, whereas in 1968 Democrats are disproportionately cross-pressured. In other years the differences between the parties are small, although the total number of cross-pressured Democrats is larger given the gap in the size of the two groups of identifiers.

8. These are the only third-party candidates for whom the like-dislike questions are asked. Note that the questions are asked about the candidates alone, not about whatever parties might have nominated them.

9. In contrast, Republicans limited to the two-candidate race are loyal to Nixon on issues at a level of 74.7 percent that is indistinguishable from the 74.9 percent they had given Eisenhower in 1952.

10. Preference for Wallace is not simply due to a dislike for the major-party candidates combined with a neutral or less negative view of Wallace: 82.9 percent of Democrats who preferred Wallace had a positive attitude toward him. But Democrats preferring Wallace *were* more likely to have already preferred Nixon to Humphrey (5.4 percent of all Democrats) or to have been indifferent to the major-party candidates (4.9 percent) than to have preferred Humphrey (2.7 percent); 9.9 percent of Democrats who preferred Wallace had a favorable image of Humphrey on issues, whereas 62.3 percent were unfavorable. Of those who supported Wallace on issues more generally, 39.4 percent had negative attitudes toward both Humphrey and Nixon, 25.7 percent were negative toward one and neutral toward the other, 20.7 percent were neutral toward both, and only the remaining 14.2 percent were on balance positive toward either of the major-party candidates.

cross-pressured respondents once the third candidate is included. Any impression of a general decline in the extent of cross-pressure over time is clearly destroyed.[11]

The implications of these results on the impact of party identification are mixed. Availability of third candidates increases the number of cross-pressured respondents, creating a possible motivation for defection that is almost as strong in 1992 and 1996 as it was in 1968 and is far higher than in the two-candidate race of 1972.[12] When we consider alternatives to voting for the major parties, the existence of so many cross-pressured respondents late in the period greatly decreases the likelihood that party would be as strong in 1996 as Miller and Shanks thought.

But the mere existence of cross-pressures tells us nothing about the impact of party on vote choice. The cross-pressured respondent must choose between party and issues, and more cross-pressured respondents certainly mean more respondents with a reason to abandon their parties. But not every respondent

11. Anderson's appeal is relatively evenly distributed across the two groups of partisans: He is preferred on issues by 9.2 percent of Democrats and 7.8 percent of Republicans, and another 12.1 percent of Democrats and 14.2 percent of Republicans are indifferent between Anderson and their own parties' nominees, preferring either candidate to the opposing parties' candidates. As for Wallace, support for Perot on issues is more skewed, this time being greater among Republicans: He is the preferred candidate on issues for 14.4 percent of Republicans in 1992 and for only 6.2 percent of Democrats; four years later the figures are only modestly different: 13.4 percent and 7.5 percent. Anderson is also distinctive in that a relatively small 39.1 percent of respondents who prefer him actually support him on issues. The others prefer him to Carter and Reagan, but only because they have negative attitudes toward those candidates. Perot is supported by 55.4 percent of those who prefer him in 1992 and by 72.5 percent of those who prefer him in 1996, suggesting that his performance in the latter year is based more on genuinely positive feelings toward him than on rejection of the major-party alternatives. Yet even his 1996 figure pales in comparison with the genuine enthusiasm of the 82.9 percent of his supporters who had genuinely approved of Wallace on issues in 1968.

12. Relatively unfavorable attitudes toward parties and candidates on issues after 1968 might have given any third-party candidate a relatively positive score on issues in those years, if neutrality toward the interloper were combined with negative attitudes toward major-party candidates. If that were the case, the results for 1968, 1980, 1992, and 1996 would be less due to peculiarities of the electorate in those years than to elite-level factors that prevented the emergence of a major challenge to the Democrats and Republicans. If we look at the simple sum of open-ended responses, major-party candidates were particularly unpopular on issues in 1980 and 1992: The population had more negative than positive things to say about them. The two other years in which there were third-party challenges, 1968 and 1996, showed a net positive evaluation of the candidates and parties, whereas 1976 and 1984, both lacking third-party challenges, had candidates who were relatively unpopular on issues. This is consistent with the situation in 1968 and 1996, when third-party voters were relatively enthusiastic about their own candidates rather than simply rejecting the major-party candidates. The years 1956, 1960, and 1952, as one might suspect, had the highest net positive candidate-evaluation scores on issues; 1972 and 1976 were the years without third-party challenges in which simultaneous dislike of the major-party candidates was relatively great.

On the Resurgence of Party Identification in the 1990s **43**

Figure 2–3. Resolution of Cross-Pressures: Party and Vote, 1952–1996

Percentage of Cross-Pressured Who Intend to Vote with Party

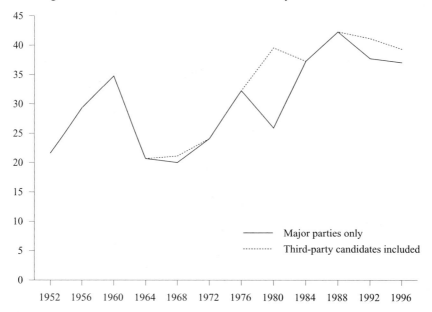

with a reason to abandon party will do so, and the respondents whose cross-pressures are due to third-party candidates might be particularly unlikely to do so. Many of those who prefer third-party candidates on issues might nonetheless vote for major-party candidates for strategic reasons: Third-party candidates have no realistic chance to be elected. The inclusion of third parties might increase the number of cross-pressured respondents, but it might also increase the percentage of cross-pressured respondents who vote with their parties rather than with their issues.[13]

The resolution of cross-pressure between party and issues is indicated in Figure 2-3, which shows the percentage of cross-pressured respondents who vote with their parties in each year. In none of the election years do a majority

13. Furthermore, the inclusion of third-party candidates may well improve the predictiveness of issues for the major-party candidates. For example, pretending that Perot did not exist creates the possibility that someone who appears to prefer Clinton to Bush in fact prefers Perot to both. In 1992, to continue with this example, only 64.5 percent of voters who prefer Clinton to Bush on issue orientation in fact vote for him, a figure no higher than for Dukakis. The reason is that some voters who prefer Clinton to Bush really do prefer Perot: If those who really prefer Perot are separated out, leaving only those who truly prefer Clinton on issues, 73.6 percent of them vote for him.

David G. Lawrence

of the cross-pressured respondents vote with their parties, but the degree to which they do so varies over time in ways that are quite consistent with the resurgence of party since 1968.

The relative impact of party and issues in determining the vote choice of cross-pressured respondents (see Figure 2-3) shows a somewhat different pattern than the stable 1950s, dealigning 1970s, and resurging 1980s and 1990s pattern shown by some other indicators. Nonetheless, this impact is quite consistent with the resurgence of party over time. Party is rather weak among the cross-pressured respondents in 1952, when only 21.6 percent of the cross-pressured respondents voted with their parties, although the impact of party increases to as high as 34.7 percent in 1960. A sharp decline in the impact of party among the cross-pressured respondents begins immediately thereafter, however, and the 1968 election, which marks the high point in the number of cross-pressures, essentially matches the 1964 low for the extent to which such cross-pressures are resolved in favor of party. Thereafter, the recovery in the impact of party among the cross-pressured respondents occurs at the same time that the number of cross-pressured respondents is falling. By 1980, party is more powerful among the cross-pressured respondents than it had been in 1960, and its strength continues to a high of 42.3 percent in 1988. The modest fall-off thereafter to 37.0 percent still leaves party as important among the cross-pressured respondents in 1996 as it was before 1988.

Most striking in Figure 2-3 is the impact of including cross-pressures due to third-party candidates. In the simple analysis of party identification and vote choice described earlier in this chapter, the inclusion of third-party candidates reduces the apparent effects of party. Because partisans who vote for a third party are necessarily defectors, their existence lowers the impact of party identification generally. But cross-pressures due to issue preferences for third-party candidates are disproportionately resolved by remaining loyal to one's party. In 1968, the effect is modest: Wallace seems to have won a considerable number of votes from partisans who preferred him on issues. But the percentage of respondents loyal to party in cross-pressured situations nonetheless rises slightly from 19.9 percent to 21.1 percent when those who preferred Wallace on issues are included. In the three other years with third-party candidates, the impact of party is far greater. In 1980, an apparent decline in the effects of party is dramatically reversed when those who preferred Anderson on issues are included: Anderson won the votes of only 35.1 percent of partisans who preferred him on issues, whereas Wallace held the votes of 51.6 percent of those who preferred him. The inclusion of Anderson raises the percentage of cross-pressured respondents who remain loyal to their party from 25.9 percent to 39.6 percent. In the Clinton years, the effects of adding Perot fall between the modest impact of 1968 and the great impact of 1980. Around 40 percent of the cross-pressured respondents vote with their parties in each year, levels extremely high in historical perspective, which suggests that the relatively large number of cross-pressured respondents in these two elections need not produce an overall decrease in the impact of party on vote choice.

Candidate Orientation

A second factor that might affect the relationship between party identification and vote choice is candidate orientation. A candidate orientation that reflects citizens' likes or dislikes for the candidates as individual personalities, as opposed to perceptions based on issue or party considerations, is unlikely to have the theoretical centrality of issue orientation. It is not necessarily linked to the great crosscutting issues that rent the party coalitions in the 1960s and 1970s; therefore, it is less likely to play much of a role in realignment or dealignment. The period covered by these elections has undoubtedly included some extremely popular or unpopular candidates who could nonetheless create cross-pressures with party identification and thereby affect the way that party affects vote choice.

Figure 2-4 shows the incidence of cross-pressures between candidate orientation and vote choice in the twelve NES surveys, just as Figure 2-2 did for cross-pressures involving issue orientation.[14] Figure 2-4 differs rather dramatically in some ways from Figure 2-2. The increase in the number of cross-pressured partisans continues through 1972, but the decline thereafter is far greater for candidates than for issues, and the level of cross-pressures involving candidate orientation in the late 1980s is far lower than it was in the 1950s. The slight increase in the Clinton years results in still substantially fewer cross-pressured votes than were present in the Eisenhower years.[15]

Including third-party candidates again has substantial effects on the number of cross-pressured respondents. Actual support for the third-party candidate

14. Candidate orientation is a simple sum of the personal preferences given in response to the open-ended like-dislike questions. The variable again has the classic advantages of open-ended questions: exhaustiveness and salience. Closed-ended questions about candidate attributes are suspect on both counts. "Feeling thermometer" questions (Funk 1999), which ask overall how warm or cold a respondent feels toward a political object, fail to limit consideration to personal (as opposed to issues and party) concerns.

15. The decline in the number of cross-pressured respondents over time is not particularly due to an increase in the number of partisans who prefer their own candidates; rather, the number of partisans with no preference on candidate orientation rises, particularly in 1988.

Figure 2–4. Party and Candidates: Cross-Pressures, 1952–1996

Percentage of Identifiers Whose Party and Candidate Preferences Differ

(or equal dislike for both of the major-party candidates) produces a fairly sizable number of respondents with a net preference for Wallace, Anderson, or Perot. Every year with a third-party candidate has a larger number of respondents cross-pressured between candidate and party than any year without a third-party candidate. Once the third-party candidates are included, the number of cross-pressured respondents behaves in a way that could certainly contribute to the decline in the impact of party in the late 1960s and 1970s; but it does not particularly suggest a basis for the recovery in the impact of party in the Clinton years.

As Figure 2-5 shows, however, these cross-pressures are again resolved in a way that reinforces the apparent impact of party on vote choice. Respondents cross-pressured between the candidate they most like and their party increasingly vote with candidate orientation between 1952 and 1972. Party is of steadily decreasing importance, even in 1952–1960, a situation not really changed by inclusion of those who prefer Wallace to their own parties' candidates in 1968.

The recovery in the impact of candidate orientation begins immediately after 1972. The rise is temporarily interrupted, rather modestly, in 1980 if we exclude Anderson; but inclusion of third-party candidates produces upward

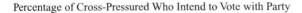

Figure 2–5. Resolution of Cross-Pressures:
Party and Candidate Orientation, 1952–1996

Percentage of Cross-Pressured Who Intend to Vote with Party

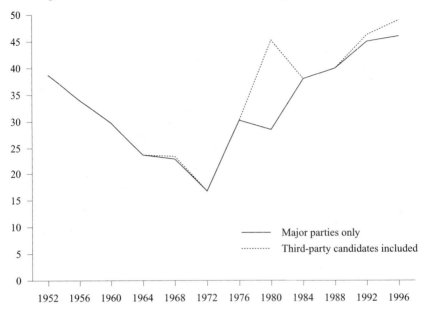

movement in the impact of party in 1980, a modest decrease in 1984 to a level approximately the same as in 1952, and a continuing increase to unprecedented highs thereafter. In 1996, regardless of how we handle Perot, party is stronger than it has ever been among the cross-pressured respondents and at least 50 percent more powerful than it was in 1964–1976.

Impact of Party Identification: Controlling for Issue Orientation and Candidate Orientation

The frequency and resolution of cross-pressures between party identification and issue orientation and candidate orientation raise the possibility that the increase in the impact of party over time is real. The extent of two-party cross-pressures declines somewhat after peaking in the early 1970s. At the same time, party becomes substantially more dominant for those who have to resolve their cross-pressures. Third-party candidates certainly are a possible cause of defection from party identification, and the availability of third-party candi-

David G. Lawrence

Figure 2–6. Impact of Party Identification on Vote Choice, 1952–1996

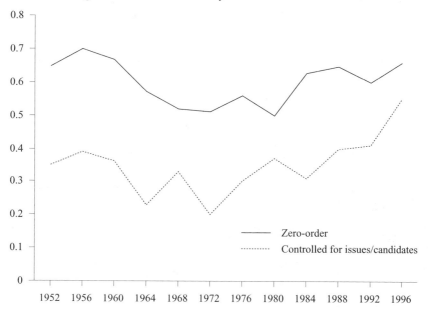

Standardized Regression Coefficients for Party

dates considerably increases the number of citizens who are torn between the party with which they identify and the issues or candidates they prefer. Cross-pressures involving third-party candidates are particularly likely to be resolved in favor of party.

Figure 2-6 presents a multivariate analysis of the impact of party by presenting coefficients that estimate the impact of party identification on vote choice both before and after controls for issue orientation and candidate orientation have been introduced.[16] Issue and candidate perceptions of Wallace, Anderson, and Perot are included.

The top curve in Figure 2-6 presents the simple bivariate relationship between the seven-point party identification variable and our defection-sensitive vote choice variable. The shape of this curve is almost entirely congruent with the associations between the two variables in Table 2-2, the simple relationship that initially indicated the divergence between strength and impact of party.

16. The coefficients are standardized regression coefficients. Ordinary least squares regression is presented because its coefficients provide a widely understood and easily interpretable estimate of the effects of the independent variables.

The lower curve reports the coefficient after measures of issue and candidate orientations have been added to the equation. For years without third-party candidates, these measures are a simple balance of Democratic and Republican preferences; for 1968, 1980, 1992, and 1996 these measures also include a full set of possible preferences for the third-party candidates.[17]

In some ways the two curves in Figure 2-6 resemble each other: An initially relatively high coefficient in 1952–1960 deteriorates thereafter, hitting a new low in 1972. Both curves then begin to rise, but the pattern of increase begins earlier, is more consistent, and is greater in magnitude for the controlled coefficient: The controlled coefficient never matches its 1972 low, whereas the zero-order coefficient does; and the zero-order coefficient barely reaches the levels of 1952–1960, whereas the controlled coefficient consistently exceeds the 1952–1960 levels in all three elections after 1984. The presence of third-party candidates has only very modest impact on the increased importance of party over time. The result for 1968 breaks the curve's general smoothness, and third-party years show a slightly smaller deviation between zero-order and controlled betas. The Anderson and Perot years form part of a general increase in the controlled beta in Figure 2-6, into which two-party races such as 1976, 1984, and 1988 fit nicely.[18]

The last piece of the puzzle about the rising impact of party over time lies in breaking down the controlled betas for different levels of strength of partisanship. Figure 2-7 reports the coefficients for party identification in equations that include issue and candidate preferences for strong, weak, and leaning identifiers separately.

17. For years without a third-party candidate, there are two variables for both issues and candidates: net Democratic preference and net Republican preference. For years with a third-party candidate, these variables are supplemented with a net preference for Wallace, Anderson, or Perot, plus a number of variables designed to reflect ties between any two of the three candidates that might produce an incentive to vote consistently or inconsistently with party. All variables involving the third-party candidates exist for Democratic and Republican identifiers separately, because the implications of a preference for the third-party candidates on our defection-sensitive vote choice variables will depend on the respondent's party identification.

18. The coefficients for the issue and candidate variables are of secondary importance here: These variables are introduced to show how including them affects the impact of party identification on vote choice. The issue and candidate measures that involve a clear preference for one of the electoral alternatives (including those for a third-party candidate) have the expected sign and are statistically significant, with the exception of Republicans who prefer Anderson and Perot (either year) on issues. A weak and not statistically significant tendency to defect exists in 1980 and 1996, and there is no effect in 1992. Of the sixteen coefficients for variables that involve ties between two of the three candidates in 1968, 1980, 1992, and 1996, fifteen take the predicted sign, but they are small in magnitude, and only ten of the sixteen are statistically significant.

David G. Lawrence

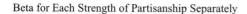

Figure 2–7. Impact of Party Identification on Vote Choice:
Different Strengths of Partisanship, 1952–1996

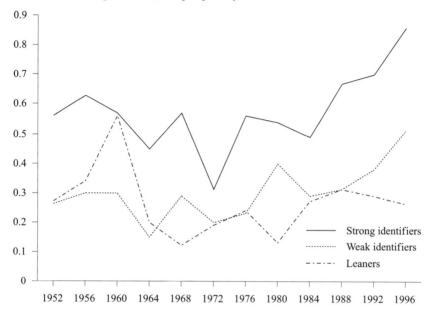

Beta for Each Strength of Partisanship Separately

The curve for strong identifiers in Figure 2–7 is an exaggerated version of the curve for the entire population. The bottoming out of impact in 1972 is followed by an irregular but clear increase that brings the beta to the level of the 1950s by 1988 and considerably exceeds it thereafter. Our conclusion about the increasing impact of party is particularly true for strong identifiers, and the impact for strong identifiers is greater than that for other strengths of identification in a way that makes sense if strong identifiers are more intense in their identification.

The curve for weak identifiers in Figure 2-7 looks more like the curve for the general population. The pattern of fall-off and recovery in impact of partisanship is clear, but the extent to which it exceeds the level of the 1950s at the end of the period is more modest. The impact of party identification on vote choice is consistently more intense for strong identifiers than for weak identifiers, and the impact of both groups' party loyalties increases over time.

The interesting group in Figure 2-7 is the leaning identifiers. The pattern of the impact of their party loyalties on vote choice differs considerably from that of the two other strengths: Its peak is in 1960, at a level that is far higher than for that of weak identifiers (and essentially the same as for strong identifiers) for that year. The decline thereafter is strong but irregular, and by the time it bottoms out in 1980 both other groups are well into their recovery. The subsequent recovery reaches its peak in 1988, never equaling the levels in 1956 or 1960, and declines in both Clinton years.

In other words, leaning identifiers do not share in the recovery in impact of party identification on vote choice over time. At a time when the impact of party is increasing for strong and weak identifiers, it changes only modestly (and somewhat erratically) for leaners. In every year through 1964, party had been more important for leaners than for weak identifiers, a rather troubling result that suggests one might have been wrong to see leaning identification as less intense than weak identification. In every year after 1976, however, once the impact of party has increased for weak identifiers while simply meandering for leaners, the coefficient in Figure 2-7 is weaker for leaners than it is for weak identifiers. Party seems to be particularly weak for leaners in 1968, 1980, and the Perot years, suggesting that the weakest of partisans are particularly susceptible to the appeal of third-party candidates.

Conclusion

The title of this chapter turns out to be far too modest: The resurgence in both strength and impact of party identification is in no sense limited to the 1990s. The decline in partisanship occurred at a rapid rate in a short period of time between 1960 and 1972, and the recovery has been going on for more than a quarter of a century. What is unique about the 1990s is that the impact of party identification on vote choice, for the population as a whole and particularly for strong partisans, has exceeded the level reached in the supposedly golden age of party dealt with in *The American Voter.*

The initial finding in this chapter was of a divergence between the rate and extent of resurgence in the strength of party identification and the impact of party identification since 1968. Strength increased modestly, a finding consistent with a modified dealignment thesis; impact increased more dramatically, to an extent more suggestive of a modified return to an era of stable party systems. My initial response to the divergence was to suggest that the latter, less consistent with system-level phenomena, was probably an artifact of the way nonvoters and third-party voters were handled. The data reported here in fact give a rather different, more complicated, and more interesting picture.

It is certainly true that the rise in strength of partisanship since the 1970s is modest. As a psychological attribute, partisanship is still considerably weaker in the electorate of the 1990s than it was in the electorate of the 1950s. But the increase in the impact of partisanship is, if anything, greater than suggested by Miller and Shanks (1996) or in the analysis with which we began. The partisan attachments that exist have even more powerful consequences for vote choice than they had forty years ago. The number of people cross-pressured between their parties and their two-party issue or candidate preferences has declined from its 1968–1976 peak to levels no higher than those of the 1950s, although bringing in third-party candidates increases them considerably. The resolution of cross-pressures is increasingly in favor of party, particularly for voters who are attracted to third-party issues and candidates. The result is a clear if irregular rise in the impact of party over time that reaches genuinely higher levels in 1996 than in the 1950s.

All this becomes clearer once we differentiate the various strengths of partisan loyalty. The general pattern is most marked for the strongest partisans, is clear for weak partisans, but is nonexistent for leaning partisans. Leaners have in two ways lowered the importance of party identification in the 1990s below what would otherwise be the case. First, they represent the only partisanship category that has increased in size since the 1950s, being on average 70.1 percent more numerous in the last three elections in the series than in the first three (in contrast, strong identifiers have declined by 16.5 percent and weak identifiers by 15.3 percent). The continued relative weakness in strength of party identification is attributable to the increased numbers of leaners. Second, the relative weakness of leaning identification as a source of vote choice helps reduce the impact of partisanship below what would be the case otherwise.

At the beginning of the twenty-first century, party is neither generally weaker nor generally stronger than in the golden age of *The American Voter.* The divergence between strength and impact cannot be resolved by saying simply that one is real and the other an illusion of some sort. If our point of comparison is the 1950s, party is both weaker *and* stronger. If our point of comparison is the late 1960s and 1970s, in contrast, such subtleties are unnecessary: For a quarter of a century, both strength and impact have been increasing. Such trends need not continue, but if they do, another three or four elections will bring strength of party identification to the level of the 1950s, and the impact of party on vote choice will be unprecedentedly high.

The deterioration of the partisan base that sustained the New Deal party system raised the specter of perpetual dealignment, an era of unstable and unpredictable election outcomes, candidate-centered elections, and divided government; and the politics of the late 1960s and early 1970s had some of the classic characteristics of a dealigned electoral universe.[19] At the system level, much evidence of dealignment continues to exist. Voter turnout remains low, third-party presidential challenges have become routine, and divided control of government seems to have a life that defies failed theories that particular parties have a lock on particular institutions. If the recovery of party is as great as the data reported in this chapter suggests, a dealigned political universe may prove to have been a brief interlude of party weakness caused by the specific tensions of American electoral politics in the mid-1960s. The tension between individual-level resurgence of party and the remaining system-level signs of partisan disaggregation may be one of the main themes of American electoral politics in the first years of the new century.

19. The volatility of American electoral outcomes was always somewhat less than initially thought: Different parties may have won successive elections, but the stability of the popular vote was no lower than in eras that have usually been considered stable. See Lawrence (1996).

David G. Lawrence

3

Evidence of Increasing Polarization Among Ordinary Citizens

Richard Fleisher and Jon R. Bond

In recent years, we witnessed an unexpected rise in the partisan behavior of policy-making elites. Beginning in the mid-1970s and accelerating in the 1980s and 1990s, party conflict among members of Congress and between the president and Congress increased considerably (Bond and Fleisher 2000; Fleisher and Bond 1996; Ornstein, Mann, and Malbin 2000; Rohde 1991). The party conflict among elites became so intense that Republicans in Congress were determined to remove President Clinton from office even though polls repeatedly showed that such a move did not have popular support. Some analysts have argued that heightened partisan polarization among elites put them out of touch with the voters, leaving many voters angry and alienated (Craig 1996; Dionne 1991; Tolchin 1996). According to this view, voters who are basically moderate and pragmatic in their political orientations have become turned off by the incessant partisan bickering in government.

The onset of increased party conflict among elites was clearly inconsistent with studies indicating that political party was becoming less important in American political life. A number of scholars argued that the nation was undergoing a dealignment. The cornerstone of the dealignment thesis was the weakening of political parties in the electoral arena. Election campaigns became candidate centered as elites running for public office were less depend-

We wish to thank the Graduate School of Arts and Sciences at Fordham University and the Department of Political Science at Texas A&M University for the support provided for this study. The Center for Presidential Studies at Texas A&M University supplied data on public approval of the president's job performance from 1988 to 1994. These organizations bear no responsibility for the interpretations and conclusions reported here. We owe special thanks to Stephen Hanna, Glen Krutz, and Mike McCleod for their assistance in the analysis, presentation, and interpretation of the data. We also gratefully acknowledge helpful comments from Frank Baumgartner, Jeffrey Cohen, Bob Erikson, Jim Gibson, Susan Hammond, Patricia Hurley, Gary Jacobson, Bryan Jones, David Lawrence, Jan Leighley, Warren Miller, and Kent Tedin.

ent on political parties to get their messages out to voters and could make appeals to voters across party lines. Scholars of electoral behavior, unable to find evidence of a realignment of the parties, instead coined a new concept, dealignment, to characterize an electorate whose attitudes and behaviors were less influenced by party affiliations.

Evidence supporting the dealignment thesis was widespread. Compared with voters in the 1950s and 1960s, those in the 1970s were less likely to declare themselves to be partisans and those that did often expressed weaker partisan attachments (Beck 1984; Burnham 1970, 1975; Ladd 1982, 1985; Ladd with Hadley 1978; Nie, Verba, and Petrocik 1979; Wattenberg 1984, 1991, 1994). As political parties became less salient to voters (Wattenberg 1984), the impact of party identification on vote choice declined and split-ticket voting increased (Ornstein, Mann, and Malbin 2000, 70–71; Stanley and Niemi 2000, 133; Wattenberg 1984, 1994, 162–166). These developments seemed to provide abundant evidence of a dealigning electorate. A recent account of contemporary electoral politics concludes, "For the moment 'dealignment' seems to be [an] accurate term to describe the American political scene" (Abramson, Aldrich, and Rohde 1999, 290).

Although parts of the argument of a general weakening in the partisan attitudes and behaviors of the American electorate are undoubtedly correct, we believe that advocates of the dealignment thesis have missed some cross-currents swirling around the American electorate. Rather than observing clear signs of a unidirectional march toward weaker partisanship, recent research offers evidence of heightened party polarization among ordinary citizens. In this chapter, we present additional evidence showing change in mass political attitudes consistent with an argument of heightened polarization among ordinary citizens.

Trends in Partisanship Among Ordinary Citizens

A careful reading of the literature on electoral behavior and public opinion provides initial cause to question whether dealignment is an adequate characterization of electoral politics. The slide toward weaker party identification, for example, seems to have stalled (Miller and Shanks 1996; Stanley and Niemi 2000, 112). Consistent with the dealignment thesis, the percentage of strong partisans (strong Democrats plus strong Republicans) declined between 1952 and 1978. Beginning with the 1980 presidential election, however, the trend reversed, and the proportion of strong partisans in the electorate began to rise.

Richard Fleisher and Jon R. Bond

From a low of 23 percent of the electorate in 1978, the percentage of strong partisans increased to 32 percent in 1996, the largest number of strong partisans in more than three decades. Furthermore, the strengthening of party identification is not limited to only one party; both Democrats and Republicans experienced increases in the percentage of strong partisans during the 1980s and 1990s.

Because strong partisans are more likely than weak partisans to express positive or negative attitudes toward the parties (Wattenberg 1991) and to vote for their parties' candidates, changes in the distribution of party identifiers reinforces our hunch that cross-currents are spawning greater party polarization in the electorate. Furthermore, the relationship between party identification and vote choice was stronger in the presidential elections of 1984 through 1996 than at any time in the past three decades (Abramson, Aldrich, and Rohde 1999, 174; Lawrence 1999; Miller and Shanks 1996). Bartels (2000) recently analyzed the effect of partisanship on voting in both presidential and congressional elections. He found that the "conventional wisdom regarding the 'decline of parties' is both exaggerated and outdated" (Bartels 2000, 35). In another study, Jacobson (2000) analyzed changes in the composition of the electoral coalitions of members of Congress over time. He argues that partisan polarization in Congress reflects electoral changes that have left the parties with electoral coalitions that are more homogeneous within party and more dissimilar across parties.

The increase in the number of partisans in the electorate and the greater effect of party identification on voting does not fully describe the changes in citizen attitudes regarding political parties. John H. Aldrich (1995) reports that the percentage of the electorate seeing differences between the Democratic and Republican Parties increased during the 1980s and 1990s. Finally, research into the policy preferences of Democratic and Republican identifiers reveals an increasing divergence in citizen attitudes on social welfare, race, and sociocultural issues (Carmines and Layman 1997).

To be sure, proponents of the dealignment thesis did not completely miss the possibility of heightened party polarization. Martin Wattenberg (1994), for one, noticed increased polarization during the 1980s. But he argues that candidates rather than political parties were the central object of the polarization. Wattenberg based this conclusion on the analysis of open-ended questions measuring what respondents liked and disliked about both the parties and the specific candidates running in the presidential election. Given the open-ended question format, respondents were unconstrained in what they could mention as being the source of such likes and dislikes. Wattenberg's (1994) analysis of these questions indicates that the gap between Democratic and Republican evaluations was greater for candidates than for parties. He concludes that if the electorate had indeed polarized, it was a reaction to specific political figures whose behavior and policy platforms were more ideologically extreme than was previously the case. The polarization of the 1980s and 1990s is not a function of a stronger role for political parties but is instead the consequence of the type of candidates nominated in an age of candidate-centered politics. In this chapter, we argue that polarization of the electorate during the 1980s, and continuing into the 1990s, extends to more than the public's response to the particular candidates running for elected office. In fact, a closer examination of Wattenberg's (1994, 161) results reveals that even when parties were the object of evaluation, citizens' views became more polarized over time.

Thus we believe that our understanding of the scope and magnitude of party polarization among ordinary citizens needs closer scrutiny. How extensive is the polarization of ordinary citizens? Does this polarization manifest itself across a number of objects (for example, parties, candidates, issues)? Has the polarization of ordinary citizens been limited to specific subgroups of the population? We seek to answer these questions in this chapter.

Increasing Partisan Polarization of the Electorate

A study of party polarization must begin with a definition of the concept. The concept of increasing party polarization can be defined as a growing gap in the way that Democrats and Republicans understand and view the political world in which they live. To determine whether voters have polarized, previous research analyzed differences in the attitudes of Democratic and Republican identifiers: The greater the difference in the attitudes of the two groups of party identifiers, the greater the polarization (Carmines and Stimson 1989; Wattenberg 1994). We adopt a similar logic.

To illuminate different elements of party polarization, we examine discord in Democratic and Republican citizens' attitudes toward several political objects: (1) presidential candidates, (2) parties, (3) issue preferences, (4) ideological self-placement, and (5) presidential approval. The analysis of candidates focuses on the most short-term component of the voter's evaluation process, whereas the investigation of parties is meant to elicit evaluations toward a political object that transcends the heat of the immediate campaign. Issue preferences and ideological self-placement measure attitudes that are thought to re-

Richard Fleisher and Jon R. Bond

quire prospective evaluations, whereas presidential approval ratings are believed to tap voters' retrospective evaluations. If Democratic and Republican attitudes toward these diverse political objects diverge over time, then we will have evidence that at least some segments within the electorate are becoming more polarized. A generally more partisan electorate would also be consistent with increased party conflict among elites. Thus, in this chapter, we build on the work of those who have studied the divergence in political attitudes by Democratic and Republican identifiers by showing that polarization increased across a range of objects including parties, candidates, prospective issue positions and ideological self-placement, and retrospective performance evaluations of the president. A finding of an electorate polarized along party lines in their attitudes and beliefs across such a wide range of objects will support the argument that political parties, as vehicles for organizing political life, are far from dead.

But even finding that Democratic and Republican identifiers have polarized across this range of objects still leaves important questions unanswered. For example, we do not know whether the divergence in the political attitudes across the party groups was limited to specific subgroups of the population. We extend the analysis of polarization to look for differences across regional, generational, and partisan subgroups. Specifically, we are interested in determining whether the polarization was limited to the South, to voters who most recently entered politics, and to those with strong party identifications. Findings showing that polarization also occurred among citizens outside the South, among older voters, and among those with weaker party attachments will be important in determining the extent of polarization among ordinary citizens.

Evaluations of Candidates and Parties

First, we explore citizen evaluations of the Democratic and Republican Parties and their presidential candidates during each presidential election from 1968 to 1996. We use the National Election Study (NES) "feeling thermometers" to measure citizen attitudes toward these objects. These items ask respondents to locate how warm or cold they feel toward the object by placing themselves on a scale of 0 (very cold) to 100 (very warm). A divergence of the mean thermometer scores of Democratic and Republican identifiers over time would indicate increased polarization toward candidates and parties.[1] Although Wattenberg (1994,

---

1. Widespread use of feeling thermometers in the voting literature indicates that they are generally valid and reliable measures of citizen attitudes about an object. Evaluations measured by feeling thermometer scores are less stable than self-declared party identification (Converse and Markus 1979). Because we are interested in whether attitudes of partisans change over time, lower

Figure 3–1. Party Polarization on Parties and Candidates, 1968–1996

Party Polarization

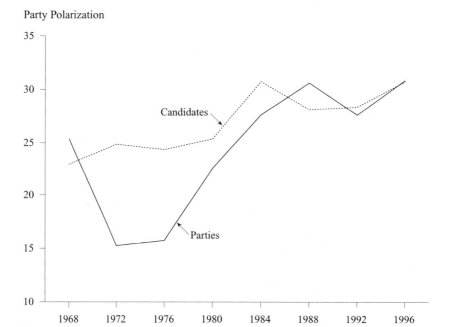

161) argues that voters polarized mainly toward candidates rather than parties, we expect increased polarization toward both objects in the 1980s and 1990s.

Figure 3-1 maps the mean party difference in feeling thermometer scores of Democratic and Republican identifiers toward the presidential candidates and the two political parties from 1968 to 1996.[2] This analysis includes strong

stability of feeling thermometers is not a problem. We assume that citizens' evaluations of political parties and presidential candidates change from time 1 to time 2. Changes in the mean thermometer rating may result from two processes: (1) Some voters may warm or cool toward the object over time, or (2) new cohorts may enter the electorate with warmer or cooler attitudes toward the object, compared with continuing voters. The source of change is not important for this analysis because we are interested only in whether the parties, as aggregations at the mass level, diverged.

2. The feeling thermometer questions for parties and candidates were not asked at the same point in every year. In 1968, 1988, 1992, and 1996 the questions for parties were asked only during the preelection survey; in 1980 and 1984 the questions were asked during both the pre- and postelection surveys; and in 1972 and 1976 the questions were asked only during the postelection survey. In 1968 and 1976 the candidates questions were asked only during the postelection survey; in all other years these questions were asked in both pre- and postelection surveys. Analysis of pre- and postelection survey results indicates that party polarization is larger when using questions asked before the election than when using questions asked after the election. When available, the results reported in Figure 3-1 are based on both pre- and postelection questions. If the parties questions were asked in both pre- and postelection surveys, we averaged the two results.

Richard Fleisher and Jon R. Bond

and weak partisans as well as independents who leaned toward one of the political parties. The inclusion of weak and independent partisans in the analysis lessens the likelihood of finding party polarization because previous research has identified these voters as more likely to have dealigned from the party system (Wattenberg 1984, 16).

Democratic and Republican evaluations of both candidates and parties diverge over time, yet the trends in polarization toward parties and candidates differ. As Wattenberg (1994) suggests, between 1972 and 1984, partisans were more polarized toward candidates than toward parties. In the three presidential elections since 1988, however, the difference in levels of polarization toward candidates and parties disappeared.

Analyzing parties and candidates separately, we find that the level of partisan polarization toward candidates increased but by a relatively small amount. Between 1968 and 1980, the difference in how Democratic and Republican partisans evaluated candidates was approximately 25 percent. In 1984, polarization toward the presidential candidates increased by approximately five or six percentage points. After a slight dip in polarization in 1988 and 1992, the scores in 1996 again reached the peak value set in 1984.

Turning to polarization toward the parties, we see a drop from 1968 through 1976, then a sharp jump in 1980. Evaluations toward parties continued to become more polarized in 1984 and 1988, declined slightly in 1992, but increased in 1996 to approximately the same level as in 1988.

A widening gap in how Democrats and Republicans evaluate the political parties could be the result of increasingly positive evaluations of one's own party, negative evaluations of the opposition political party, or some combination of the two. Figure 3-2 presents the average party evaluations of Democratic and Republican identifiers from 1968 to 1996. This analysis shows that voter evaluations toward the political parties widened as a result of increasingly negative feelings toward the opposition party rather than a warming trend toward one's own party. This tendency is true of both Democratic and Republican identifiers. Respondents' evaluations of their own parties remain basically stable during the entire time period. In contrast, Republican evaluations of the Democratic Party began to decrease in 1984; the drop in Democratic evaluations of the Republican Party began in 1980. It may be only coincidence, but the decline in evaluations of the opposition party took place during a period when negative campaigning increased sharply. In their analysis of negative campaign practices, Stephen Ansolabehere and Shanto Iyengar (1995, 113) argue that attack advertising "was fueling the polarization of American politics."

Figure 3–2. Democratic and Republican Identifiers' Evaluation of Own and Opposition Parties, 1968–1996

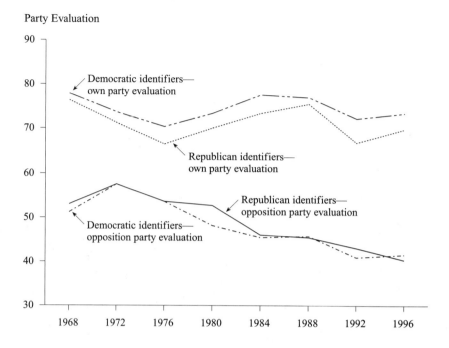

Although we do not have measures linking citizen evaluations of the parties to negative advertising, our results indicating a drop-off in support for the opposition party with no change in the evaluation of one's own party are consistent with that observation.

Over time, therefore, voters became more polarized toward political parties and to a lesser extent toward candidates. Furthermore, in contrast to the picture painted by Wattenberg (1994), by the late 1980s and early 1990s the electorate was about as polarized toward parties as toward candidates. We turn next to an investigation of party differences in issue preferences and ideological self-placement, objects thought to evoke prospective evaluations.

Prospective Issue Preferences and Ideological Self-Placement

We examine the preferences of party identifiers on policy questions asked in the NES presidential elections surveys from 1972 to 1996. Unlike the feeling thermometer questions that were analyzed in the preceding section, the analysis of issue preferences allows us to see whether the attitudes of Democratic

Richard Fleisher and Jon R. Bond

and Republican identifiers have been diverging on some of the major policy issues of the times. Survey research into attitudes on policy questions has used
many different formats, including differences in the number of possible responses that individuals may select. In order to keep constant the maximum
possible numerical difference between Democrats and Republicans, we limit
the analysis to those questions using the NES seven-point scale. For each policy question, voters were asked to place themselves on a scale consisting of
seven possible choices and anchored at the extremes (points one and seven) by
a statement of policy position. Given that we want to examine whether the policy preferences of Democratic and Republican partisans have changed over
time, it is extremely important that the number of possible answers to the questions remains constant.

The questions in each survey covered a diverse range of issues dealing
with both domestic and foreign policy issues. Some issue questions were asked
in every survey; others appeared in less-than-complete series. Issue polarization is calculated as the average difference in issue position of Democrats and
Republicans across the set of policy questions asked in a given year.[3]

The bottom curve in Figure 3-3 presents the average issue polarization
score in presidential elections from 1972 to 1996. Again, we see evidence of
increasing party polarization over time as the gap between Democrats and Republicans nearly doubled. The gap in the average issue position of Democrats
and Republicans increased from about one-half of a scale point in 1972 to
nearly a whole scale point in 1996. For example, on the question of whether
government should guarantee a job and a good standard of living, the difference between the average Democrat and the average Republican was approximately three-fourths of a point on a seven-point scale. In 1988 and 1992 the
partisan gap on this question had increased to greater than 1.1 and in 1996 to
1.25. Thus the evidence indicates that Democrats and Republicans diverged on
this important policy question. These results are consistent with those of other
studies. In their analysis of mass opinions, Benjamin I. Page and Robert Y.
Shapiro (1992) find that across a wide range of issues the opinions of party
groups grew increasingly different from each other over time. Edward G.
Carmines and James A. Stimson (1989, 167–168) present evidence of partisan
polarization on the issue of race beginning in 1964 and increasing through

3. Specifically, issue polarization was measured as the $[ABS(Di - Ri)/N]$, where Di and Ri
are the average Democratic and Republican scores on issue i and N is the number of issues analyzed in the year. The questions and years in which they were asked are given in the appendix to
this chapter.

Figure 3-3. Party Polarization on Issues and Ideology, 1972–1996

Party Polarization

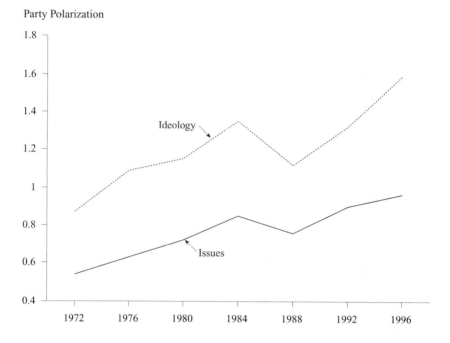

the 1970s and 1980s. Carmines and Geoffrey C. Layman (1997) report increasing polarization on social welfare, race, and sociocultural issues.

To further explore the growing divergence between Democratic and Republican identifiers, we examine the ideological self-placement of respondents. Although some people incorrectly identify themselves as liberal or conservative, a recent examination of the literature on mass ideology points to a strong connection between how individuals define themselves ideologically and positions they take on a host of specific issues (Jacoby, in press). The question asking respondents to identify their ideological position on a seven-point scale has been asked in every NES survey since 1972. At the extreme points of this scale, respondents can label themselves as either strongly conservative or strongly liberal. We calculated the difference in the average ideology score of Democratic and Republican identifiers in each survey (Figure 3-3, top curve). Using this measure of ideological self-placement, increasing polarization is indicated if the ideological positions of Democratic and Republican respondents grew farther apart over time.

Richard Fleisher and Jon R. Bond

Once again, the evidence is clear. Looking at Figure 3-3, we see that the ideological self-placement of party identifiers grew farther apart over the time period covered by this study, reaching its highest point in 1996. More specifically, ideological polarization increased in every presidential election between 1972 and 1984, declined somewhat in 1988, and resumed its upward climb in 1992. Based on the analysis of data not presented in the figure, evidence indicates that the widening gap was created by movement of both parties' supporters. During the 1990s, Democratic identifiers were somewhat more likely to identify themselves as liberal and Republicans were more likely to label themselves as conservative. But Republicans moved more to the right than Democrats moved to the left. A score of 4.0 is the midpoint on the seven-point scale, indicating that the respondent did not identify as either liberal or conservative. Between 1972 and 1988 the average Democratic identifier was slightly left of center, scoring 3.8 on the seven-point ideology scale. In 1992 and 1996 this score dropped to 3.6, indicating that the average Democratic identifier shifted only slightly in the liberal direction. The Republican shift to the right started earlier and is more pronounced. In 1972 the average Republican scored 4.6 on the ideology scale. Republican conservatism increased to almost 4.9 in 1976 and has not dropped below 4.9 in any election since. The score exceeded 5.0 in 1980, 1984, and 1996, reaching a peak of almost 5.2 in 1996.

Presidential Approval Ratings

Finally, we examine the gap in presidential performance evaluations of Democratic and Republican identifiers to see if citizens have become more polarized toward an object thought to evoke retrospective evaluations. The analysis relies on the Gallup presidential approval question that reads, "Do you approve or disapprove of the way [the incumbent] is handling his job as president" (Edwards with Gallup 1990). Figure 3-4 plots the average annual difference in Democrats' and Republicans' approval of the president's job performance from 1953 to 1996.

Once again we find evidence of increasing party polarization beginning in the 1980s and extending to the 1990s. The president's partisans, of course, are more likely to approve of his job performance than are those who identify with the opposition. But the gap in Democratic and Republican evaluations of the president widened over time. From 1953 to 1980 the difference in partisan approval ratings of presidential performance averaged about 35 percent. After 1980, partisan evaluations of presidential performance clearly changed: From

Figure 3–4. Difference in Presidential Approval of Democrats and Republicans, 1953–1996

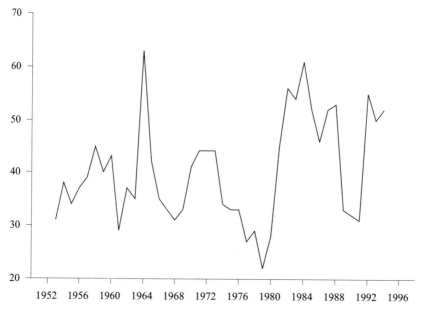

Partisan Difference in Presidential Approval

Source: Edwards with Gallup (1990). Data for 1988 to 1994 provided by the Center for Presidential Studies at Texas A&M University.

1981 to 1994 the average difference in partisan evaluations of the president jumped to 48 percent. During Reagan's two terms in office, the partisan gap in annual presidential performance evaluations averaged 52 percent and was never less than 45 percent. Although Democrats and Republicans were less polarized during the first three years of the Bush presidency (the mean difference was about 32 percent), the partisan gap increased to 55 percent in 1992 and remained above 50 percent during Clinton's first term in office.

To be sure, presidential approval ratings measure more than the partisan orientations of respondents. A vast literature demonstrates that changes in real-world conditions, most notably in the economy and in world affairs, can send the president's approval ratings either higher or lower.[4] The results presented in Figure 3-4 suggest that the real-world events that influence presidential approval are increasingly being interpreted through stronger partisan filters that

4. The literature on presidential approval is much too voluminous to cite in its entirety. Readers interested in the subject can explore the material presented in Brody (1991).

Richard Fleisher and Jon R. Bond

leave Democrats and Republicans with very different perceptions regarding the president's performance in office.

Subgroup Differences

The evidence presented thus far clearly shows that, during the 1980s and 1990s, partisan identifiers expressed increasingly divergent ideologies and issue positions as well as assessments of candidates, parties, and presidents. But citizens differ in the intensity of their party identification, the region where they live, and their age. We do not know whether these variables will condition the impact of partisan identification on the attitudes analyzed.

In this section, we examine the effect of three variables that may condition the trend toward increasing party polarization. First, we analyze whether the trend toward greater party polarization describes only strong party identifiers or whether voters of all intensities of partisanship became more polarized. Given the increase in the number of strong partisans in the population, the findings described earlier in this chapter could be due to the change in distribution of partisanship. In addition, a finding that strong party identifiers are polarizing whereas weaker supporters are not would lend credence to the view that some citizens could dealign from the party system while others become more partisan in their views.

Second, regional differences may exist in changes in partisanship. The dealignment thesis was developed in part because scholars were unable to document a partisan realignment nationally; however, convincing evidence indicates a regional realignment in the South as African Americans began to exercise their voting rights and conservative southern whites shifted their allegiance from Democrat to Republican (Aldrich 1995; Rohde 1991). Because a strong realignment in one region might produce the limited partisan divergence observed nationally, we need to examine whether this polarization is limited to southern voters or whether partisans from other regions of the country are experiencing a similar polarization.

Finally, Warren E. Miller and J. Merrill Shanks (1996) present evidence showing generational cohort effects in partisanship and voting behavior. They note that during the 1970s, members of the newest generational cohort were less partisan in their attitudes and behavior than were members of older cohorts. During the 1980s, however, they find signs that this cohort is beginning to move in a more partisan direction. The issue of polarization across age cohorts has important consequences for our understanding of the developments of the past three decades. Since the New Deal generation was more strongly

Figure 3–5. Partisan Differences in the Evaluation of Candidates and Parties, by Strength of Partisan Identification, 1968–1996

Differences in Feeling Thermometer Scores

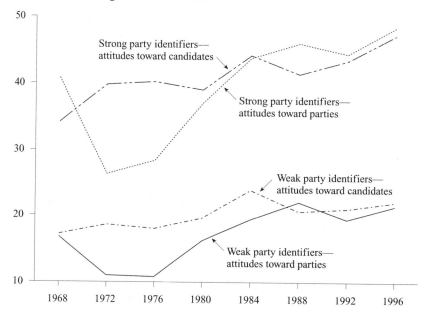

partisan than the post–New Deal generation, we might suspect that the increase in polarization would come disproportionately from the ranks of the newer cohort. Citizens who came of political age in the midst of Watergate, Vietnam, and the aftermath of these events are likely to be weaker partisans or independents than are respondents of earlier generations (Miller and Shanks 1996). Findings of greater party polarization during the 1980s and 1990s may indicate movement among the age cohort that was seen as being most dealigned from the party system. Thus we need to explore whether polarization describes some age cohorts more than others.

Figures 3-5 and 3-6 show the level of polarization toward presidential candidates, political parties, issues, and ideology by strength of partisanship. Over time we observe that partisans of all intensities became more polarized in the 1980s and 1990s. Not surprisingly, the absolute level of polarization is greater for strong partisans than for weak partisans. But the trend toward increasing party polarization across all of the objects is clear even for the weakest partisans. The attitudes toward the parties, candidates, issues, and ideological self-

Richard Fleisher and Jon R. Bond

Figure 3–6. Partisan Differences in Issues and Ideology, by Strength of Partisan Identification, 1972–1996

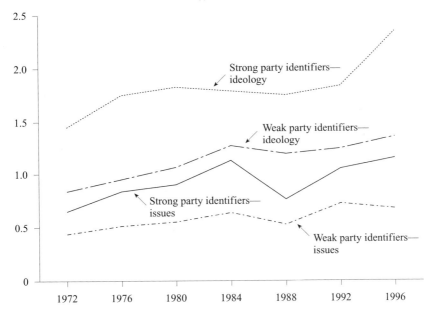

Partisan Differences in Issues and Ideology

placement of Democrats and Republicans who were only weakly attached to their political parties diverged.

Finding increasingly divergent attitudes among weak partisans is particularly noteworthy, suggesting that the elevated partisan polarization is not due entirely to the increased number of strong partisans. Furthermore, because even the weaker partisans are polarizing, elected politicians who act in a more partisan and ideological fashion are not necessarily out of step with the less partisan members of their constituencies. If only strong partisans were polarizing, then elected officials might have had to make a difficult choice: reflect the polarized views of those who are most likely to vote and contribute money and time to their campaigns or respond to the less partisan preferences of the weaker identifiers who make up a larger percentage of the electorate. Our findings, however, indicate that the tradeoff is not quite so sharp. Given that our evidence indicates an increasing polarization on the part of weak partisans, elected officials who acted in a more partisan manner were moving in the same direction as weak partisans as well as strong partisans.

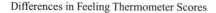

Figure 3–7. Partisan Differences in the Evaluation of Candidates and Parties, by Region, 1968–1996

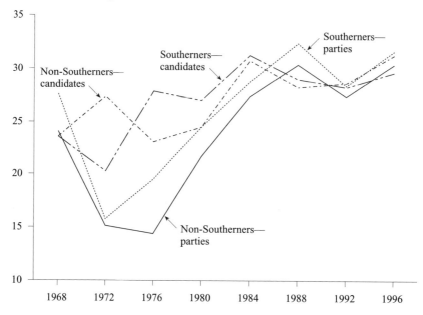

Differences in Feeling Thermometer Scores

To examine whether the polarization in mass attitudes was limited to only southerners, we reexamined the change over time in the partisan polarization of respondents' attitudes regarding parties, candidates, issues, and ideology, this time controlling for whether the individual resided in the South. Figures 3-7 and 3-8 present these results. We see that the trends toward greater polarization in attitudes on the part of Democratic and Republican identifiers are not limited to the South. The trends showing increased party divergence toward the four objects are similar for both regions. Citizens in both the South and non-South were less polarized during the 1970s and then became increasingly polarized through the 1980s and into the 1990s. This finding suggests that the realignment in the South contributed to greater polarization, but it cannot account for the entire pattern.

Finding that polarization is not a regional phenomenon is important for understanding the heightened levels of party unity by members of Congress. Not only did elites polarize during the 1980s and 1990s, but regional differences within the parties have all but disappeared. The results presented here il-

Richard Fleisher and Jon R. Bond

Figure 3–8. Partisan Differences in Issues and Ideology, by Region, 1972–1996

Partisan Differences in Issues and Ideology

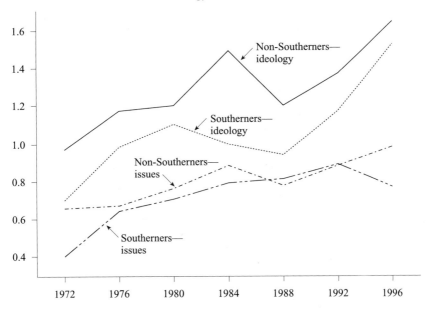

luminate why elected elites from all regions of the country acted in a more partisan fashion: The constituents who elected them were also diverging in both the South and the non-South.

Finally, to analyze the degree of party polarization across generational groups, we used year of birth to place respondents into one of two cohorts: New Deal (birth year 1912 to 1947) and post–New Deal (birth year 1948 and later).[5] Figures 3-9 and 3-10 show the trends in polarization toward parties, candidates, issues, and ideology for the different age cohorts from 1968 to 1996. Once again we see that this control does not change the basic finding: Republicans and Democrats in each age cohort were more polarized in the 1980s and 1990s than during the 1970s. Between 1980 and 1984, partisan polarization increased for both cohorts on each of the objects. Thus Miller and Shanks (1996) were right in pointing out that those who were members of the

5. A number of respondents were born before 1912, but because the number of these pre–New Dealers drops considerably in recent elections, we analyze only those in the New Deal and post–New Deal cohorts.

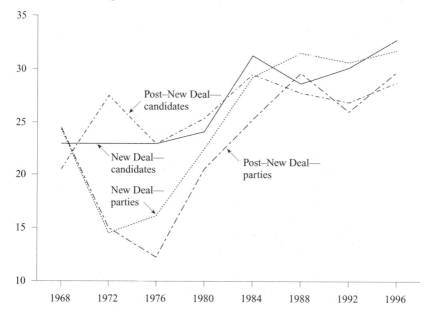

Differences in Feeling Thermometer Scores

post–New Deal cohort entered politics in a weakened partisan state given the effects of Vietnam and Watergate but became more partisan during the Reagan years and beyond. Our results also show that even partisans in the New Deal cohort, whose political attachments were formed much earlier than was the case for the post–New Deal cohort, held more divergent attitudes in the 1980s and 1990s than they did in the 1970s.

Conclusions and Speculations

After decades of decline, the partisan behavior of policy-making elites began to rise, slowly during the 1970s and then more rapidly in the 1980s and 1990s. Furthermore, elites became more polarized on a variety of indicators: party votes, ideological preferences, and presidential support. Increasing partisanship on the part of elites was at odds with a general view of American politics built on evidence of partisan decline in American politics. This view suggested that the policy-making behavior of elites was out of step with the views of vot-

Richard Fleisher and Jon R. Bond

Figure 3–10. Partisan Differences in Issues and Ideology, by New Deal/Post–New Deal, 1972–1996

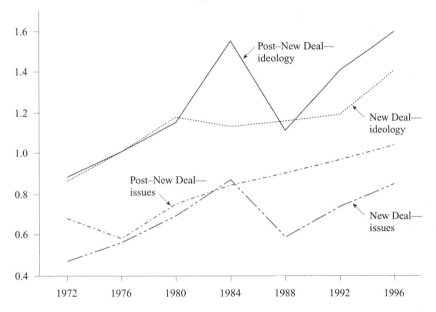

Partisan Differences in Issues and Ideology

ers whose support was necessary to return them to office. In addition, according to some accounts, heightened levels of party conflict were responsible for greater voter anger and alienation. In this chapter, we have presented evidence demonstrating that in the aggregate, elites were not alone in displaying greater partisan polarization. The views of party identifiers toward a variety of political objects—candidates, parties, issues, ideological self-placement, and presidential performance—show a growing divergence. The analysis reveals that polarization is not limited to only the most partisan elements of the electorate, as even weak and independent partisans polarized. Our findings also show that growing polarization is not limited to the South or to any particular generational group.

When combined with research showing greater levels of party polarization on the part of delegates to the national nominating conventions (Stone, Rapoport, and Abramowitz 1994), this evidence produces a different view of American politics over the past several decades than the dealignment thesis suggests. American politics in the 1980s and 1990s became more partisan and ideological. This characterization is true not only of policy-making elites but also of citizens. Research showing that some citizens do not fit very well into a system of heightened partisanship is undoubtedly true. Our point is that it is not universally true.

Although this analysis suggests that policy-making elites did not become more partisan while the other elements of the political system were becoming less so, sorting out the causal sequence in the connection between citizens and elites is difficult. The causal connections may flow from three processes. First, mass attitudes may lead elite behavior, as elites respond to changes in partisan attitudes of citizens. Second, the causal direction may be reversed, with the mass following partisan cues provided by elites. Finally, elite behavior and mass attitudes may move simultaneously in response to some influence in the environment.

Although limitations in our data preclude a precise comparison of the timing of changes in mass attitudes and elite behavior, we can offer some speculation about the sequence. The data suggest that elites in Congress made the initial move toward greater party polarization, beginning in the 1970s. Evidence of increasing polarization at the mass level did not show up until after 1980. But once citizens moved toward greater polarization, elites seemed to have taken sustenance from this and polarized even more. Thus there may be grounds to argue for a relatively simultaneous influence of mass and elite polarization in which each actor's more partisan attitudes reinforced the other.

If elites did move first toward greater polarization beginning in the 1970s, the reasons for this movement remain somewhat unclear. Two developments may have contributed to the increase in elite polarization at that time. First, changes in southern electoral politics brought on by the 1965 Voting Rights Act contributed to the development of a viable Republican Party in the region. With the implementation of the Voting Rights Act in the late 1960s and 1970s, African Americans in the South entered the electorate in large numbers for the first time since Reconstruction. But whereas black voters during Reconstruction supported the party of Lincoln, in the 1960s blacks weighed in almost exclusively in the Democratic Party. Responding to this change in their constituency, southern Democrats in Congress moved to the left (Fleisher 1993; Rohde 1991). At the same time, the most conservative white southern voters began to leave the Democratic Party, contributing to the election of an increasing number of conservative southern Republicans to Congress. Redistricting in 1992 provided an additional boost to the Republican Party in the South. Efforts to maximize the number of African Americans elected to Congress removed

Richard Fleisher and Jon R. Bond

large blocs of reliably Democratic voters from the constituencies of white Democratic incumbents. A side effect of drawing districts to elect more black representatives to Congress was the defeat of several moderate white Democrats by conservative Republicans in 1992 and 1994 (Hill 1995).

Second, changes in the Republican Party reduced the number of liberal Republicans elected to Congress. Beginning with the Goldwater revolution at the 1964 Republican convention, and reinforced by Reagan's electoral success in 1980, the party machinery was taken over by hard-line conservatives.[6] Moreover, activists who support the party with money, labor, and votes became more conservative, making it much harder for liberal candidates to raise campaign resources and win Republican primaries. Both Aldrich (1995) and Gerald C. Wright (1994) argue that members of Congress responded to the policy preferences of party activists in their states and districts.

During the late 1970s a group of junior Republicans sought to sharpen the philosophical differences between the parties and to embarrass the Democratic Party leadership. Newt Gingrich of Georgia, Vinny Weber of Minnesota, Robert Walker of Pennsylvania, and a host of other young Republicans, dissatisfied with the accommodationist politics of more senior Republicans, began to use their resources to attack the Democratic Party. Democrats, more homogeneous than ever, responded in kind. The Speaker of the House, armed with a set of weapons left over from the reforms of the 1970s, began to act in a highly partisan manner. The developments in the South leading to the election of fewer conservative Democrats made it easier for elected Democrats from all over the country to coalesce around a common platform. A more unified Democratic Party, facing two conservative Republican presidents, prepared for party warfare. The Republican Party, having gained strength from the election of conservatives from the South and the disappearance of the "liberal wing" elected largely from the Northeast, was also ready for the state of war. Increasingly, battles were fought across the partisan caucuses rather than inside them. The findings that their core constituents also held increasingly partisan attitudes increased the resolve of politicians in both parties to aggressively engage in partisan warfare.

6. Republican and Democratic Party activists who attended state party conventions in 1988 were more polarized on issues than were convention delegates in 1980 (Stone, Rapoport, and Abramowitz 1994). Data reported by Stanley and Niemi (2000, 71) suggest that delegates to the national party conventions became more polarized ideologically in the 1980s and 1990s. Although activists in both parties are more ideologically extreme than rank-and-file voters, Republican convention delegates shifted further to the right in the 1980s than Democratic delegates shifted to the left.

Thus we believe that the movements toward a politics of polarization began with the behavior of elected elites who saw it as being in their interest to act in a more partisan fashion. Elected elites, pursuing a goal of reelection, could move in a more partisan direction only if such movements did not jeopardize their electoral positions. The contribution of this chapter is to report that there is indeed evidence of a polarization in mass political attitudes that elected elites would need to sustain a long period of partisan warfare. This logic suggests that elites will continue to act in a highly partisan manner as long as they suffer no ill effects at the polls. The evidence to date indicates that the public is not only willing to reelect such elites but is fully along for the ride.

Richard Fleisher and Jon R. Bond

Appendix: Variables Used to Measure Polarization on Issues

	1972	1976	1980	1984	1988	1992	1996
Progressive Taxation	V178	V3779					
Government-Guaranteed Jobs	V172	V3241	V1110	V414	V323	V3718	
	V613	V3758		V1048			
Government Health Insurance	V208	V3273		V1058	V318	V3716	V0479
Social Service Spending			V291	V375	V302	V3701	V0450
				V1028			
Busing	V202	V3257	V1133	V1074			
Help Minorities	V629	V3264	V1062	V382		V3724	V0487
Status of Blacks					V332		
Status of Minorities					V340		
Legalize Marijuana	V196	V3772					
Rights of Accused	V621	V3248					
Women Equality	V232	V3787	V1094	V401	V387	V3801	V0543
Urban Unrest		V3767				V3746	
Defense Spending			V281	V395	V310	V3707	V0463
USSR			V1078	V408	V368		
Central America				V388			
				V1039			
Inflation	V190		V301				
	V598						
Vietnam Withdrawal	V184						
	V590						
Pollution	V214						
Campus Unrest	V678						
Crime							V0519
Jobs/Environment							V0523
Environmental Regulations							V0537

Note: Entries refer to NES variable numbers. See NES Codebooks. The National Election Studies are available through the Inter-University Consortium for Political and Social Research, Ann Arbor, Michigan.

4

Party Politics and Personal Democracy

Matthew Crenson and Benjamin Ginsberg

In the nineteenth century the United States was exceptional for the vitality of its democratic institutions—especially its political parties. The country may have been slow to abolish slavery, but it was first to achieve universal voting rights for white males, and by mid-century, when European states were taking their first hesitant steps toward mass democracy, America's dynamic party organizations were routinely mobilizing 70 to 80 percent of the electorate in presidential campaigns. Outside the South, even midterm congressional contests typically pushed turnout past 60 percent (Chambers and Davis 1978, 180–185; Kleppner 1982, 18–19).

American politics is no longer exceptional for its feats of grassroots mobilization. In the midterm elections of 1998, for example, barely a third of registered voters went to the polls. Candidates are spending more than ever to turn out their supporters. They are employing mechanisms of mass communications to project their voices and images across a vast electronic electorate. But the citizen response has grown progressively weaker. Behind the receding waves of electoral mobilization, a new kind of American exceptionalism is emerging, marked by rates of voter participation significantly lower than the ones that prevail today in those same European nations that once stood by and watched while America built the world's premier popular democracy.

Voting is the most common means of citizen participation, and the contraction of the electorate is the most obvious sign of the diminished role that citizens play in American politics. But the decline of citizen activism extends beyond the voting booth. The absence of nineteenth-century opinion polling makes it difficult to trace forms of popular participation other than voting, but strong indicators point to a general decline in popular politics since the end of the nineteenth century (McGerr 1986). Furthermore, evidence from the last 30 or 40 years of the twentieth century suggests, at best, stagnation in political activism. Contributing money to political organizations is the only activity to register an unambiguous gain since the 1950s, and it is unclear whether we should regard such financial donations as a sign of active involvement in politics or as a substitute for it (Rosenstone and Hansen 1993, 61; Verba, Scholzman, and Brady 1995, 72–73, 531).

American democracy is not dead. It has, however, undergone a transfiguration, and so has American citizenship. These changes are not the results of some vast conspiracy to deprive the general public of its place in politics. In fact, twentieth-century political reforms have given citizens unprecedented access to the political process. The introduction of primary elections, the use of referendum and recall, sunshine laws (requiring that decision-making processes be open to the public), and legislative mandates requiring agencies to give public notice and hold public hearings before making policy changes all would seem to have made the government more responsive to citizens than ever before. Through ACTION, VISTA, Americorps, and the Peace Corps, the government has sponsored the activism of citizens committed to a vision of the public good, and it has extended the idea of citizenship itself to cover many circumstances of life once regarded as purely private. Gender, race, age, sexual preference, and physical handicap have become bases for claims that we make on the public. According to Michael Schudson, "[A] dimension of citizenship has come to cover everything," and he adds that the new political dimensions of life in the United States may compensate for the "slackening of voter turnout" (Schudson 1998, 229).

But the new opportunities for citizen involvement have changed the nature of citizenship itself. The proliferation of opportunities for individual access to government has substantially reduced the incentives for collective mobilization. For ordinary Americans, this means that it has become standard practice to deal with government as an individual customer rather than as a member of a mobilized public. At the same time, Americans of more than ordinary political status find that they can use courts, administrative procedures, and other political channels to achieve their ends without organizing a political constituency to support them and their aims. In short, elites have fewer incentives to mobilize non-elites; non-elites have little incentive to join together with one another. The two circumstances have operated in combination with one another to produce a new politics of individualized access to government and a new era of *personal democracy.*

The manifestations of this personal democracy are subtle and wide ranging. Consider, for example, the recent transformation of civic education in the United States. Its emphasis used to be the preparation of children for active participation in public decision making. Pupils participated in debates. The not-so-hidden curriculum concentrated in particular on the electoral process. Students held elections to choose team captains, class officers, and student government representatives. They even held mock elections that paralleled real elections.[1]

Schools have not abandoned all of these rituals. But there is a pronounced shift from these electoral exercises to so-called student service learning. Maryland was the first state to make it a requirement; others are rushing to do the same. Elementary and secondary school students are expected to volunteer for public service jobs with charitable, civic, and public interest groups. Traditional civic education tried to teach students that they could help to govern the country just as they governed their classrooms, teams, and schools. Service learning imparts a fundamentally different set of lessons about citizenship. It is no longer about the collective activity of governing. Students, often acting alone, perform work of possible benefit to the public, but it is frequently work that the government has abandoned or is not prepared to pay for. One study finds that over half of all service-learning students report that they have worked in environmental or beautification projects, where they may not even be providing assistance directly to other human beings. But the principal and intended beneficiaries of these programs may be the students themselves, rather than the service recipients. The service-learning experience is supposed to be personally rewarding and bolster self-esteem (Blyth, Saito, and Berkas 1997, 42–43).[2]

The civic activities of young adults (ages 18–24 years) reflect a similar shift toward service activities. Since the mid-1970s, voter participation among young people has declined by more than twelve percentage points while their participation in quasi-public and private volunteer organizations such as Americorps or the Jesuit Volunteer Corps has grown substantially (Crowley 1999, A28). In a study of local activists, Nina Eliasoph (1998) found parallel tendencies among adults in general. Activists tended to avoid politics in favor of community service projects. Talking about political issues, they believe, is wasteful because such talk seldom arrives at consensus on clearly defined conclusions. Perhaps more important, they were convinced that political issues

---

1. One of the authors served as a stand-in for Adlai Stevenson at his elementary school's mock election during the 1952 presidential campaign. Like the real Stevenson, he lost—badly.

2. Only 19 percent of service-learning students interviewed in one study indicated that their activities were political in nature—for example, involving efforts to change laws or collecting signatures on petitions (Wang, Greathouse, and Falcinella 1998).

were unlikely to yield to the efforts of community volunteers such as themselves. They tended to concentrate instead on community service projects through which they knew they could make a difference—especially projects aimed at the welfare of children. Not only were such efforts likely to be noncontroversial, says Eliasoph, but the volunteers "took a 'focus on children' to mean 'a focus on private life.' That meant that the only real changes regular citizens could make were changes in feelings" (Eliasoph 1998, 61). Not least important were the feelings of the activists themselves, whose personal satisfaction depended on the conviction that they were making a difference.

What passes for citizenship today often inverts the feminist dictum that the personal is political. It has transformed the political into the personal. Political activity should feel empowering. It should enhance self-esteem. It should not engender confusion, ambiguity, or frustration.

An all-too-easy diagnosis of the new, service-oriented citizenship would locate its origins in a more comprehensive feel-good culture of self-gratification and self-esteem. But that would overlook the authentic sacrifices made by volunteers who perform tasks useful to their communities. And it would ignore the more authoritative efforts of political elites to recast the meaning of American citizenship: "Ask not what your country can do for you; ask what you can do for your country." President Kennedy's inaugural exhortation bore fruit in the Peace Corps and, later, in VISTA. The National Community Service Act of 1990 would embrace an even wider population of volunteers, and it supplied more than $200 million to fuel President Bush's thousand points of light. President Clinton followed this initiative in 1993 with his half-billion dollar Americorps program.

These programs unquestionably inspire worthy people to worthy deeds, but they also represent a government-sponsored shift in our conception of citizenship. Rather than make demands of government, we now fulfill them ourselves, and in doing so we gain the personal satisfaction and certainty that we have performed a service and made a difference.

While citizens have been encouraged to think of themselves as public servants, the more conventional public servants employed by the federal government have also been encouraged to adopt a new perspective on the citizens they serve. This new perspective emerges in the 1993 Report of National Performance Review, the manifesto of the Clinton administration's campaign to reinvent government. The report is one in a long succession of studies designed to improve the functioning of the federal bureaucracy. Its predecessors emphasized the democratic accountability of public bureaucracy. That was one of the first points made by the First Hoover Commission in 1949: "The President, and under him his chief lieutenants, the department heads, must be held responsible and accountable to the people and the Congress for the conduct of the executive branch." The statement is hardly controversial. But, as James Q. Wilson observes, nothing like it appears in the Report of the National Performance Review overseen by Vice President Gore (Wilson 1994, 668). The subject of democratic accountability is scarcely mentioned. Nor do citizens figure in the report. They have been transformed into customers, and the report's explicit objective, as declared by the vice president, is "to make the federal government customer friendly" (Gore 1993, 43).

There is nothing undemocratic about this aim. The customer, after all, is always right, and the vice president's point is that federal employees should strive to meet the needs of their customers and to treat them with respect—in other words, to make the government more responsive to its citizens. But a crucial difference exists between citizens and customers. Citizens are members of a political community with a collective existence created for public purposes. Customers are individual purchasers seeking to meet their private needs in a market. What is missing from the experience of customers is collective mobilization to achieve collective interests, and the omission is not just a matter of changing semantic fashions along the Potomac. The emerging tendencies in civic education and administrative terminology have something in common with one another. They do not portend the downfall of democracy but the advent of a new individualized democracy in which citizens are less likely to engage in collective action because they can get what they want on their own. It is a personal rather than a public democracy, and it marks the passing of popular mobilization in American politics.

Personal Democracy and Party Politics

The advent of personal democracy has had major consequences for the character and behavior of political parties in the United States. Competing political factions once built party organizations to crush their foes by outmobilizing them in the electoral arena. Today's political parties, by contrast, serve as competitive vehicles for forces that neither view the electoral arena as politically decisive nor necessarily conceive all-out popular mobilization to be a desirable political strategy. As a result, contemporary political parties are organized as much to wage institutional struggle as for electoral mobilization and, moreover, engage in a number of practices calculated to circumvent or reduce rather than expand popular political participation. Thus institutions originally created by the likes of Thomas Jefferson and Andrew Jackson to bring ordinary citizens into the political process have, in the contemporary era, become associated with patterns and practices that diminish the political role of the average American.

American political parties in the nineteenth and early twentieth centuries were led by machine politicians whose chief goals were electoral success. These party leaders were famously pragmatic, willing to champion whatever issues and adopt whatever positions promised to bring victory at the polls. The parties were the archetypes for the vote-maximizing model of political competition developed by Anthony Downs in the 1950s—a model still at the core of rational choice theory today (Downs 1957). Although reformers charged that political party leaders were indifferent to issues, the pragmatism of their leadership meant the nineteenth century parties were very open to new issues, albeit as means rather than ends. Witness that during the nineteenth and early twentieth centuries, conflicts over matters such as the tariff, internal improvements, slavery, banks, monetary policy, and immigration generally spilled over into the electoral arena as opposing forces sought to secure victory in Washington, D.C., by outmobilizing and outpolling their foes throughout the country.

Political machines came under attack by the late nineteenth century Progressive movement and, again, by the New Politics movement of the 1960s and 1970s. In both eras, coalitions of issue-oriented activists who lacked the ability to outmobilize machine politicians sought, instead, to drive them from power through other means. Activists sought, first, to create privileged avenues of access to the courts and bureaucracy that would allow them to circumvent the electoral arena dominated by their opponents (Ginsberg and Shefter 1999). Both Progressive and New Politics groups then sought to reconstitute the party system to make it possible for upper-middle-class activists like themselves to seize control of political party machinery for their own purposes. To this end, the Progressives introduced the direct primary election, whereas New Politics forces brought about the adoption of the so-called McGovern-Fraser rules, which substantially increased the influence of liberal activists in the Democratic Party (Shefter 1994).

As a result, today's political parties are dominated not by pragmatic machine politicians, but by coalitions of issue-oriented advocates concerned more with policies and programs than simply winning elections. For these politicians, electoral mobilization is one of several strategies rather than an end in and of itself. Indeed, in recent decades, some of the most important party bat-

Party Politics and Personal Democracy

tles have involved institutional struggle through the courts, bureaucracy, and media, or what Ginsberg and Shefter call "politics by other means," more than through competition in the electoral arena (Ginsberg and Shefter 1999). Watergate, the Iran-Contra imbroglio, and the Clinton impeachment are prime cases in point.

Mobilization and Its Alternatives

Political historians have dubbed nineteenth-century American political campaigns as "militarist" in style (Jensen 1971, chap. 6). Competing political parties were well organized and active in virtually every constituency in the nation. Voters in each precinct were "drilled" by party "captains" who received support and information from a disciplined and well-financed party organization. A rabidly partisan press disseminated news that sometimes amounted to little more than party propaganda (Summers 1994). Throughout the country, hundreds of thousands of party workers marched from house to house on election day, handing out leaflets, helping voters go to the polls, and occasionally offering financial incentives to those voters who needed a bit of extra assistance in making up their minds (Ostrogorski 1902). Millions of citizens attended campaign rallies, listened to speeches, marched in parades, and actively took part in American political life (Campbell 1972, 263–337).

Political competition in nineteenth-century America was not solely a matter of electoral mobilization. After all, the country's first impeachment crisis occurred during the 1860s, and criminal indictments and prosecutions, such as those of the Whiskey Ring and Tweed Ring, were important weapons in political struggle throughout the century. Moreover, particularly in the South, extralegal violence, perpetrated by groups such as the Ku Klux Klan, played a major role in resolving political conflicts (Kousser 1974). Nevertheless, all-out voter mobilization in national elections was a central strategy for forces seeking to control the government and to influence national policy.

The nineteenth-century pattern of lively public involvement is a far cry from the manner in which politics is conducted in contemporary America. Since the 1950s, voter turnout in the United States has been extremely low, averaging slightly more than 50 percent in presidential contests. Fewer than 49 percent of eligible voters cast their ballots in the 1996 presidential election, the lowest electoral turnout since 1924. In midterm congressional elections, more than two-thirds of eligible voters stay home. Generally speaking, affluent and well-educated Americans continue to vote. Except among younger persons, presidential election turnout among college graduates averages close to 80 per-

Matthew Crenson and Benjamin Ginsberg

cent. Less affluent and less well-educated Americans, in contrast, have been increasingly marginalized in the political process. Among individuals with less than a high school education, for instance, voter turnout has dropped from close to 50 percent in the early 1970s to barely 30 percent in the most recent presidential race (U.S. Bureau of the Census 1998).[3]

Competing political forces in contemporary America obviously have not given up seeking to appeal to voters. Indeed, politicians are currently spending enormous sums on election campaigns. Parties and candidates may have spent as much as $2 billion competing for popular support in the 1996 national, state, and local races (Feld 1999). Much of this money, however, is typically spent on television advertising during the final month of the campaigns. This advertising is aimed primarily at middle-class Americans who are already registered and likely to vote. Sophisticated polling techniques allow candidates to target specific slices of this truncated and already-mobilized audience with political advertising designed to appeal to their particular interests (Schier 2000). With the growth of computerized databases and greater candidate familiarity with the potential inherent in Internet advertising, targeted or customized campaigning is certain to become even more important in the years to come (Milbank 1999).

In sharp contrast with the nineteenth-century pattern, neither party makes much of an effort to defeat its opponents by attempting to mobilize the tens of millions of poorer and less well-educated Americans who are not currently part of the electorate (Nelson 1999; Shogan 1998). Indeed, many candidates work to further depress turnout through the use of negative advertising, which disparages the opposition and is designed to discourage both nonvoters and their opponents' established supporters from coming to the polls (Ansolabehere and Iyengar 1995). The prevalence of negative campaigning and smear tactics is one reason that many Americans claim to be too disgusted to participate in politics (Dionne 1991; Drew 1999; Nye, Zelikow, and King 1997). Only the occasional political outsider such as Minnesota Governor Jesse Ventura makes any real effort to bring nonvoters into the electorate (Canon 2000, 3). Neither of the established parties even supports electoral reforms such as the elimination of voter registration requirements and a shift from weekday to weekend voting—the norms throughout Western Europe. The European experience suggests that these two changes alone would appreciably boost electoral turnout.

3. The most current data are regularly posted on the Census Bureau's web site: http://www.census.gov/population/socdemo/voting/history/vot23txt.

The parties' failure to engage in all-out efforts to mobilize the more than 60 million Americans who could vote in presidential elections but do not is especially striking given the bitter political struggles of the 1980s and 1990s and given that neither major party has been able to win a decisive edge in the electoral arena since the 1960s. Despite the huge sums candidates and parties have spent campaigning for the support of existing voters, the results have been inconclusive, and control of the government has been divided for the most part since 1970.

As an indication of the intensity of contemporary partisan struggles, party divisions in Congress, as evinced by patterns of roll call voting, have achieved levels previously reached only in the nineteenth century. At the same time, partisan struggles between Congress and the White House have reached a degree of ferocity virtually without precedent in American history. A Democratic Congress drove Republican president Richard Nixon from office and sought to do the same to Ronald Reagan. A Republican Congress impeached, but failed to convict, Democratic president Bill Clinton. Significantly, though, these ferocious elite struggles have not led either party to endeavor to mobilize more voters. Instead, participation has continued to decline.

This pattern of popular quiescence alongside intense elite struggle contradicts what might be called the neoclassical theory of political participation. As developed by Key, Schattschneider, and Duverger, the neoclassical theory asserts that in a democratic polity, high levels of elite conflict will inevitably lead to increased rates of mass participation as contending forces engage in competitive efforts to mobilize political support. V. O. Key (1942) credited Thomas Jefferson with setting the stage for large-scale popular mobilization in the United States when he built local party organization and "lined up the unwashed" to defeat his Federalist foes. The Federalists followed suit, albeit reluctantly, and built party machines to mobilize the "unwashed" for their cause. E. E. Schattschneider (1960, ch. 4) referred to this phenomenon as "expanding the scope of the conflict" and claimed that it was a central feature of democratic political processes. He argued that popular mobilization was most likely to be initiated by the losers in inter-elite struggles who hoped to change the outcome by enlarging the universe of participants. French political scientist Maurice Duverger, for his part, asserted that the process of mass mobilization was most likely to be initiated by elites representing groups further down the social hierarchy and then emulated by their more upscale competitors. He called this phenomenon "contagion from the left" (Duverger 1963).

American political practices during much of the nineteenth century and

Matthew Crenson and Benjamin Ginsberg

portions of the twentieth century seemed to be generally consistent with the neoclassical model. The Jeffersonians, Jacksonians, and Republicans all expanded the suffrage and brought new groups into the political process in an effort to overwhelm their opponents at the polls. During the 1930s the New Dealers sought to solidify their political power by increasing participation on the part of working class and ethnic voters. As recently as the 1960s, liberal Democrats strove to defeat the Republicans and overpower conservative forces within their own party by enacting the Voting Rights Act, which enfranchised millions of African Americans in the South, and by securing passage of the Twenty-sixth Amendment, which gave the vote to young people.

Contemporary American political patterns, however, seem less consistent with the neoclassical model of political participation. An astonishing two-thirds of those eligible to vote failed to take part in the November 1998 national elections even though the Democratic and Republican Parties were, at that very moment, locked in a momentous battle over the president's impeachment. Indeed, despite their bitter fights, contending elites deliberately refrained from mobilizing legions of new supporters. The unwashed, at least those living outside the Capital Beltway, were left to their own devices. "I don't think we ought to play to that crowd," said Rep. John Lindner of Georgia, chairman of the House Republican campaign committee, when asked if the GOP should seek to bring new voters to the polls in 1998 (Nelson 1999; Shogan 1998). Interestingly, just a decade earlier, Democratic presidential candidate Walter Mondale's advisors told him that the idea of mobilizing new voters was "backward thinking." Democrats refrained from engaging in large-scale voter registration efforts even though the polls indicated that, among Americans already registered and likely to vote, Mondale faced nearly certain defeat at the hands of Ronald Reagan.

Politicians have always been afraid to mobilize new voters. Key, Schattschneider, and other neoclassical students of participation failed to take full note of the fact that contending elites and parties have generally viewed expanding the universe of participants as a strategy fraught with frightful risks and painful uncertainties. Even in an era of scientific opinion polling, the political leanings and partisan loyalties of new participants are always uncertain. Democrats in the 1960s, for example, pushed to drop the voting age to 18, only to discover that, on balance, young voters helped the Republicans in the 1970s and 1980s.

Moreover, even if they remain loyal to the political party that mobilized them, new participants are likely to bring with them new aspirants for leadership positions within that party. Political leaders who successfully line up the unwashed may find themselves watching the final victory of their cause from the sidelines. The popular forces brought into politics by the Jeffersonians, for example, dismayed their distinguished patrons by demanding and, ultimately, seizing control of much of the Republican Party machinery—eventually giving rise to Jacksonian democracy. For these reasons, expanding the scope of the conflict is a dangerous strategy and is seldom undertaken lightly. Lord Derby famously and accurately called the Second Reform Bill, expanding England's suffrage in 1867, a "leap into the dark."

Today, both political parties fear the potential consequences of a strategy of mobilization. Republicans are concerned that an expansion of the electorate might lead to an influx of poor and minority voters who would not be likely to support the GOP. Among some Republican conservatives, moreover, a view has evolved that many ordinary Americans have fallen prey to a moral and intellectual weakness that renders them unfit to participate in the process of government. Versions of this notion of the public's lack of moral fiber were put forward by some conservative intellectuals and commentators to explain why most Americans seemed unwilling to support the GOP's campaign to impeach President Clinton (Didion 1999).

As for the Democrats, expansion of the electorate might benefit the party as a whole. An influx of tens of millions of new voters, however, would represent a substantial risk for current officeholders at the national, state, and local levels. Even if these new voters remained loyal to the Democratic Party as an institution, they might not support the party's current leadership. Moreover, various liberal interests allied with the Democrats, such as upper-middle-class environmentalists, public interest lawyers, antismoking activists, and the like, could not be confident of retaining their influence in a more fully mobilized electoral environment. Though it is seldom openly admitted, some liberal intellectuals and activists have little interest in increasing participation among working-class and lower-middle-class whites, whom they see as opponents of abortion rights and proponents of school prayer and unrestricted handgun ownership (Lasch 1995).

Almost all American politicians purport to deplore the nation's low levels of voter turnout. Even modest efforts to boost voter turnout, however, inspire little support in Washington, D.C., or in most state capitals. For example, the so-called Motor Voter Act, signed into law by President Clinton in 1993, was bitterly opposed by most Republicans (Dewar 1993). Congressional Democrats, for their part, were willing to delete portions of the bill that were most likely to maximize registration among the poor, such as the provision for automatic registration for all clients at welfare offices. Many Democrats had been happy to see a previous version of Motor Voter vetoed by President Bush in 1992. At any rate, the Motor Voter Act has had little effect on the size or composition of the electorate. Thus far, few of the individuals registered under the act have gone to the polls to cast their ballots. In 1996 the percentage of newly registered voters who appeared at the polls dropped (Baker 1996). Mobilization of voters requires more than the distribution of forms. To bring tens of millions of new voters to the polls, political parties and candidates would have to engage in old-fashioned, door-to-door electioneering. This is a task they currently seem unwilling to undertake.

Who Needs Citizens?

The declining place of mass political mobilization and the narrowing political role of American citizens have done nothing to diminish the ethical elevation of citizenship itself. Citizenship, in fact, seems to have become an embodiment of the virtues and values in which American society is alleged to be deficient—civic consciousness, the sense of community, and responsibility to others. Among academics, a recent "explosion of interest in the concept of citizenship" is partly a response to a perceived deterioration in the practice of citizenship (Kymlicka and Norman 1994, 352). The new requirements for community service in public school systems are being introduced to reinvigorate a sense of public mindedness supposed to have been weakened by a market-driven society that mobilizes consumers rather than citizens. One of the more recent eulogies for the lost virtues of citizenship comes from a representative of the television industry, an institution often blamed for the erosion of America's civic community. Television news anchorman Tom Brokaw's best-selling book *The Greatest Generation* honors an entire generation of citizens who endured the hardships of the Depression and the hazards of World War II (Brokaw 1998). They are the measure of what we have lost and the model of what we should have become. In a sense, they are modern America's counterparts for the fallen soldiers glorified in Pericles's famous funeral oration, the citizen-heroes who sacrificed themselves for the sake of Athens.

We are witnessing a radical divergence between the moral conception of citizenship and the political conduct of citizens. The mismatch is widely acknowledged and conventionally attributed to deficiencies in the moral, cultural, or social resources of today's citizens (see Bellah et al. 1985; Mead 1986;

Putnam 1996), which prevent them from acting on behalf of interests larger than their own. But self-interestedness, as Peter Riesenberg (1992) points out, has been the constant companion of citizenship. Even Pericles recognized the intimate connection between the public sacrifices of citizens and their private interests. Political communities had to offer inducements to inspire good citizenship: "For where the prize is highest, there, too, are the best citizens to contend for it" (Thucydides 1960).

States offer "prizes" for citizenship because they have need of citizens. In classical antiquity, the extension of citizenship rights often followed escalation in the need for military manpower—especially foot soldiers. Otto Hintze (1975) notes that at the beginning of the twentieth century a similar connection existed in modern states between dependence on citizen-soldiers and the extension of suffrage. The existence of militia forces was associated with the early onset of democracy, and even in more centralized and authoritarian systems, Hintze argues, universal military service eventually led to universal suffrage, if only after several generations (Hintze 1975; Fox 1991, 189).

Armies, of course, had to be equipped, provisioned, paid, and pensioned—all of which enlarged the state's need for taxpayers—and the need for taxpayers gave states another incentive to extend the rights of citizenship. Long before American colonists demanded that representation accompany taxation, England had begun to recognize taxpayers as citizens. The step was taken not just to part taxpayers more peacefully from their money but also to increase the wealth available to be taxed. Property rights, the right to practice a trade or engage in commerce, and the right to secure those rights through the courts helped to enhance the prosperity of taxpayers and expand the state's revenue base (Sacks 1994, 7–66; Sayer 1992). In absolutist France, the transformation of taxpayers into citizens occurred later, but more suddenly, when a revenue crisis forced Louis XVI to summon the Estates-General for the first time in centuries (Tilly 1992, 74–75, 253–298). Within a few years, almost everybody in Paris was addressing everybody else as "citizen."

The modern states of Europe invented modern citizenship not just because they needed standing armies and the money to pay for them but also because the very existence of the state defined the conditions for citizenship. The modern state was a membership organization to which people belonged directly as individuals, not indirectly through their membership in families, clans, tribes, guilds, or status orders. The state itself replaced this jumble of premodern political jurisdictions as the single, paramount object of political allegiance (Brubaker 1992, 41; Sayer 1992, 1398–1399).

Understood in this way, the connection between the modern state and modern citizenship is tautological. The definition of citizenship is implicit in our definition of state. But citizenship was more than a vertical relationship between subject and state; it also implied a relationship among fellow citizens, a common tie of blood, belief, or culture that united them into a political community. Beyond that, citizenship also has behavioral implications—a role in governing the state and the support of state authority. These were the activities denoted by Aristotle's definition of the citizen as one who rules and is ruled. The benefits of rulership were the prizes that citizens won for being of service to the state, and as Pericles observed, the more valuable the prizes, the higher the standards of citizenship were likely to be. His ancient observation, as well as the modern state's cultivation of citizen-soldiers and taxpayers, suggests an alternative to the view that the recent decline in the role of American citizenship is a product of the citizens' personal characteristics, their cultural values, or their access to social capital.

Citizens become politically engaged because states and political elites need them and mobilize them. If they remain passive, politically indifferent, or preoccupied with private concerns, the reason may be that our political order no longer provides incentives for collective participation in politics. The state may no longer need citizens as much as it once did, or perhaps citizens have become a nuisance to political elites, or it may be that citizen prizes have gotten too expensive for the state to bear.

Citizens, of course, do not disappear simply because they have become institutionally inconvenient. A political system engaged in the collective demobilization of citizens will fashion other arrangements for the political management of its population. In general, American institutions operate increasingly to disaggregate and depoliticize the demands of citizens. The reinvention of American government has reinvented citizens as customers. This reinvention offers so-called stakeholders easy access to the decision-making process as a low-energy alternative to collective mobilization. It emphasizes private rights at the expense of collective action. It promotes arrangements for policy implementation that encourage individual choice rather than the articulation of public interests. It reduces the occasions for citizens to congregate around opinion leaders, and it weakens the incentives for political entrepreneurs to organize public constituencies. The reinvention of American government has begun to privatize not only many of its own functions but also the public itself. American politics has entered the era of personal democracy.

Citizen Government in America

The essential and original claim of American exceptionalism was not just that we were different from other nations but also that we had a different way of being a nation. The United States was a community of political belief, not blood and soil. Political scientist Hans Morgenthau—no sentimentalist—detected something almost spiritual at the core of the country. Unlike other nations, he argued, the United States did not gradually arrive at a conception of its national mission by reflecting retrospectively on the course of its history. "The rule that action precedes reflection in the discovery of the national purpose suffers but one complete exception. The United States," Morgenthau wrote, "is the only nation that has reversed the sequence. The awareness of its purpose was not an afterthought. The United States was founded with a particular purpose in mind" (Morgenthau 1964, 11).

John Winthrop provided a classic illustration of the anticipatory purposefulness that Morgenthau saw in American politics. In the middle of the Atlantic, on the deck of the ship *Arbella,* Winthrop—soon to be the first governor of the Massachusetts Bay Colony—preached a sermon to the fellow travelers who would soon become the first citizens of that colony. His subject was the purpose of their errand in the wilderness, an errand not yet begun. Winthrop, of course, had a religious purpose in mind as well as a political one, but it was also a universal purpose that spoke to all humankind and not to a narrow sect. In the most famous passage of his sermon he urged his shipmates to "consider that we shall be as a city on a hill, the eyes of all people are upon us" (Mitchell 1931, Vol. 2, 295). But in a less prominent place, before he reached the summit of his homily, Winthrop reflected on the nature of the religious bonds that would solidify the Puritan political community: "[T]hough we be absent from each other many miles . . . yet we ought to account ourselves knit together by this bond of love" (Mitchell 1931, Vol. 2, 292).

From the outset, the American polity was no mere territorial community; it was not defined by spatial propinquity. It was a compact among fellow believers. Although it remained for centuries an Anglo-American nation, it would eventually surrender much of its ethnic distinctiveness as well. Americans claimed to be citizens of a nation defined by shared and universally valid purpose or principle. Long after it had ceased to be a Puritan purpose, it still retained something of its original religious flavor. To G. K. Chesterton (1922, 7), the United States was the nation with the soul of a church. In Gunnar Myrdal's

(1944) formulation, Americans became the people of "the Creed." They shared a set of beliefs that was supposed to set the nation's existence on a different plane than other nations', and although writers such as Samuel Huntington (1981) and Louis Hartz (1955) found much that was troublesome in the creed, hardly anyone denied its power (see also Lipset 1996, 19, 31).

But a political community organized around ideas might redefine or simply dissolve itself much more easily than one rooted in blood and soil. Although all nations may be "imagined communities" (Anderson 1983),[4] some are more imaginary than others. During the Civil War, the United States demonstrated that it could imagine itself out of existence. Although we face no such dramatic rupture today, the bonds of American citizenship are sufficiently exiguous that they can be redefined in ways that drastically change the role and political attachments of the American people.

The exceptionalist vision of Americans as a people united only by democratic purpose may have been a patriotic conceit, but in the nineteenth-century republic little else held the citizens together as a nation. Even coercive efforts to preserve the country, like the Civil War, could scarcely have succeeded without an army of volunteers devoted to the cause of the Union. In an earlier departure from the exceptionalist creed, President Jefferson acquired the territory of Louisiana without first securing the consent of its inhabitants. They were citizens by purchase, not by principled belief. The tenuous nature of the government's hold over its new territorial acquisition made national authorities especially deferential to the inhabitants and heavily reliant on their willingness not only to transfer their loyalties from Paris or Madrid to Washington, D.C., but also to take on the work of governing. To facilitate such cooperation the government agreed that courts in the most heavily populated section of the Louisiana Purchase would follow the Continental civil code rather than the English common law (Meinig 1993, 12–17).

Nineteenth-century American citizens helped to perform the work of government and in return gained a voice in government. Their service as soldiers, administrators, and taxpayers helped to integrate them into the political order, but it also earned them the legal and political rights of citizens. Today, government has found ways of raising military forces, administering public policy, collecting taxes, and winning popular acquiescence that do not require much citizen involvement or voluntary mobilization. As a result, the acquisition and

---

4. The term "imagined communities" has been made familiar by Benedict Anderson (1983).

exercise of power by government institutions and political elites no longer revolves around popular participation and support as much as it once did.

The United States was not the only nation that relied on citizens to perform the tasks of government. Throughout the West, citizens were enlisted to enhance the administrative, extractive, and coercive capabilities of states. And, as in the United States, they received in return a variety of benefits including legal rights, pensions, and perhaps most notably the right to vote. The history of suffrage is often written so as to suggest that the opportunity to participate in national politics was wrung from unwilling rulers after bitter popular struggles. Yet, as Schattschneider observed, the difficulty with which voting rights were secured in the United States has often been overstated (Schattschneider 1960, 100). Political elites learned that it was worthwhile to accept the extension of suffrage even though it seemed to pose a risk to their own power. Allowing citizens the opportunity to take part in national politics enhanced the state's ability to wage war, raise revenues, and administer the government.

What distinguished the United States from European regimes of the nineteenth century was the exceptional extent of its reliance on citizen government. It had no choice. Alexis de Tocqueville reported that he had found nothing in America that a European would regard as government (de Tocqueville 1960, Vol. 1, 72–73). No professional civil service had survived from an earlier era of royal administration. Scarcely any standing army existed. The country's territory extended to remote regions in which the only government was what the citizens provided themselves. It was no wonder that American government was exceptional for its attentiveness to citizen sensibilities and its professed dedication to the creed of popular sovereignty. It was more democratic than other states of the time partly because it was exceptionally dependent on the good will, cooperation, and work of its people.

A Short History of Personal Democracy

The routine operations of American government once relied on the large-scale mobilization of the public to a far greater extent than they do today. Conceptions of political democracy that focus on parties, elections, and pressure groups tend to overlook this fading dimension of popular sovereignty. But the complete citizen, as Aristotle observed, plays two roles—ruling and being ruled—and these roles have been bound to one another. The more that government rule depended on citizen cooperation, the more that government submit-

Matthew Crenson and Benjamin Ginsberg

ted to the rule of citizens. As government has learned to manage the public business without the public, it has also diminished the occasions for the kind of popular mobilization that demands the reshaping of public policy or the changing of political institutions.

Some of the first steps toward the demobilization of American citizens date to the Progressive era, when reformers sought to eliminate waste and incompetence from government by abolishing patronage and crippling the political party organizations that mobilized working-class, immigrant voters who offended the Progressives' "public-regarding" conception of citizenship (Shefter 75–81). The Progressives' conception of an autonomous citizen independently evaluating candidates and policies was an early anticipation of personal democracy. But some of the most significant discouragement to the collective mobilization of citizens followed the end of World War II, perhaps the last and greatest summons to citizen duty in the nation's history.

They were expressions of the postwar conservative reaction against the New Deal. The Administrative Procedure Act of 1946 and the Taft-Hartley Act of 1947 were intended to curb the authority of New Deal regulatory agencies by holding them to formal standards of rule making and adjudication. The ostensible purpose of these acts was to prevent the interest groups under regulation from "capturing" or taking control of the agencies that were supposed to regulate them. The chief concern of congressional conservatives at the time was the privileged status of labor unions with respect to the National Labor Relations Board. To counter such interest group influence in the regulatory process, Congress tried to open the administrative rule making to the public at large by means of requirements for public notice and comment. To avoid bias in particular cases, the Administrative Procedure Act attempted to construct a firewall between an agency's rule-makers and its administrative law judges. Finally, Congress decreed that an agency's decisions could be appealed to the courts (Cass 1986, 377–378; O'Brien 1997).

In the effort to eliminate factional bias from the regulatory process, Congress also reduced the incentives for citizens to mobilize and form interest groups. After the Administrative Procedure Act, pressure successfully exerted on an agency's rule-makers did not necessarily extend to its adjudicators. Also, because the rule-making process was now open to the public at large, the need to organize groups and mobilize constituencies in order to gain access to it was not as great, especially because unfavorable decisions could be appealed from regulatory agencies to the courts.

The postwar regulatory reforms were eminently democratic, at least in a formal sense (O'Brien 1997, 50). It could be argued, in fact, that they opened government more fully to the participation of its citizens because of their notice and comment provisions and the opportunity to appeal agency decisions to the courts. The Taft-Hartley Act was explicitly justified as a measure that would protect individual workers from undemocratic labor unions as well as from the unfair labor practices of their employers. But because the new regulatory regime facilitated individual access to policy making, it reduced the value of collective mobilization.

The legalistic mode of administration imposed by the postwar conservative reaction was extended, in the 1960s and 1970s, to types of policies that the conservatives could hardly have anticipated—civil rights, occupational health and safety, environmental protection, and consumer protection (O'Brien 1997, 61; Sterett 1992). A further step in the progress of legalistic policy making was the use of public interest lawsuits as instruments of regulation. The civil rights movement had used litigation to advance its aims since the 1940s—but it did so, in part, because the denial of voting rights to African Americans and their minority status meant that blacks were seriously handicapped in the usual arenas of democratic decision making. Litigation was, like the resort to civil disobedience, a way to overcome electoral disabilities. In the 1970s, however, public interest groups emerged whose chief democratic disability was not minority status but rather the very breadth and diffuseness of the disorganized constituencies they claimed to represent. They devoted less energy to mobilizing their potential supporters than to litigation. Aided by responsive federal judges, these new public interest groups employed lawsuits against federal agencies—such as the Environmental Protection Agency—to establish regulatory standards that the agencies were then required to enforce (Melnick 1983).

A so-called advocacy explosion ensued. Groups claiming to represent diffuse population groups such as consumers, children, the disabled, the elderly, or the public in general opened offices in Washington, D.C., not just to conduct traditional lobbying activities aimed at Congress or the federal bureaucracy but also to litigate on behalf of their constituents. The relationship between the constituencies and the organizations claiming to speak for them, however, was often quite tenuous. Litigation required money, research, and expertise but not the political mobilization of a popular following. The membership of these groups sometimes amounted to nothing more than a mailing list of faceless contributors who had never met with one another to discuss the group's political objectives or strategies. A few highly influential groups, in fact, were sup-

Matthew Crenson and Benjamin Ginsberg

ported by foundation grants or by legal fees won in court cases, and some received funding from the federal government itself (Berry 1993, 31–32).[5]

The legalization of national policy making accentuated an emphasis on individual rights that has always been inherent in American ideas about citizenship. Public interest lawsuits aimed not only to assert those rights but also to invent new ones, and in the process they changed the character of national political discourse. Mary Ann Glendon (1991) argues that the language of rights is a conversation stopper. It "puts a damper on the processes of public justification, communication, and deliberation upon which the continuing vitality of a democratic regime depends" (Glendon 1991, 171). The successful assertion of a right trumps all other arguments. In some instances, of course, political argument can be stimulated by the contest between competing rights or by the attempt to extend a recognized right to a new situation. Once established, however, a right can be invoked without engaging in the collective action that awakens and renews the common ties of citizenship.

The vast increase in interest group litigation since 1970 (Koshner 1998), and the rights-based politics that followed from it, may help to explain a contemporary curiosity of American politics. By all accounts, the population of Washington lobbyists and interest groups has grown rapidly since 1970, to unprecedented levels, but no corresponding increase in group membership has occurred among Americans at large. One possible reason for this disparity may be that some of the newest interest groups have begun to target ever-narrower interests (Schier 1999, 15–17). But an explanation with even longer reach is that contemporary interest groups tend to concentrate more on litigation, research, polling, fund-raising, and media relations and less on mobilizing popular support. The handful of Washington-based interest groups that have extensive grassroots memberships, such as the National Rifle Association and AARP, are connected with the vast majority of their constituents only by mail (Skocpol 1999, 68). The interest group struggle in Washington, like the clash of party elites in Congress, becomes increasingly disconnected from the mobilization of citizens, and the scope of citizenship itself narrows.

While Washington interest groups floated free from the constituencies they claimed to represent, the federal government seemed to fasten itself more firmly to the grassroots. "Maximum feasible participation" was the controversial watchword of federal policy. Requirements for citizen participation spread

5. On government and foundation funding of interest groups, see Greve (1987) and Skocpol (1999).

from one national program to another (Crenson and Rourke 1987). Public bureaucracies and private interest groups seemed to be moving in opposite directions, but they were both dancing to the same music. Like the conservative reforms of the postwar era, they were opening the administrative processes of
regulation and policy implementation to outside forces—to citizens, and, like
their conservative precursors, they accomplished almost exactly the opposite.

Maximum feasible participation usually achieved only minimal mobilization of the public. In the Community Action Program, the Model Cities Program, and other antipoverty ventures of the federal government, the chief effect of participatory administration was to absorb and dissipate the political
pressures generated by urban protest movements, often by coopting the actual
or incipient leaders of those movements (Cloward and Piven 1971; Crenson
1974; Kerstein and Judd 1980). The participatory programs also lacked substance. After all, to allow for policy making by the people, official policy-makers had to refrain from issuing precisely designed programs with clearly artic-
ulated objectives. The immediate result, as Theodore Lowi pointed out, was
that "the absence of central direction and guidance simply deprives the disappointed of something to shoot against. This is a paternalism that demoralizes"
(Lowi 1969, 234–235).

It was also a formula for policies that would be difficult to justify and defend when under attack, precisely because the policies and their purposes were
not clearly or compellingly defined. When the Reagan tax cuts made deficit re-
duction the organizing purpose of federal politics in the 1980s, the last vestiges
of community action were swept away, along with the revenue-sharing and
block-grant programs of the 1970s (Conlan 1998, 168–169). They suffered
from the same political disabilities as their participatory predecessors—
vaguely defined objectives and weak or politically diffuse clienteles.

What replaced them was a new conservative policy regime that preached
the virtues of the market not just as a substitute for big government but also as
an instrument of big government. Privatization and vouchers were supposed to
free the public sector of bureaucratic inefficiency and unresponsiveness. But
they also represented a new stage in the erosion of citizenship. Vouchers and
programs of choice were designed so that public policies could be disaggre-
gated into private decisions. Under a school voucher system, for example, parents dissatisfied with the kind of education their children receive need never
complain or join with other parents to protest. They can simply choose to send
their children to a different and more satisfactory school.

An undercurrent in twentieth-century American politics flows through

Matthew Crenson and Benjamin Ginsberg

movements and measures strikingly at odds with one another. The postwar conservatives who backed the Administrative Procedure Act and the Great Society liberals who launched the war on poverty will never be mistaken for ideological soulmates. They are connected, however, by a shared political sensibility that ties them not only to one another but also to the Progressives who preceded them and the Reagan-Bush conservatives who followed. This sensibility is a tendency to individualize democracy—an inclination to provide citizens with personal access to politics, policy making, and administration, and by so doing to reduce the frequency and the need for collective action.

Personal democracy lowers the political barriers that citizens used to breach only by collective assault. Freedom of information policies, sunshine laws, mandatory public hearings, public notice and comment requirements, quotas for citizen representation on boards and committees, public agency hotlines, and policies of choice—these and other arrangements permit citizens to play politics alone. Yet the principal effect of these apparently benign arrangements for personal democracy is to shrink the role of citizens in American politics. Organizational entrepreneurs and elites who once mobilized followers in order to earn a place among the government's power-holders and policy-makers now discover that they can achieve similar or better results through litigation, or that by claiming to speak on behalf of a diffuse and otherwise voiceless constituency, they can qualify as stakeholders whose presence is essential to the legitimacy of federal policy. When popular mobilization ceases to be a favored strategy among leaders, citizens are left to their own devices—of which there is no shortage these days. But they generally lend themselves only to an attenuated kind of citizenship. It seldom results in political mobilization for collective ends; more frequently the outcome is individual action for improved service or personalized treatment. One alternative for citizens is community activism designed, not to raise political issues or reshape public policy, but to produce public goods and services directly—cleaning up the environment, for example, or serving meals in a homeless shelter. This dimension of personal democracy may be personally rewarding and certainly helpful to needy people or the local community at large, but it does not represent an exercise of political democracy. A nation of citizens, once illuminated by democratic purpose, has disintegrated into a thousand points of light.

PART TWO

The Parties as Electoral Organizations

5

American Political Parties: Still Central to a Functioning Democracy?

L. Sandy Maisel

One must be struck by certain ironies as one looks at the role of American po-litical parties at the dawn of a new millennium. On the one hand, parties have some evident weaknesses; no close observer can fail to recognize that certain basic functions that parties perform in our system—for instance, the role of mobilizing citizens to participate in politics—are not now performed as well as would be the case in a more ideal system. On the other hand, for a democracy such as ours to function effectively, the role of parties is still vital, and this nec-essary centrality, a position once clearly in evidence, is recognized by even the critics of our current parties. In this chapter, I develop both sides of that dilemma about the role of parties in the decades ahead.

The Role of Parties in the "Golden Age"

My first assertion in this chapter is that parties have been central to the func-tioning of American democracy. Of course, we are not just at the dawn of the new millennium, but, equally important to some, we are about to mark the 100th anniversary of the founding of the American Political Science Association (APSA) and the 50th anniversary of the publication of the APSA's groundbreak-ing committee report on political parties (American Political Science Association 1950). Those two events mark an interesting time to begin this examination.

I would like to thank John Bibby, Paul Herrnson, Steven Schier, and Walter Stone for comments on an earlier draft of this chapter. I am also grateful for the comments of the participants at the Fordham Conference and of the editors of this volume. I also would like to acknowledge the help of my research assistants, Cathy Flemming and Rebecca Ryan. The data from the Candidate Emer-gence Study was made possible through a grant from the National Science Foundation (SBR-9515350).

Writing almost 100 years ago, Lord Bryce's observations of our democracy, as a foreigner visiting our shores, were nearly as perceptive as de Tocqueville's had been a century before that. Bryce noted that as institutions for mobilizing citizens, political parties served the role of overcoming significant impediments to an effectively functioning participatory democracy: constraints on citizen time, competing demands for citizen leisure time, and the complexity of political issues (Bryce 1909, 237–240, 331–356; see also Schier 2000).

Bryce was observing American politics during the Progressive era, as reforms were being instituted that would undermine the strength of political parties. But he was most struck by what American politics looked like during the time period in which parties were central to American democracy, a period that most observers claim extended into the 1890s. At the end of the nineteenth century, one could claim with good reason that American political parties were viewed as an essential, vital aspect of the functioning of our political institutions (Silbey 1991, 1998).

Why was this so? In recent years scholars have invested a good deal of time and effort into understanding the circumstances in which political parties are strong. John Aldrich has argued that parties are instruments that serve the needs of politicians:

> My basic argument is that the major political party is the creature of the politicians, the ambitious office seeker and officeholder. They have created and maintained, used or abused, reformed or ignored the political party when doing so has furthered their goals and ambitions (Aldrich 1995, 4).

But factors other than their utility to politicians have been seen as important in understanding party dominance as well. Among the factors to which Aldrich points are the rules that govern the regime and the party role in it (see also Maisel and Bibby 2000) and the "historical setting," a broad phrase encompassing the competitive situation, the issues at play, the means of political dialogue, and other factors (Aldrich 1995, 5). Martin Shefter (1994) and John Coleman (1996) stress the policy environment for its role in contributing to the strength of parties. They essentially argue that parties will dominate when issues divide the electorate in a way that is consistent and meaningful to most citizens.

What can be concluded about the so-called golden age of parties is that a combination of circumstances evolved with the result that American politics could not be understood or appreciated without acknowledging the primary roles that parties played. The major issue of the day—the tariff—divided the

L. Sandy Maisel

parties and the electorate along class lines and reinforced regional and ethnic cleavages. The rules under which politics were fought gave the parties a principal role in choosing candidates, in running campaigns, and in governing. Politicians, in response to their own ambitions, found parties useful in winning office, in passing policies they favored, and in enhancing their personal power. The parties cemented citizen loyalties by providing material incentives and social benefits that were each important in the daily lives of the average American.[1] Citizens responded to these parties by giving their enthusiastic loyalty to the parties that championed their views on the most important policies of the day, a loyalty they expressed through long-term commitment and turnout at the polls.

The argument is thus that parties served a key role in the effective functioning of a participatory democracy. Citizens related to one party or the other. The parties expressed views on the issues of the day that mattered most to the citizens. Citizens knew about the party positions and turned out to vote for candidates who advocated their views.[2] Those in government attempted to implement policies that reflected the positions they had taken in campaigns. And for our purposes, parties did what Lord Bryce observed—they overcame the problems inherent in participatory democracy by making politics part of what citizens did for leisure, reducing the time politics consumed by reducing a range of choices to a rather simple one, and simplifying the task of understanding government policies by squaring off on the fundamental issues that concerned most citizens.

Abuses by Parties and the Progressive Response

What went wrong? The problem was that the golden age of partisan politics was in fact tarnished. As parties became more powerful, and as they were serving the needs of a public not consumed with politics, they were also becoming less than exemplary institutions. Corruption was widespread. Patronage was often tied to graft. The partisan press, so useful in communicating party views,

1. Unfortunately, we do not have survey data to compare the ways in which citizens of this era felt about political parties with the ways in which today's citizens respond. Stone has pointed out the interesting converse to that data gap: We do not know how observers of politics in the golden era of parties would view partisan divisions in our time. Although these questions are interesting and in some ways troubling, we are left to deal with the best observations we can obtain for each time period.

2. Of course, in giving this very abbreviated argument, I am ignoring the fact that participation was restricted by gender and race throughout most of the nation for most of this time.

frequently distorted public issues in order to increase sales. Political machines dominated city government, socializing immigrant groups to be sure but often short-circuiting the citizenship process so that newly indebted immigrants could convert their gratitude into votes. One could argue that parties began to limit political discourse, restricting alternatives that might alienate some of their voters. Party power depended on electoral victory; other goals became secondary. (See Erie 1985; Schier 2000; Schudson 1998.)

The reaction to this aspect of party power was the reformist zeal of the Mugwumps and the reforms of the Progressive era. The story of these reforms is familiar and has been told in many places (see McGerr 1986). From the point of view of parties, the progressive reforms instituted change after change that limited their ability to control the process: widespread adoption of the secret ballot to prevent parties from knowing for whom their supporters were casting ballots; improvement in registration systems to regularize access to the ballot; civil service reform to remove many government jobs from partisan control; corrupt practices acts to make explicitly illegal some of the actions in which parties had been involved; implementation of the direct primary to remove control of the nominating process (and thus recruitment of officeholders) from the hands of party officials; direct election of U.S. senators to transfer to the voters an important prize previously controlled by the party dominating a state's legislature; nonpartisan governments in many municipalities to handle what many felt to be routine governmental functions without partisan interference; and the institution of initiative, referendum, and recall provisions to permit citizens to retain control over policy making even after elections had been contested (Maisel 1999, 51–52).

How can one evaluate the results of these reforms? That depends, of course, on the criteria one uses. First, these reforms accomplished their stated goals. The power of party bosses to control the political process abated. These reforms played a key role in the weakening of party as the central fixture in American politics. Other factors contributed to this trend as well. The expansion of the role of the federal government during the New Deal meant that government officials, not party bosses, provided jobs and welfare for those unable to manage on their own. Political communications, once carried out largely on a personal basis, moved to the realm of mass media, first to radio and then to television. Thus, during the first half of the twentieth century, parties declined for a variety of reasons.

Second, the consequences of these reforms were not seen by the Progressives and their allies. Jump ahead fifty years. By the time of the APSA report

(American Political Science Association 1950), scholars and activists alike were dissatisfied with the role that political parties were playing in our system of government. Parties were seen by the members of the APSA committee as an institutional vehicle that could be reformed in order to serve more fruitfully the needs of a participatory democracy. Whether the responsible party model was ever an appropriate one for American democracy is not the point. The fact that parties, once central to the system but by mid-century weakened, were seen as a vehicle for governmental reform is more relevant. Further, it can be stated without much controversy that the weakening of parties seen by mid-century continued through the last half of the century. Of course, one must acknowledge that Broder's (1971) lament, *The Party's Over,* has not come to pass. Rather, as organizations parties have proven to be quite adaptive institutions. Today they provide resources, both financial and professional, that are important to candidates' campaigns. Through the use of soft money and issue ads, they help to define the issues in campaigns in certain highly competitive regions. But these roles are reactive to the new context of candidate-centered campaigning (Bibby 1998b; Herrnson 1998b; see also the other articles in Maisel 1998).

Thus we see an evident dilemma as we look to the future of political parties. They are moving in two apparently opposite directions. Even with the significant adaptations noted earlier in this chapter, parties and party leaders are not looked to as building blocks of the electoral process. Choose your own standard of judgment—self-reporting of party identification by voters or strength of party identification among those who do identify, ticket splitting, party switching among the political elite, control over campaigns, control over political communication, ability to discipline their own officeholders, breadth and strength of organization, centrality to the process—by these criteria or many others, parties continue to appear weak and far from central to the electoral process.

Difficulties Evident in the Electoral Process Today

How then might parties be still central to a functioning democracy? *The argument is that just as parties are weak, so too is the state of our participatory democratic system.* For a representative democracy to function effectively, citizens must be given meaningful choices at the polls. Our representative democracy rests on the consent of the governed. Citizens can give their consent to the policies passed by those in office only if they have the opportunity and take the opportunity to review the performance of those in office. Frequent elections are meaningless in the absence of competition. Thus one measure of the health of a democratic system is the extent to which citizens are given a meaningful choice. Another measure is the extent to which citizens participate in that choice.

Even with all of their flaws, political parties in their heyday contributed to these important aspects of democracy. The parties controlled access to the ballot and guaranteed that competition existed. They did so because that was viewed as the most important aspect of their role. Parties benefited when their candidates won office, controlled the spoils of victory, and implemented the policies they advocated.

But more than that, parties involved citizens in the electoral process. As I noted earlier in this chapter, party politics was relevant for most citizens, because the parties split on the key issues of the day and because they affected voters' daily lives in basic ways, serving as an important element of the community's social fabric. Parties mobilized citizens in many ways. Citizens saw the relevance of the issues raised and had a stake in the success of the party that claimed their allegiance. A deep sense of loyalty developed between voters and party leaders. In addition, involvement in party politics during campaign season was part of the leisure activities in which citizens partook—in a way that would be totally alien to even the most politically active citizens today.

The contrast between the functioning of parties in the so-called golden era and the ways in which they work today could not be more stark. One hundred years ago party leaders controlled the nominating process; their most important function—and ultimately that on which all else depended—was to contest for office. Today, throughout the nation, party nominations are determined by direct primary; in some states, party rules prohibit party officials from involvement in the nominating process. In most states the role of parties in determining nominees is minor and informal (Morehouse 1998).

One hundred years ago the parties provided a simple, coherent set of reasons for their supporters to maintain loyalty. The issues before the nation were less complex than they are today, the major parties divided on the issues of the day, and the parties connected directly with the people. Today candidates voice their own issue positions, often at odds with those of others in their parties, still more often nuanced to appeal to their particular constituents. Rather than appealing to citizens based on issue differences, the leaders of the two major parties strive to capture the middle-ground, to offend as few possible voters as possible by issue positions.

L. Sandy Maisel

One hundred years ago parties mobilized their followers through personal contact at the precinct, ward, or, in rural areas, town level. Party workers knew all of the voters and knew their preferences. The job of the party workers was to get their supporters to the polls. Incentives were both tangible and intangible. Voters knew that the tangible incentives from their parties depended on their parties' officeholders winning elections. Social networks and peer pressure also led citizens to vote; civic participation was expected and was a clear societal norm. Today political communication is through the mass media or through computerized, impersonal mailings. Citizens do not know local party workers, often because party positions in their localities are vacant. Certainly party workers who do exist do not provide important rewards to party loyalists. Politics no longer provides the social network for many citizens; leisure time is filled by other pursuits—sports, church, family, television, movies, and the like. (On these points see Nie, Junn, and Stehlik-Barry 1996; Rosenstone and Hansen 1993; Schier 2000.)

Broad-based partisan mobilization has been replaced by narrowly defined issue-specific activation (Schier 2000). Whereas once the parties tried to mobilize all of their followers to vote for their slate of candidates, now special interests, making narrower appeals to carefully selected audiences, try to convince only those who support their positions to participate. Turnout is down. Programmatic discussion has given way to narrow appeals based on specific interests or to broad appeals based on either character or capturing the middle-ground and offending as few as possible. Satisfaction with and trust in government have declined.

To cite just three indices:

1. Voter turnouts in presidential and congressional elections remain well below what they were at the beginning of the twentieth century and considerably below what they were even in the 1950s.
2. In National Election Study surveys in the 1990s, more than 70 percent of the respondents agreed with the statement, "Public officials don't care what people like me think," and 60 percent of the respondents thought, "Government is run by a few big interests looking out for themselves."
3. Competition for the right to govern has decreased drastically. In the 1998 congressional election, more than 98 percent of the incumbent representatives seeking reelection did so successfully. But more than that, ninety-four incumbents were returned to office without any major

party competition whatsoever. In addition, another thirty-nine incumbents won with over 75 percent of the vote in the general election. Out of more than four hundred incumbents seeking reelection in 1998, only thirty received less than 55 percent of the vote; among those thirty were the five who lost in that election. The 1998 election was not an aberration. It merely extended a trend that has existed and has been commented on for some time. Although slightly more competition exists for more visible offices—governor and U.S. senator—there is even less competition for seats in most state legislatures and for seats in county legislatures and on city and town councils.

A number of factors are obviously at work here—and one could not argue that weakening parties are the only cause of this lack of competition. But two aspects of this phenomenon, which is a serious problem for our democracy, deserve attention.

First, candidates run on their own, frequently building their own organizations distinct from that of the party and often taking great pains to avoid association with a party. Candidate-centered organizations have been encouraged by (1) the weakening of party allegiance among the electorate and of party organization, (2) by the means through which citizens receive political communications, and (3) by campaign finance laws that require individual candidates to form their own committees, that restrict the role that party can play, and that encourage the role of special interest groups.

Second, party organization plays a limited role at best in recruiting candidates for office. The role is limited because party organization in many areas is weak or nonexistent, because parties can offer potential candidates few incentives to encourage them to run, and because national party rules have restricted what the party committees most concerned with campaigns for federal office are permitted to do.

These two developments have shifted the process through which ballot positions are filled from one of *party recruitment* to one of *candidate emergence*. However, it is difficult to pinpoint when this shift occurred. The timing of this shift varies from locality to locality and from office to office, but there is no doubt that it has occurred.

Discussions of systemic reform have gone on elsewhere. Certainly the literature on changes in political communication is more than adequate to make the point (see, for example, Ansolabehere and Iyengar 1995; Ansolabehere, Behr, and Iyengar 1993; and Kerbel 1998). Similarly, campaign finance reform

L. Sandy Maisel

has been an issue atop the agendas of those dissatisfied with the ways our elections have been run for decades. In fact, during the Carter administration the prestigious designation HR1 was reserved for a campaign finance reform measure in 1977. The history of the failure of campaign finance reform has been well documented (see Corrado et al. 1997; Mutch 1988; see also Chapter 7 in this volume).

Strengthening Parties to Address the Problems of Today's Politics

What about the weakness of party organization as a contributing factor to both the lack of competitiveness in American elections and the lack of citizen interest in those elections? Although there is widespread agreement that party organization is weak today, perhaps less agreement is found concerning what would constitute strong parties in the modern context. Certainly no one would argue that we should return to the antidemocratic, smoke-filled rooms of the past. But is it possible to strengthen party organization so that the parties can perform the important, central functions they once performed in our system (at least more effectively than today)? If so, what would constitute strong parties in that context?

The first prerequisite would be to have some influence on the selection of candidates running under their labels. Second, parties would need some additional control over the functioning of elections in order to regain strength. Third, party messages would need to be consistent (and differentiated) at least on major issues. Fourth, parties would have to be able to play an active role in implementing major parts of their programs. The argument is not that these enhanced roles for parties need to be absolute, but each needs to be altered so that parties are in a stronger position than they are now. (For a similar view of elements of strong parties, see Ware 1988). This is not an argument for a responsible party model. Rather, it is an argument for a *relevant party model.*

The most important of these aspects—and the focus of the remainder of this chapter—is the potential impact on state and local nominations. To the extent that parties affect state and local nominations, officeholders have a stake in the party. That is, if state and local party activists are influential in an officeholder's first nomination or if they are seen as influencing an officeholder's ability to achieve renomination, then elected officials will care about what the party activists think and do. The chances of the other criteria being met increase when party becomes more relevant to officeholders.

Table 5-1. Contact by Party Committees

	Named Potential Candidates (percent) (Largest n = 452)	State Legislators (percent) (Largest n = 875)
National Party Committees	8.2	3.2
National Congressional Campaign Committees	15.7	4.9
State Party Committees	22.2	8.8
Local Party Committees	34.7	14.4
Any Party Committee	40.7	18.7

Source: Candidate Emergence Study, Potential Candidate Survey.

Some years ago John Frendeis, James Gibson, and Laura Vertz (1990) demonstrated that the existence of functioning local party organizations had important consequences for electoral competition. My work with Walter Stone shows that party organization retains significant influence in encouraging strong potential candidates to run for office. In the summer of 1997, we surveyed a group of potential candidates for the U.S. House of Representatives whom we identified in a random sample of 200 congressional districts throughout the nation.[3] The Candidate Emergence Study asked potential candidates a series of questions regarding the likelihood that they would run for the House and the factors that entered into their decisions. The analysis of the data is ongoing, but some of the results to this point are suggestive of the role that political parties can play in the recruitment process.

The pool of potential candidates in the 200 congressional districts comprised individuals who were identified by one or more of the informants in their districts as someone who would be a strong candidate for Congress, regardless of whether the individual had ever expressed interest in running or been mentioned as a possible candidate. State legislators whose districts were located in the 200 congressional districts in the sample were added to this list of named potential candidates. For analytical purposes two separate datasets were created, one consisting of all potential candidates named by those in our informant pool (including potential candidates who happened to be state legis-

3. The Candidate Emergence Project has been described in great detail elsewhere (see Maisel and Stone 1997; Stone and Maisel 1999; Stone, Maisel, and Maestas 1998; these and other papers are available on the Candidate Emergence Study web site at http://www.socsci.colorado.edu/CES/home.html).

L. Sandy Maisel

Table 5–2. Total Contacts by Party Committees

	Named Potential Candidates (percent) (n = 452)	State Legislators (percent) (n = 875)
No Contacts	59.3	81.3
Contacted by One Organization	16.8	9.9
Contacted by Two Organizations	12.8	6.4
Contacted by Three Organizations	5.8	1.0
Contacted by Four Organizations	5.3	1.4

Source: Candidate Emergence Study, Potential Candidate Survey.

lators) and one consisting of all state legislator respondents (including those who were named by our informants).

A battery of questions was asked seeking respondent assessment of the likelihood that he or she would run for the U.S. House of Representatives in 1998, in the next three to four terms, or in the foreseeable future. For much of the analysis this battery of questions has constituted the dependent variable.[4] The independent variables about which respondents were questioned included contacts by various party officials. In addition to asking about the national parties, the national congressional campaign committees, state parties, and local parties, indices were created to measure multiple contacts, and a dummy variable was used to measure whether the respondent had been contacted by any party organization.

Table 5-1 shows the frequency with which the respondents were contacted by party organizations. Table 5-2 shows the numbers of organizations that contacted the respondents. Some conclusions are clear. First, as one would expect, the more local the committee, the more likely that a respondent was contacted. More than one in three of the named potential candidates and one in seven of the state legislators representing voters in the sampled congressional districts were contacted by local party officials about running for the House. By contrast, far fewer were contacted by either the national party organization or by the state party.

Second, an impressively large number of the named potential candidates (more than two in five) were contacted by some level of party organization;

4. For other aspects of the analysis, "chances of winning" has been used as the dependent variable. For still other projects, different questions have been used as appropriate.

American Political Parties

Table 5-3. Correlations with Likelihood of Running in 1998

	Named Potential Candidates [n]	State Legislators [n]
National Party Committees	0.2332* [299]	0.0173 [762]
National Congressional Campaign Committees	0.1841* [308]	0.0502 [765]
State Party Committees	0.1512* [324]	0.941* [771]
Local Party Committees	0.1553* [330]	0.1174* [776]
Any Party Committee	0.1800* [407]	0.1103* [820]
Cumulative Party Contact	0.2449* [407]	0.1086* [820]

Source: Candidate Emergence Study, Potential Candidate Survey.
* $p < .01$

nearly one in five of the state legislators reported some contact. Third, although the norm was for only one organization to contact a potential candidate (if any made contact at all), nearly a quarter of the named potential candidates (and almost 10 percent of the state legislators) were contacted by more than one organization. Further analysis remains to be done, but the implication is that party organizations make a concerted effort to contact the most appealing potential candidates in order to convince them to run.

Of course the relevant question for this analysis is the extent to which these contacts were successful in convincing potential candidates to run for the House. Table 5-3 presents an initial answer to this inquiry, exploring the question of the relationship between a potential candidate's likelihood of running for the House in 1998 (scored on a seven-point scale) and the various measures of party contact.

Table 5-3 reveals a statistically significant ($p<.01$) relationship between the likelihood that a potential candidate will run for the House and that potential candidate's having been contacted by party officials in all cases except two (the national organizations contacting state legislators). The strength of the relationship varies among the types of contacts. It is strongest when named potential candidates are contacted by more than one party organization—and when the named potential candidates are contacted by the national party organization. These bivariate relationships, while highly suggestive, are just that—suggestive. Much more analysis needs to be done to understand, for example, which of the potential candidates were most likely to be contacted by which level of party organization (if at all) or to unravel the nature of the relationship between contact and likelihood of running. The nature of the contact, the expectations of the potential candidate for organizational support, the strength of the party organization, and other variables clearly enter into this relationship.

The argument then is that party organizations can have an impact on recruiting quality candidates for Congress and by extension for other offices. As the offices become more local in scope, the local organization is the likely point of contact. Clearly most local organizations—and all party organizations for most offices—do not play this role effectively. But it is there to be played, and it can be effective.

To be sure, the national parties are playing this role for some seats in Congress. Both national congressional campaign committees and those in leadership positions in the House were concerned about the challengers running in 2000, because control of the House was at stake. In strategizing, both parties see congressional elections as local in nature. To determine which races they will attempt to influence, the parties use poll-derived studies of the vulnerability of incumbents. They encourage potential candidates by offering various types of campaign support, both that paid for by soft money at the party level and financial contributions or help in raising money by party leaders.[5] However, they have neither the resources nor the power to take these steps in every race throughout the nation. Thus they concentrate on only a relatively small number of seats seen to be "in play," all but guaranteeing little or no competition in the other seats.

Although stronger state legislative party organizations and state legislative leaders play active roles in recruitment in some areas, the extent of party influence in recruiting candidates below the national level seems at best to parallel the situation in recruiting candidates for Congress. That is, candidates are recruited for seats seen as likely to be hotly contested. But many seats go to one party or the other by default, because the state and local parties do not find any candidates, much less credible candidates.

The potential role that parties can play in effectively extending competition goes beyond encouraging qualified strong candidates to run for office. One

5. I thank Paul Herrnson for suggesting how these party efforts conform with my argument (see Herrnson 1988, 1998, 2000).

of the most important tools taken away from parties by the progressive reforms was control over the nominating process. If parties cannot control nominations—or at least strongly influence them—then party encouragement of potential candidates may be for naught. And potential candidates surely see this.

No clearer example of this can be presented than the case of the special election to fill the California congressional seat left vacant by the death of Democrat George Brown. Ten candidates filed for the special election in the fall of 1999, for a seat that was thought to be highly competitive. The Democrats feared that their party would be split between Brown's widow, Marta, and state senator Joe Baca; Baca's lukewarm position on gun control was a key issue in that race. The Democratic leadership felt that each was a strong candidate but that a united party was crucial. Republican leaders, including Rep. Thomas M. Davis III of Virginia, chair of the National Republican Congressional Committee, felt that the strongest Republican candidate was Superior Court Judge Linda M. Wilde, who had lost to Brown by fewer than 1,000 votes in 1996. But Davis and others were unsuccessful in efforts to convince the 1994 GOP nominee, Rob Guzman, and the 1998 nominee, Ella Pirozzi, who was raising money for a rematch with Brown in 2000 at the time of his death, to step aside for Wilde. As a result, Wilde stepped aside.[6]

Party efforts to derecruit can be as important as efforts to recruit. The 2000 U.S. Senate race to succeed Sen. Daniel Patrick Moynihan, D-N.Y., was characterized early on by GOP efforts to clear the nomination path for New York City's mayor Rudolph Guiliani, thought to be the Republican most likely to capture the seat against First Lady Hillary Rodham Clinton. When Guiliani dropped out of the race unexpectedly, party leaders made similar efforts on behalf of the eventual nominee, Long Island congressman Rick Lazio. In Ohio, party leaders worked hard, and successfully, to discourage controversial talk-show host Jerry Springer from seeking a seat in the U.S. Senate in 2000.

Is it possible to determine when party officials do and do not play an effective role in the nominating process? Some variables can be singled out for further testing. The most important factor is the willingness (and in some cases the ability under party rules) of party officials to be involved in the nominating process.

6. The California example also points to the influence of changes in state laws that impede parties' roles in the nominating process. At the time California operated under a so-called blanket primary, in which all names appear on one ballot and voters can essentially cast ballots in the Democratic primary for some offices and the Republican primary for others. This form of ballot makes it more difficult for party activists and loyalists to exert influence over their parties' nominations.

The first step in this effort is the commitment to involvement. The second step is the recruitment of strong potential candidates to convince them to run. The third step is the effort to smooth the path to nomination for those candidates.

To achieve the first step, party organization must exist. For years there was no Republican Party organization throughout much of the South. Most seats, especially those below the level of statewide office, went by default to Democratic candidates. The rejuvenation of the GOP in the South started at the top, but one clear sign of success has been the ability of southern Republicans to fill slates and win seats for lower-level offices (for example, state legislators or county officials). Where party organization does not exist, the likelihood that party will play its most basic role—contesting offices so that the citizenry has some choice—diminishes quickly.

Some party organizations are prohibited, by party rule, from intervening in primary contests. That restriction places party officials in a bind. Part of their role, almost by definition, is to guarantee that their slate is as full as possible. But they cannot even guarantee help to the candidates whom they recruit if those candidates are challenged for a nomination, much less can they guarantee them the nomination. Therein lies a serious problem for party organization at the dawn of the new millennium.

The reformist zeal to rein in parties was so strong and the image of party leaders among the electorate so tainted at the turn of the last century that party leaders today are often unable to perform what should be their most vital function in our democracy, the recruitment of candidates for office. Party leaders who are so restricted often must let the nomination process take care of itself. In so doing, they allow many seats to go uncontested, weak candidates to win nominations without serious opposition in other cases, and qualified candidates to go unrecruited and unencouraged, even if they are contemplating a contest.

What can be done to alter this situation? Some steps are already being taken. Legislative leaders are setting up their own organizations to recruit candidates for key seats. This has been seen at the national level for some time. The experience of GOPAC, a political action committee established by Rep. Newt Gingrich, R-Ga., is instructive here, but so too is the collaboration between House Minority Leader Richard Gephardt, D-Mo., and the Democratic Congressional Campaign Committee as they sought candidates for the 2000 election. It is becoming more and more true at the state level. But again, this kind of enterprise is selective; organizations concentrate only on those seats deemed winnable, not on guaranteeing competition throughout a state or region. Although these efforts are commendable, they do not allow the system to meet the minimum requirements for an effectively functioning participatory democracy.

Other steps are being taken in various parts of the country. No one would encourage reforms that would lead back to domination by party bosses or to nominations decided in secret in the proverbial smoke-filled rooms. But a number of states do permit party organizations to play a formal role in nominating contests. In many states pre-primary party conventions play some role in the process. The role may be to guarantee access to the primary ballot (as in New Mexico, Colorado, and New York) or to place the convention choice in a preferred position on the ballot (as in Rhode Island, North Dakota, and Delaware). Connecticut calls for convention (or party caucus) nominations, unless the choice is challenged by a candidate who has not prevailed at the party meeting. Party endorsements have official status in eight states and unofficial but important status in at least five more.

In addition, local party units often play key endorsing roles in other states. The states with a strong party role in the nominating process tend to be highly competitive two-party states. The party rules all but guarantee a strong party organization, because the organization has an important function to perform (see Maisel 1999, chap. 7). In the late 1980s, Malcolm Jewell and David Olson pointed out that parties with formal roles in the nominating process were not equally successful in guaranteeing that the parties' choices won the primaries (Jewell and Olson 1988, 96–98; see also Jewell and Morehouse 2001). The point is that rules of this type give the party a stake in seeking and supporting strong candidates—and that leads to improvement of the process.

Conclusion

Although American political parties appear to be weaker now than they were in their heyday, they still have important roles to play, if our political system is to function as well as it might. The dilemma about the future for political parties—that is, which of the two trends, resurgence or decline, will prevail—will be resolved according to whether parties can emerge to play a relevant role. Neither advocacy of a pure strong party model nor acceptance of an archetypal weak party model seems appropriate. Rather, what is called for is a relevant party model. Parties have taken some steps in this direction, but many more steps remain if the goal of an effectively functioning democracy is to be obtained.

L. Sandy Maisel

First, few would argue against the proposition that American political parties appear to be weaker than they once were. The relevant question is the standard of strength one should apply. If the standard is the strong or responsible party model familiar to students of party theory (and present in many parliamentary governments), our party system falls far short. But if one adopts a more pragmatic standard, one could argue that American parties have adapted quite well to a changing political context. They behave strategically in allotting their resources, and their role is an important one for maintaining competitive elections.

One could extend that argument further. As mentioned earlier, the lack of two-party competition stands as one piece of evidence that the electoral system today fails to meet democratic ideals. Some would argue that those ideals are met throughout the nation as a whole, even if they are not met in every district. The partisan split in the House of Representatives is extremely close; congressional elections in swing districts are extremely hard fought as control of the House is at stake. Much the same can be said for the Senate. Fewer and fewer state houses are dominated by one party or the other; split state houses or divided government in the states has become more common (Fiorina 1996). Presidential elections and gubernatorial elections in most states are also hotly contested, with neither party eliminated before the campaigns begin. As a result of these factors, competition for control of the national government and of most state governments is intense. Looked at in this way, citizens can use the ballot box to instruct their elected officials as to their desires.

However, this view of effective competition to ensure democratic control over the government accepts that only some citizens should have a say in the outcome. Other citizens have no direct control, though their votes offset each other. That conception of democracy fails the basic test of citizen participation, of obtaining consent of the governed. It is a view of representation that ignores the nexus between representative and constituent. It is a view that leads to increased public cynicism and disdain for politics.

Thus we return to the role of parties as these organizations might function in the twenty-first century. How can they be relevant in an evolving electoral context? How can they effectively expand their current roles to be more central to the functioning of American democracy?

Parties perform many of the functions they have traditionally performed but often do so poorly. That is to say, parties provide a framework for an overall organization. The national party conventions name the parties' nominees for president and vice president, who adopt platforms that state party positions. State and local parties try to fill ballot slates and to organize campaign activities for all of their candidates. And the parties certainly provide the structure for organizing government at the state and national levels. But these roles involve little independent input by party officials. They are carried out because they must be carried out. Little of substance is involved in the parties' roles in these functions.

Parties have adapted to a changing political context by taking on some new roles, particularly as a provider of campaign funds and a broker bringing together candidates who need financial support and interests that might provide that support and bringing together political consultants with specific expertise and candidates in need of that expertise (Bibby 1998b; Herrnson 1998b; Sorauf 1998). In so doing, they have made themselves relevant to their candidates.

But that kind of relevance is different from relevance to the democratic process. The roles parties have adopted are important for self-preservation, so that the parties do not become the dinosaurs of the political process. But can they make a positive contribution to that process?

The argument here is that they can—and that the key to their playing a central role in the current political environment lies in political recruitment. It is important to differentiate roles when noting that parties are weakening in some ways and becoming stronger in others. Recruitment is one role on which they must concentrate if they are to reassume a central position in a democracy.

In the current environment the party role in recruitment is far different from what it was in the past. In the past, parties controlled access to the ballot. They recruited candidates and guaranteed those candidates the party nomination. Today no guarantees can be given; parties have only limited power to influence nominations, and that power varies from state to state. Moreover, candidate-centered campaigns imply that candidate emergence has replaced candidate recruitment. Most candidates today are self-starters, not brought up through the ranks by party leaders.

The relevant party role in recruitment in this context takes on three aspects. The first aspect is recognition that an important party role is to guarantee, to the extent possible, that strong candidates run for all offices. As more and more districts become competitive, fewer and fewer seats are safe for either party; strength of candidacies is important in the outcome. The second aspect, following directly on the first, is the assumption that the party role is to encourage, in every possible way, good candidates who are considering running. The Candidate Emergence Study clearly shows that many strong potential candidates consider races for public office but in the end decide not to run. It also shows that party encouragement helps potential candidates tip the scales toward running but that parties are not very active in encouraging potential candidates. A clear opportunity exists for an enhanced and highly relevant role.

The third aspect is necessary to make this role possible. Parties need to increase the resources available to them to encourage potential candidates to run. Doing so would involve changes in party rules, changes that would set up mechanisms for party endorsement of potential candidates before nomination. Such mechanisms exist in some states—and those states are more successful in fielding strong slates of candidates.

It is difficult to argue for an enhanced role for political parties in an era generally viewed as anti-party. In addition, one must be concerned about who controls a party organization if one thinks it should have more strength. If party organizations are controlled by fringe elements in the party, then their domination might lead to less, not more, competition in general elections. If that were the case in both parties, the result could be increased tension in the polity. The assumption here is that an increased role for party organization would mean that traditional elements in the party would have a stake in participating. Party then could play a more central role in defining the issues of the day, in structuring campaigns, in mobilizing the electorate, and ultimately in seeing that the electoral process represents our best effort to give the consent of the governed to policies passed by our elected officials.

If citizens see the importance of electoral competition to their stake in our democracy, they should not resist efforts by state and local parties to take the steps necessary so that they can encourage strong potential candidates to run in an effective manner. By so doing, they would take a large step toward the creation of a more relevant role for parties in the politics of the twenty-first century.

6

Policy Coherence in Political Parties: The Elections of 1984, 1988, and 1992

William Crotty

Political parties do many things. For some, practitioners and theorists alike, winning elections is their chief goal. For others, such a minimalist and instrumental objective is not enough. They see political parties in the context of the parties' performance within a democratic system and emphasize the parties' duties of representation and accountability, especially in terms of the policy choices offered and, once in office, implemented. This for them is a crucial linkage function that distinguishes between parties of little sustained relevance—campaign organizations to promote individual candidacies—and parties that are viable agents of democratic choice and governance.

To fulfill the policy-based conception of a party system, the parties would have to do the following:

- Offer voters clear choices on issues
- Represent and commit to distinctive policy options
- Move in office with coherence and unity to achieve the major policy initiatives emphasized in campaigns

This conception of a principal focus for American political party accountability is not new. Arguably it has been around for a century or more. The most forceful, contentious, and influential statement of this broad perspective would have to be the conception of party responsibility found in *Toward a More Responsible Two-Party System* (American Political Science Association 1950). This American Political Science Association (APSA) report argued for disciplined parties with capabilities for policy formulation and responsiveness, in both elections and public office, to the concerns of its members. In effect, parties would approximate the like-minded coalitions so often discussed and would have the will and resources to move beyond campaign rhetoric in providing policy guidance and leadership to the mass public, fulfilling what many would consider a prime tenet of democratic representation.

The assumptions of the APSA report include the following:

A. Popular government in a nation of more than 150 million [now an estimated 275 million] people requires political parties which provide the electorate with a proper range of choice between alternatives of action. In order to keep the parties apart one must consider the relations between each and public policy. The reasons for the growing emphasis on public policy in party politics are to be found, above all, in the very operations of modern government.

B. The crux of public affairs lies in the necessity for more effective formulation of general policies and programs and for better integration of all of the far-flung activities of modern government.

C. An effective party system requires, first, that the parties be able to bring forth programs to which they commit themselves and, second, that the parties possess sufficient internal cohesion to carry out these programs.

D. The fundamental requirement of accountability is a two-party system in which the opposition party acts as the critic of the party in power, developing, defining and presenting the policy alternatives which are necessary for a true choice in reaching public decisions. The opposition most conducive to responsible government is an organized party opposition.

E. Party responsibility means the responsibility of both parties to the general public, as enforced in elections.

F. Party responsibility includes also the responsibility of party leaders to the party membership, as enforced in primaries, caucuses and conventions (American Political Science Association 1950, 1–2).

The APSA report begins—and I think this is both important and overlooked—with an assessment of party conditions at the time the report was published. This assessment reads:

Historical and other factors have caused the American two-party system to operate as two loose associations of state and local organizations, with very little national machinery and very little national cohesion. . . . [E]ither major party, when in power, is ill-equipped to organize its members in the legislative and the executive branches into a government held together and guided by the party program. Party responsibility at the polls thus tends to vanish. This is a very serious matter, for it affects the very heartbeat of American democracy. It also poses grave problems of domestic and foreign policy in an era when it is no longer safe for the nation to deal piecemeal with issues that can be disposed of only on the basis of coherent programs (American Political Science Association 1950, v).

The parties of the day were parochial, boss-led, clientelistic, personalized, locally based, patronage-driven, often corrupt (or ethically challenged), and policy starved. To my knowledge, no one in critiquing the APSA report has made extended reference to the politics of the time, against which the report was reacting. The report's authors envisioned—or at least chose to propose for discussion and consideration—a quite different model of a national party system. Clearly the report's creators were not unmindful of the political environment of their day and were, in fact, offering an alternative conception—more a political vision, given the party operations of the 1930s and 1940s—that put forward both goals to seek and criteria to assess the parties' performance at that time.

The general outline is clear enough: The report called for parties that were cohesive in structure and purpose and accountable in office. The parties were to offer policy choices of consequence to the electorate and then act on their commitments once in office. In subsequent elections voters could hold parties accountable for their efforts to realize the policy objectives to which they committed. The opposition party had the duties both to present alternative policy proposals and to conscientiously monitor the actions of the ruling party.

The APSA report made other assumptions as to the organization of the parties; the structures to be created or reinvigorated; the role of the national party leadership, including a hand in selecting congressional candidates (much along the British lines of party nominations); and the significance of the parties and their representatives in American society.

Although a call was made for agencies of policy formulation within the parties and thus an intraorganizational set of devices for including the views of party members in some aspects of party decision making, neither the APSA report nor the writings of its principal architect, E. E. Schattschneider (1942, 1948), were overly concerned with intraparty democracy as such. Both stressed party cohesion but through leadership initiatives, and both approached elections as a competition between major contenders for the right to govern (American Political Science Association 1950). The two parties in this scenario would be policy-sensitive instruments but otherwise not conceptually distinct from a competing teams model of democratic accountability. This would be sufficient to achieve the ends sought. In many ways it represents a curiosity, given the policy-making and structural changes favored, in achieving a broad-based sense of democratic representation.

Reaction and Reassessment

The APSA report has been influential—the number of related studies and assessments to date attest to its impact. It introduced what I would call a welcome debate as to what could (or should) be expected from a party system in the modern state.

At the same time, the APSA report was severely criticized as being unrealistically visionary, out of touch with the American experience, neglectful of the structure and demands of the American electoral system and calendar, and supportive of objectives unattainable in this country. Several factors argued against the conception of a party system as envisioned by the report's authors: constitutional governing structures; a large, heterogeneous, and changing population; the legendary openness and looseness of party structures as well as the contrasting and uncoordinated operations at different strata; the weak-to-nonexistent formal ties with the parties' base membership; the lack of cohesion and coordination among party units and agencies, including the contrasting (and often conflicting) objectives sought by legislative and executive party branches; the evolution of parties as elite-based instruments of political convenience; the lack of will, or perception of the need to change, among party leaders; and the inability to discipline party members effectively—whether candidates, officeholders, or supporters—at any level (see the arguments in White and Mileur [1992] and sources cited therein).[1] The report might be seen as a wishful and idealized, if harmless, exercise by some; for others, it was more an object of derision and ridicule, clear evidence of how far political science was removed from the realities of everyday political life in the United States.

Since the APSA report's publication, a number of works have assessed and reassessed its objectives and its relevance. It is not my intention to review here the body of these studies, although selective reference to research findings that touch on issues relevant to the report's assumptions and of broad concern to the analysis that follows is helpful for establishing the contours of the research.

1. A guide to the basics relevant to this discussion would include Ceasar 1979, 1982; Crotty 1978, 1980, 1983; Crotty and Jackson 1985; Crotty, Jackson, and Miller 1999; Everson 1980; E. Kirkpatrick 1971; J. Kirkpatrick 1976; Polsby 1983; Polsby and Wildavsky 1996; Pomper 1971, 1980; Ranney 1956, 1975; and Shafer 1983.

Relevant Explorations of the Model

Early on, Herbert McClosky, Paul J. Hoffman, and Rosemary O'Hara (1964) compared party followers and leaders, focusing on national convention delegates and finding a congruence of views among the groupings, with Democrats closer to their issue base than Republicans. This study set the tone for others to follow.

A more comprehensive series of studies in the wake of the party reform movement of the early 1970s, initially by Jeane Kirkpatrick (1976) and later by Warren E. Miller and M. Kent Jennings (1986), among others, reaffirmed the distinctive policy differences between the parties. The elite focus again was on delegates to the national conventions, with findings of a greater congruence between delegates and party identifiers in the Republican Party (J. Kirkpatrick 1976) during the 1972 election year. Later findings of differences in intensity and direction within and between parties and supporters demonstrated variations in the closeness of fit in individual election years. The key here would appear to be the contrasting policy orientations between the parties and, although it can change from election to election, the fit between policy options of the base party members and their representatives to the national convention.

Other aspects from the APSA report, and related calls for a responsible party system, received attention—although not a direct motivation for the research undertaken in the studies. For example, Miller (1988) found that contrary to much that had been assumed, written, and accepted as general wisdom, delegates selected in primaries—agencies emblematic of the opening of party decision making—were not only less likely to be the divisive force within a party as had been argued but were closer to party norms on issues than those chosen through the more regular and controlled party channels of local and state caucuses and conventions.

The most consistent development of the policy strains separating (or uniting) leaders and followers over time has been the quadrennial surveys of elites by John S. Jackson III and colleagues (1978, 1982). Jackson's research and data make a direct contribution to the analysis in the next section.

American political parties have evolved significantly since 1950 in terms of their organizational structure and resource base. The parties of today are not the parties of the post–World War II period, although difficulties related to competing demands and lack of coherence in approach continue to exist. In fact, it is reasonable to assume that the political parties are in worse shape and under more pressure than they were five decades ago, as a result of the development of television, the obsessive need for increased spending, the declining intensity in party identification, a candidate-centered political environment, ticket splitting, and a more ideologically driven national agenda.

The parties have selectively, and hesitantly, experimented with developing institutions relevant to achieving some of the basic objectives of the APSA report. One proposal, a critical one, was for a national policy council to determine party positions. The council was to contain representatives of all elements of the parties' coalitions, including spokespersons elected from the mass membership. In one sense, the national conventions perform this function and in tandem with the congressional parties' legislative agendas are as close as we come to realizing a body that articulates broad policy commitments. There is, of course, little connection or consultation between the two. The Democrats, in the rush of reform fever, instituted a short-lived national policy convention to meet during the off-year congressional elections. This development made party professionals uneasy and was soon abandoned.

The inability to settle on any such party-inclusive, policy-formulating mechanism speaks to the nature of the problem of policy congruence within a party. Jackson writes:

> There are simply too many political obstacles—too much attachment to the status quo, too much fear of the unknown, too much threat to established power bases—in so drastic a change as the creation of a really viable party council represents. Party reforms are generally driven by the perception among elites of a political threat to which they must respond to ensure organizational maintenance and survival. The political crises that have propelled other organizational changes have not been deep enough or of sufficient magnitude to cause the elites to support so radical an approach (Jackson 1992, 70).

Jackson and others quite correctly see the parties as elite-driven institutions that serve primarily electoral needs. If accurate, the congruence of views between the elite that make the policy decisions and the parties' membership is incidental to the parties' operations. Yet the relationship—with the emphasis on substantive concerns rather than the structural means for integration—are critical to the parties' roles in sustaining a vital and policy-responsive democratic system. The formal ties may be weak and, at best, indirect between the party constituents and their leadership. The broad question is do they exist in some form of policy basis? Do the parties' candidates represent anything more than their own desires for office? Despite the considerable obstacles, do the parties constitute policy vehicles that offer voters clear choices on major issues, positions that accurately reflect their basic constituents? Does such a relationship exist in an era as stressful and unfriendly to party vitality as the contemporary period?

This relationship is developed in the analysis presented in the next section. The assumption is that accountability and representativeness are best achieved through the party system in terms of coherence of views between the party base and elites in addressing society's most prevalent concerns. The manner in which this coherence evolves—whether through structural adaptations of the parties' bureaucracy or, most prominently, through nominating procedures intended to select the candidates most sympathetic to the parties' base—is not of concern here. The congruity of views between elite and mass party identifiers and the consistency of these views over time is presented as the key linkage for an accountable and responsive party system. Such an issue-relevant association would give meaning to the principal concerns of the parties' bases in the electorate and offer voters a choice of consequence in elections. If such is the case, then despite any potential structural barriers and beyond the ambitions and motivations of candidates, it can be argued that the parties are doing their jobs reasonably well and performing the services to society that justify their political preeminence.

Analysis of Policy Coherence in Political Parties

Three presidential elections were chosen for analysis: those of 1984, 1988, and 1992. The three elections offer a range of differences in outlook. The 1984 presidential election produced a stark contrast between the Democratic challenger, former vice president Walter Mondale, a protégé of Hubert Humphrey and more than likely the last of the pure New Deal candidates to run for the presidency, and his opponent, President Ronald Reagan, a government minimalist and classic Republican conservative, whose administration's ambition was to eliminate federally funded social programs to the greatest extent possible. A clearer contrast in terms of party positions is unlikely to be found.

The 1988 election matched Reagan's vice president and presumptive keeper of the flame, George Bush, against Massachusetts Governor Michael Dukakis, a newcomer to national politics. Bush implicitly promised to temper some of the harsher aspects of the Reagan administration's approach to social programs while upholding the main tenets of Reagan Republicanism in keeping spending in check and taxes low. (His famous pronouncement to the Republican National Convention was, "Read my lips. No new taxes.")

William Crotty

Dukakis was defined successfully by the Bush campaign as a "tax and spend liberal." Though not incorrect, Dukakis's chief contribution and the focus of his campaign was as a New Democrat technocrat, interested primarily in the efficient and economic administration of government and delivery of its services.

Bill Clinton took much the same approach (if anything, in more explicit terms) in 1992. His game plan and campaign strategy in the general election closely followed Dukakis's (with a greater emphasis on appealing to moderates and in neutralizing white southern defections to the Republican Party). Clinton, however and in contrast to Dukakis, came to the campaign as a centrist with well-established credentials (he was a cofounder of the middle-of-the-road Democratic Leadership Council), and he was far more successful than Dukakis in establishing his own terms of reference in the campaign. He did not allow the opposition to define him politically, and, as one example, he kept a clear distance from many traditional Democratic and liberal constituencies. His appeal was to the middle-class, mainstream voter.

Clinton's opponent, President George Bush, was immensely popular, coming off the apparently fully successful Gulf War. Bush, however, proved to be unexpectedly vulnerable on domestic economic policy, an area he was accused of ignoring and one he had difficulty in adequately addressing during the campaign. The Clinton campaign pursued this advantage mercilessly.

The three campaigns then span a variety of candidacies and programmatic emphases. They consequently offer a range of testing points in determining the relationship between party followers and leaders on core measures of policy and the consistency—or lack of it—in the two parties' positions over time.

The data used in this analysis compare national convention elites to mass party identifiers. The assumption is that the turnover in convention membership each quadrennial election year is substantial—approximating 75 percent. If a consistency in elite–mass party views is found given this turnover and the differing electoral climates, then it can be fairly assumed that a core of policy beliefs is passed on from one cross-section of party and candidate supporters to the next and that these positions fairly define the party's commitments.

The same would be true for the party's base. Party identifiers are likely to change relatively slowly in their views. The challenge is to demonstrate a coherence between their views and those of the candidate-centered elites that dominate the national convention membership in a given presidential election year.

The data for the elite views are from studies of national convention delegates in 1984, 1988, and 1992 conducted by Jackson and associates. The data

Table 6–1. Activists' Ideological and Issue Positions*

	1992		1988		1984		Average Scores Three Elections	
	D	R	D	R	D	R	D	R
Ideology	1.45	2.7	1.56	2.67	1.64	2.66	1.55	2.68
Welfare Policy	2.62	5.64	2.5	5.14	2.83	4.99	2.65	5.26
National Health Insurance	2.23	5.76	2.62	5.47	3.19	5.7	2.68	5.64
Defense Spending	2.38	3.94	2.78	4.5	2.99	4.74	2.72	4.39
Aid to Minorities	2.59	5.12	3.14	4.73	3.39	5.08	3.04	4.98

Note: D = Democrats; R = Republicans.

* The lower the score, the more liberal; the higher the score, the more conservative. The ideology measure included these choices: liberal (1), moderate (2), or conservative (3). A seven-point scale was used for the issue positions.

for the party identifiers are taken from the National Election Studies conducted by the Center for Political and Social Studies at the University of Michigan. The late Warren E. Miller was the primary investigator for the years analyzed (1984, 1988, and 1992). The review of party support scores is taken from congressional votes compiled by Congressional Quarterly (Stanley and Niemi 2000).

The focus of the analysis is on the following two dimensions:

1. Correspondences in policy positions between elite activists and mass party identifiers
2. The degree of party cohesion in supporting policy programs in Congress, an indicator of the parties' unity in advancing their programs once in office

Policy Congruence

The basic focus of the analysis rests on the association between party activists and identifiers in relation to policy. The tables in this chapter present the ideological positioning and average issue support scores on matters of direct relevance to each party's coalitions. By looking at activist positions and ideology on welfare policy, national health insurance, defense spending, and aid to minorities, we see substantive differences (Table 6-1). First, the range of variation within parties is relatively modest for the areas examined. Put another way, a broad consistency exists in party positions across the three presidential election years, regardless of nominee or the political context of the individual races.

William Crotty

Table 6–2. Party Identifiers' Ideological and Issue Positions*

| | 1992 | | 1988 | | 1984 | | Average Scores Three Elections | |
	D	R	D	R	D	R	D	R
Ideology	1.8	2.56	1.92	2.59	1.85	2.54	1.86	2.56
Welfare Policy	3.37	4.56	3.39	4.51	3.45	4.61	3.4	4.56
National Health Insurance	2.89	4.19	3.5	4.54	3.57	4.46	3.32	4.4
Defense Spending	3.79	3.92	3.61	4.46	3.6	4.55	3.67	4.31
Aid to Minorities	4.65	5.12	4.1	4.92	3.69	4.94	4.15	4.99

Note: D = Democrats; R = Republicans.

* The lower the score, the more liberal; the higher the score, the more conservative. The ideology measure included these choices: liberal (1), moderate (2), or conservative (3). A seven-point scale was used for the issue positions.

Second, Democratic activists are consistently more liberal than are Republicans in ideology and on the core issue positions examined. There are no exceptions (that is, specific issues in a given year reversing support scores). Third, and of less importance, there is, as would be expected, some variation both in the intensity of support in both parties for policy areas over time and among issue areas within the parties in given years. These variations tend not to be great. The major differences are between party activists (in survey terms and averaging the scores: 2.77 for Democrats to 5.07 for Republicans; the lower the score, the greater the support for a liberal position). The party activists disagree on core issues, the differences are consistent over time, and the magnitude is substantial.

Table 6-2 presents the positions of identifiers on the same set of measures. Again, Democratic Party followers are more liberal than are Republicans in ideology and in each of the policy areas examined. Limited variability over the three elections within parties and on each issue in given years is again evident.

The two most significant observations, however, are the consistent policy (and ideological) differences between the parties—representing contrasting coalitions of reasonably like-minded individuals—and the more centrist positioning of followers compared with activists. The latter can be shown in general outline in Table 6-3.

Table 6-4 summarizes, by presidential election year, the differences in policy congruence between party activists (national convention delegates) and party identifiers for the three elections. The lower the absolute difference, the

Table 6-3. Ideological and Issue Positioning of Activists and Members, by Party

	Democrats		Republicans	
	Party Activists	Party Members	Party Activists	Party Members
Ideological				
Self-Placement Average	1.55	1.86	2.68	2.56
Issue Position Scoring	1.77	3.64	5.07	4.57

Note: The lower the score, the more liberal the placement.

better the fit (that is, the closer leaders and followers are on the policy dimensions examined). The closest correspondence in the Democratic Party between delegate and mass identifiers was with the New Deal candidacy of Mondale in 1984, and the greatest coherence in views in all the election years was on national health insurance. Correspondingly, the greatest division between delegates and followers in the Republican Party occurred over national health insurance. In each election year and for the period as a whole, the Republican delegates were close in their core views to the party's base in the electorate.

The centrist/technocratic candidacies of Clinton and Dukakis showed greater variation, particularly evident on issues such as aid to minorities and welfare reform, two staples of the Clinton program in particular. In each year,

Table 6-4. Policy Coherence Between Activists and Mass Party Members, by Year and Party*

	1992		1988		1984		Over Three Elections	
	D	R	D	R	D	R	D	R
Welfare Policy	0.76	1.08	0.89	0.63	0.62	0.38	1.55	2.68
National Health Insurance	0.64	1.57	0.72	0.93	0.38	1.24	0.58	1.25
Defense Spending	0.87	0.02	0.83	0.03	0.61	0.21	0.77	0.09
Aid to Minorities	1.68	0.44	0.96	0.18	0.3	0.59	0.98	0.4
Average	0.86	0.65	0.85	0.44	0.48	0.6	0.73	0.56

Note: D = Democrats; R = Republicans. The smaller the value of the absolute difference, the better the fit between party delegates and party followers.

* The figures indicate the differences in means between activists and followers.

William Crotty

Table 6–5. Party Votes on Budgetary Resolutions, 1985–1996

	Total		Democrats			Republicans		
Year	Yes	No	Yes	No	%*	Yes	No	%*
1985	250	168	229	29	89	21	139	87
1986	258	170	234	15	94	24	155	87
1987	245	179	228	19	92	17	160	90
1988	215	201	212	34	86	3	167	98
1989	319	102	227	24	90	92	78	54
1990	263	157	157	96	62	106	61	63
1991	218	208	218	34	87	0	174	100
1992	239	181	231	25	90	8	155	95
1993	209	207	209	47	82	0	159	100
1994	243	183	242	11	96	0	172	100
1995	223	175	222	11	95	0	164	100
1996	238	192	8	191	96	230	1	99
			Average		88%			90%

Note: Bernard Sanders, I–Vt., is counted as a Democratic Party vote.

* Percent of total party members voting to support party position.

the Democratic Party was attempting to move closer to the political center and the concerns of middle-class America and away from an identification with groups and issues it believed unpopular with mainstream voters. This approach appears to have created some tensions within the party's coalition.

Policy Implementation in Office:
The Congressional Party and Issue Voting

The political parties do act upon their policy agendas once elected to public office. The clearest example of this is the behavior of the Democratic and Republican Parties in Congress. Three sets of data can be used to establish the argument, covering the periods immediately after the elections analyzed (1985–1988, 1989–1992, and 1993–1996).

Table 6-5 presents the first of the indicators of support for party factions: party cohesion scores in budgetary votes, presumably the most critical bill for any administration and one of the more important decisions for legislators. Table 6-6 includes congressional vote scores for presidential programs under both Republican (1985–1992) and Democratic (1993–1996) administrations. Table 6-7 gives the party unity scores for the same periods.

In terms of budgetary votes, the two parties voted overwhelmingly (88 percent on average for Democrats, 90 percent for Republicans) with their par-

Table 6–6. Party Voting for President's Programs, 1985–1996
(percent)

President	Year	House		Senate	
		Democrat	Republican	Democrat	Republican
Reagan	1985	31	69	36	80
	1986	26	69	39	90
	1987	26	64	38	67
	1988	27	61	51	73
Bush	1989	38	72	56	84
	1990	26	65	39	72
	1991	35	74	42	83
	1992	37	75	33	75
Clinton	1993	80	39	87	30
	1994	78	49	88	44
	1995	75	22	81	29
	1996	74	38	83	37
	$\bar{X}$ Difference	73	68	67	74

Source: Norman J. Ornstein, Thomas E. Mann, and Michael J. Malbin, 1998. *Vital Statistics on Congress.* Washington, D.C.: Congressional Quarterly Inc., Table 8–2, pp. 209–210 and the sources cited therein.

ties in favor of their positions. Likewise, although the scores are not as high and the legislation more varied, members of both parties supported presidents of their parties or opposed the policies of presidents of the opposing parties two-thirds to three-quarters of the time over the years examined. Finally, the party unity scores for both Democrats and Republicans are impressively high, averaging over 80 percent for the period.

The evidence presented here appears persuasive. A reasonable conclusion is that the congressional parties do act as like-minded policy coalitions in support of their parties' programs once in office. The pattern is clear: The parties implement the broad policy programs associated with them when given the chance. In this regard, they are more cohesive, disciplined, and policy responsive than many observers have given them credit for being.

Conclusion

Much can be (and has been) criticized about the performance of American political parties. Critics, many sympathetic to the contributions of parties to a

Table 6–7. Party Unity Scores in the U.S. House of Representatives and the U.S. Senate, 1985–1996 (percent)

	House		Senate	
Year	Democrat	Republican	Democrat	Republican
1985	86	80	79	81
1986	86	76	74	80
1987	88	79	85	78
1988	88	80	85	74
1989	86	76	79	79
1990	86	78	82	77
1991	86	81	83	83
1992	86	84	82	83
1993	88	87	87	86
1994	88	87	86	81
1995	80	91	81	89
1996	80	87	84	89
Average:	86	82	82	82

Source: Adapted from Norman J. Ornstein, Thomas E. Mann, and Michael J. Malbin, 1998. *Vital Statistics on Congress.* Washington, D.C.: Congressional Quarterly Inc., Table 8–4, pp. 211–213 and the sources cited therein.

democratic order (such as the authors of the APSA report), have nonetheless questioned the viability of parties and even their relevance in a technologically driven information age in which many fundamental social, economic, and political institutions face a rethinking and, more than likely, a restructuring. The parties' declining memberships and the rise in prominence of independents and issue-based voting are believed by some to imperil fundamental party operations. Even the most ardent supporters of the party identifier school acknowledge the rise in importance of issue voting and the weakening of party identification, although they do not see these changes as the threats to party vitality that others might.

> [W]hat we observe in voters' attitudes and perceptions is the result of relatively stable, enduring political orientations being activated by the events surrounding the election and the election campaign itself. Campaigns come and go, but voters' partisan and policy related predispositions change only slowly (Miller and Shanks 1996, 385).

Others see the situation in starkly different terms. Wattenberg writes:

Policy Coherence in Political Parties

[S]trength of party identification no longer has the depth of meaning it once did. The significance of the rise of neutrality is not so much that it partially explains the decline of party identification as that it indicates an even sharper decline in party relevance than the rise in the percentage of Independents would lead us to expect (Wattenberg 1998, 179).

[T]he general emphasis of media campaigns on candidates rather than parties has served to make them less institutionally relevant and salient to the mass public (Wattenberg 1998, 111).

Although the two parties may be increasingly irrelevant to the electorate in their decision making, "PACs [political action committees] threaten to further displace the party organizations as a useful tool for political candidates" (Wattenberg 1998, 109). Because some analysts see parties principally as vehicles to serve the election needs of political elites, their decreasing value for candidates, combined with their weakened public impact, would be a severe, and potentially critical, blow.

Political scientists are not alone in their concerns. Political commentator and journalist E. J. Dionne Jr. writes:

[F]ree elections in a two-party system inevitably encourage polarization; voters who like some things about liberals or Democrats and some things about conservatives or Republicans end up having to choose one package or the other. . . . [E]ach side will always try to polarize the electorate in a way that will leave a majority standing on its side. But if free elections leave so many in the electorate dissatisfied with where they have to stand and push large numbers out of the electorate entirely, then it is fair to conclude that the political process is badly defective.

. . . After the election is over, parties have to govern. By putting such a premium on false choices and artificial polarization, our electoral process is making it harder and harder for electoral winners to produce what they were elected for: good government (Dionne 1991, 15).

Dionne believes that American voters would "be powerfully attracted to a political movement devoted to using government to ease their economic insecurities and to expand their capacity to seize the opportunities of a new era. They would welcome a debate focused less on 'big' or 'small' government and more on 'better' or 'more appropriate' government" (Dionne 1996, 337).

There is even the broader problem of governing in the new age with the sense that traditional institutions, and most prominently in this context the political parties, are "unable to address critical problems because our historic conception of government is inappropriate to the new realities of the postindustrial era" (Dodd 1995, 263).

I have assessed one aspect of party operations in three quite different presidential elections. Based on this assessment, I can offer several conclusions that I find encouraging:

1. Political parties offer voters choices of consequence in major issue areas of national concern.
2. The parties consist of a coalition of the like-minded on core issues of critical concern to them and their constituencies.
3. Once in office, in this case in Congress, party members act in a coherent manner to support their parties' policies, and they do try to implement these policies (as measured through the party unity and support scores for the parties in the House and Senate).
4. These conclusions can be taken as positive signs of a party system performing functions of representation and accountability in the contemporary era.

7

Parties and Campaign Finance

Victoria A. Farrar-Myers and Diana Dwyre

As campaigns became more candidate-centered than party-centered endeavors, many observers sadly concluded that political parties no longer played a central and vital role in American elections. As early as 1950 the authors of the American Political Science Association report *Toward a More Responsible Two-Party System* expressed concern that the parties' role in campaigns had diminished (American Political Science Association 1950). Journalist David Broder declared in 1971 that *The Party's Over* (Broder 1971). Political scientist Nelson Polsby (1983) discussed the mostly negative *Consequences of Party Reform,* and William Crotty (1984) wrote of *American Political Parties in Decline.*

As other parts of this book demonstrate, in some ways the parties have declined. With respect to their financial role in campaigns, however, political parties in the United States have come to play a significant yet different role than they had in the past. Many scholars who have examined the organizational and financial activities of parties since the 1970s have concluded, as Xandra Kayden and Eddie Mahe Jr. (1985) did, that *The Party Goes On* or, as Larry J. Sabato (1988) did, that *The Party's Just Begun.* Paul S. Herrnson's (1988) study of party organizations in the 1980s documents much of this financial and organization resurgence of parties.

In this chapter we discuss how and why political parties as organizations have increased their role in elections by supplying numerous resources, both cash and material, to assist their candidates in running more effective candidate-centered campaigns. Then we consider the parties' role in and response to recent efforts to reform the system that governs the financing of federal elections.

The Institutionalization of National Party Organizations

The rise of candidate-centered politics left the parties with a greatly diminished role in their candidates' campaigns. Candidates and their personal campaign organizations came to perform many of the campaign activities that the parties once did. For example, candidates tend to "emerge" rather than be recruited by the party. Candidates raise much of their own money and pay their own campaign consultants. And they communicate directly with voters through television, radio, mass mailings, and the World Wide Web, often without ever identifying themselves as a Democrat or a Republican. Indeed, given the decline in the level of relevance that voters attribute to parties (Wattenberg 1990), candidates often believe that they will fare better without advertising their partisanship.

Moreover, the Federal Election Campaign Act (FECA) of 1971 and its amendments greatly diminished the parties' financial role by limiting contributions and expenditures and forcing the parties to separate their federal election activities from their state and local party activities, thereby significantly curtailing state and local party participation in federal elections. The FECA also created a regulatory environment ripe for the proliferation of political action committees (PACs), which soon became the primary source of funds for congressional candidates. The amount of money a House or Senate candidate can collect from possibly hundreds of PACs easily eclipses the amount that parties are permitted to give to and spend on behalf of a candidate. Consequently, as candidates began to conduct more self-sufficient campaigns, they became less dependent on their parties for the organizational and financial assistance that parties once provided.

The Watergate scandal was the catalyst for many of the campaign finance reforms that so negatively affected the parties. The scandal also led to huge Republican losses in the 1974 and 1976 elections and to a large drop in the number of voters who identified with the Republican Party (Herrnson 1998b, 55). In reaction to these losses, Republicans made a concerted effort to revitalize their national party committees financially and organizationally. Later the Democrats also were motivated to reinvigorate their party organizations after that party lost the White House and the Senate to the GOP in 1980. As Herrnson argues, the "crisis of competition" that each party experienced was a catalyst for the institutionalization of the national party organizations (Herrnson 1998b, 55–57). Indeed the parties emerged out of their crises as stronger, more professional, and wealthier political organizations.

By *institutionalized national parties* we mean, for example, that the parties now have a permanent organizational presence; are financially sound; and have large, professional staffs that specialize in a variety of campaign activities such as opposition research, media, polling, and fund-raising.[1] Perhaps the most significant aspect of this institutionalization is the parties' success in raising money and using it to help their candidates and strengthen their organizations. Although the national parties no longer play as large a role in some areas of their candidates' campaigns, such as recruitment and communicating with voters, the parties have reconfigured themselves to play a meaningful role in candidate-centered campaigns. As John H. Aldrich notes, "[T]he parties as organizations have adapted to the changing circumstances, and a new form of party has emerged, one that is 'in service' to its ambitious politicians but not 'in control' of them as the mass party sought to be" (Aldrich 1995, 273). In documenting the institutionalization of the parties' Washington committees, Herrnson concludes, "[N]ot only are parties no longer in decline, but they are in fact flourishing in today's cash-oriented, technologically sophisticated world of campaign politics" (Herrnson 1988, 30).

The Washington Party Committees' Financial Boom

By the mid-1980s, the parties' Washington committees had significantly enhanced their fund-raising and expanded and professionalized their party organizations. Each party has three national party organizations: the party's national committee and its two Hill committees—a House campaign committee and a Senate campaign committee. The parties' Washington committees are the Democratic National Committee (DNC) and the Republican National Committee (RNC); the Democratic Congressional Campaign Committee (DCCC) and the National Republican Congressional Committee (NRCC); and the Democratic Senatorial Campaign Committee (DSCC) and the National Republican Senatorial Committee (NRSC). After the 1970s, first the Republican and then the Democratic Party national committees became more professional, more financially sound, and more helpful to their candidates.

Although the circumstances were ripe for parties to find some way to adapt to the new candidate-centered politics in part because each had suffered such large electoral defeats, this conducive environment alone cannot account

1. See Herrnson (1988) for an excellent analysis of this transformation of the Washington party committees to institutionalized party organizations.

Victoria A. Farrar-Myers and Diana Dwyre

for the financial and organizational resurgence of the national parties. Talented party-building entrepreneurs, such as RNC chairman William Brock in the late 1970s and DCCC chairman Tony Coelho in the early 1980s, recognized and acted on these opportunities to strengthen their parties as organizations.[2] These party-building entrepreneurs, much like policy entrepreneurs in Congress, sought to initiate dynamic change. They knew that the dramatic shift to candidate-centered campaigning required an equally dramatic change in their organizations if parties were to regain a meaningful position in federal elections. Their success is seen most clearly in the financial success of their parties' Washington committees. Table 7-1 shows the significant growth in the parties' financial strength from 1976 to 1998. The amounts are listed in constant 1998 dollars to control for the effects of inflation. The table lists the national party committees' hard money receipts, which are funds raised in accordance with limits imposed by the FECA. These funds are called *hard money* because they must be raised and spent within the hard limits of the law, as opposed to *soft money,* which is not subject to such stringent regulations. We discuss both types of funds in greater detail later in this chapter.

Table 7-1 also reveals the great financial gap between the two parties. The Republican Party's superior fund-raising success is partly the result of getting an earlier start than the Democrats. The Republicans developed highly successful direct-mail fund-raising programs soon after they were so badly beaten in the 1976 elections. The GOP's appeals for contributions were all the more powerful because the Republicans were the minority party in both chambers of Congress and had lost the White House. Attacking the Democrats in power proved to be a profitable strategy in the late 1970s as well as after 1992 when Bill Clinton won the White House (see Table 7-1). Indeed, negative fund-raising appeals, like negative campaign ads, often are more successful than solicitations that ask contributors merely to help maintain the status quo (Godwin 1988; Herrnson 1998b). Moreover, as Herrnson points out, the "greater wealth and homogeneity of their supporters also makes it easier for the Republican committees to raise money" (Herrnson 1998b, 57). Even though the Democrats significantly improved their fund-raising by the mid-1980s, due in large part to party entrepreneurs such as DCCC chairman Tony Coelho, they have never been able to catch up to the Republicans. Indeed the GOP committees raised more in 1980, $238.2 million (in constant 1998 dollars), than the Democratic

2. Kolodny (1998) offers a thorough analysis of the importance of party-building entrepreneurs in revitalizing the House and Senate campaign committees. See especially Chapter 6. See also Herrnson (1988).

Table 7-1. National Party Hard Money Receipts, 1976–1998 (in millions of constant 1998 dollars)

Party	1976	1978	1980	1982	1984	1986	1988	1990	1992	1994	1996	1998
Democrats												
DNC	37.5	28.3	30.5	27.9	73.1	25.6	72.1	18.1	76.4	46.0	107.1	61.4
DCCC	2.6	7.0	5.7	11.0	16.3	18.3	17.2	11.3	14.9	21.3	27.3	24.8
DSCC	2.9	.8	3.4	9.5	14.0	19.9	22.5	21.8	29.6	29.0	31.7	35.1
Total	43.0	36.1	39.6	48.4	103.4	63.8	111.8	51.2	120.9	96.3	166.1	121.3
Republicans												
RNC	83.4	85.5	153.9	142.1	166.1	124.6	125.4	85.7	99.2	96.1	194.5	99.9
NRCC	34.7	35.3	40.2	98.0	91.5	59.2	47.5	42.2	40.0	31.6	79.6	69.7
NRSC	5.2	27.3	44.1	82.6	128.2	128.1	90.8	81.2	84.0	7.9	64.8	51.7
Total	123.3	148.1	238.2	322.7	385.8	311.9	263.7	209.1	223.2	135.6	338.9	221.3

Source: Federal Election Commission press releases. The 1998 figures include funds raised up to twenty days after the general election; all other figures are year-end reports. All figures are for "hard money" receipts only.

Note: DNC = Democratic National Committee; DCCC = Democratic Congressional Campaign Committee; DSCC = Democratic Senatorial Campaign Committee; RNC = Republican National Committee; NRCC = National Republican Congressional Committee; and NRSC = National Republican Senatorial Committee.

committees have in any year before or after that (see Table 7-1). As we will see later in this chapter, this resource difference between the two parties influences each party's view of the campaign finance system and proposed campaign finance reforms.

This infusion of funds allowed the parties to find their place in the new candidate-centered political environment. Yet although the parties now have more money to give to candidates, the FECA limits the amount they can contribute to or spend on behalf of their candidates. For example, a party's national, congressional, and state party committees can each give $5,000 to a House candidate for each election (primary, runoff, and general election). Senate candidates may receive a combined total of $17,500 from their national and senate campaign committees, and their state parties may contribute an additional $5,000. On the presidential level, the parties' role has been greatly diminished by the public funding provisions of the FECA that prohibit presidential candidates who accept public funding from receiving contributions from other sources, even from their parties. Table 7-2 lists the federal contribution limits established by the FECA.

In addition to these limited cash contributions, parties may spend hard money on behalf of their candidates by making *coordinated expenditures,* which are expenditures made in coordination with a candidate's campaign on items such as polls, campaign ads, or issue research. The coordinated expenditure limits are indexed to inflation, so that the amount a party may spend on behalf of a House candidate has increased from $10,000 in 1974 to $ 33,780[3] in 2000. The coordinated expenditure limits for Senate candidates vary by state population and also are adjusted for inflation. The 2000 Senate limits range from $135,120 in the smallest states to $3,272,876 in California. In 1996 the national party committees each were permitted to spend just under $12 million on behalf of their presidential nominees; in 2000 the limit was $13.7 million. Each of the two major parties also was permitted to spend up to $13.5 million on their 2000 nominating conventions (Federal Election Commission 2000).

The parties prefer coordinated spending over direct contributions to their candidates, primarily because the parties have more control over how the money is spent. Inexperienced candidates often do not spend their campaign resources in the most efficient and effective manner. Candidates and their campaigns, however, sometimes resent the parties telling them what to do and how

3. For states with only one congressional district, the coordinated expenditure limit is $67,560.

Table 7-2. Federal Campaign Contribution Limits

			Recipients			
Donors	Candidate Committee	PACs	Local Party Committees	State Party Committees	National Party Committees	Special Limits
Individuals	$1,000 per election	$5,000 per year	$5,000 per year combined limit		$20,000 per year	$25,000 per year overall limit
Local Party Committees[a]	$5,000 per election combined limit	$5,000 per year combined limit	Unlimited transfers to other party committees			
State Party Committees (multicandidate)[a]	$5,000 per election combined limit	$5,000 per year combined limit	Unlimited transfers to other party committees			
National Party Committees (multicandidate)[b]	$5,000 per election	$5,000 per year	Unlimited transfers to other party committees			$17,500 to Senate candidate per campaign[c]
PAC (multicandidate)	$5,000 per election	$5,000 per year	$5,000 per year combined limit		$15,000 per year	
PAC (not multicandidate)	$1,000 per election	$5,000 per year	$5,000 per year combined limit		$20,000 per year	

Source: Federal Election Commission (1996).

[a] State and local party committees share limits unless the local party committee can prove its independence.

[b] A party's national committee, Senate campaign committee, and House campaign committee are commonly called the national party committees and each has a separate limit. See the Special Limits column for the exceptions.

[c] The Senate campaign committee and the national committee share this limit.

to spend their money, because they believe they know more than party officials and political consultants from Washington, D.C. about the conditions in their own districts or states. Yet the parties, with their many years of experience in winning elections, usually have a better idea of what works best under particular circumstances.

The Republican and Democratic Party committees often use coordinated expenditures to take advantage of the benefits of economies of scale by providing services that might be too costly for individual candidates. For example, national-level polling data can be collected in a way that reveals regional differences in order to help House and Senate candidates. The party committees also built professional television and radio production studios and encourage their candidates to use these facilities to make their campaign ads for a fraction of the cost they would pay at a private studio. Additionally, the national party organizations help their candidates raise money from PACs and individuals; direct them to professional media, polling, and fund-raising consultants; provide opposition and issue research; compile voter lists; conduct candidate and consultant training sessions; and run generic television and radio ads designed to benefit everyone on the party ticket (messages such as "Vote Republican, For a Change"). All of these party-sponsored services are possible because of the parties' enhanced resource base and increased professionalization.

Since 1996 the parties also have been permitted to make *independent expenditures* to benefit their candidates. An independent expenditure is an expenditure made for or against a candidate but without consultation with the candidate. These expenditures must be fully disclosed to the Federal Election Commission (FEC), but independent expenditures have no limit. Party independent expenditures are somewhat controversial because the Supreme Court ruled in the case of *Colorado Republican Federal Campaign Committee v. Federal Election Commission* (518 U.S. 604 [1996]) that parties could function independently from their own candidates, an interpretation some observers say is unrealistic (Biersack and Haskell 1999, 166). During the 1995–1996 election cycle the Democrats spent $1,472,058 on independent expenditures for federal candidates and the GOP spent $10,349,747; during the 1997–1998 cycle the Democrats spent $1,485,113 and the Republicans spent $283,182 on independent expenditures (Federal Election Commission 1999). As you can see from the great drop in Republican independent expenditures, the GOP leaders decided that this spending method was not the best use of their hard money resources. Indeed, Republican party leaders have noted that it was a great effort to spend money completely independently of their candidates in 1996 when they set up a totally separate office with separate staff to assure that there was no coordination with candidates in making those expenditures.

An important feature of party campaign finance during this financial boom period is that both parties became more strategic in the distribution of campaign funds by directing their money in a manner more consistent with their primary goal of maximizing the number of House and Senate seats they control. Therefore, since the mid-1980s the parties have increasingly directed more money to open-seat candidates and challengers with a good chance of winning and limited their donations to incumbents, most of whom can easily raise enough campaign cash from PACs and individual contributors (Dwyre 1994; Sorauf 1998, 229–230). Some incumbents do receive party assistance, however. Party donations to incumbents in close races, and to Democratic incumbents from the inner city who have trouble raising campaign funds in their districts, are investments consistent with the parties' seat-maximizing goal, for it is just as important not to lose any seats as it is to gain new ones (Sorauf 1998, 229). Given this more strategic distribution of party resources, parties have become for many congressional candidates the largest single source of campaign funds, and, as Frank J. Sorauf notes, since party money is now "used more efficiently, [it accomplishes] more per dollar than money from alternative sources" (Sorauf 1998, 229). Indeed most PACs favor incumbents of the party in power, because they want to ensure access to those who are most likely to win and to be in a position to affect the outcome of policy debates. Yet because incumbents collect money from so many other PACs as well as from many individuals, the impact of any one PAC contribution is relatively small.

Party Soft Money and Issue Advocacy

The hard money contributions, coordinated expenditures, and independent expenditures discussed in the preceding section tell only part of the story. As mentioned briefly earlier in this chapter, hard money refers to money raised and spent in amounts limited by the FECA. For instance, an individual may give up to $20,000 and a PAC may give up to $15,000 per year to a national party committee. Moreover, the FECA prohibits hard money contributions to parties or candidates from corporations, labor unions, national banks, government contractors, and foreign nationals who do not have permanent residence in the United States. These limits and source restrictions on hard money have motivated parties to look for other ways to raise and spend funds to help their candidates win. One way parties have enhanced their financial role is with so-

Victoria A. Farrar-Myers and Diana Dwyre

Table 7-3. National Party Soft Money Receipts, 1992–1998 (in millions of constant 1998 dollars)

Party	1992	1994	1996	1998
Democratic (DNC, DCCC, and DSCC)	42.2	54.0	127.1	89.4
Republican (RNC, NRCC, and NRSC)	57.9	57.7	146.7	111.3

Source: Federal Election Commission (1999, 1).

Note: DNC = Democratic National Committee; DCCC = Democratic Congressional Campaign Committee; DSCC = Democratic Senatorial Campaign Committee; RNC = Republican National Committee; NRCC = National Republican Congressional Committee; and NRSC = National Republican Senatorial Committee.

called soft money (that is, nonfederal funds), money that is not subject to the same contribution and source limitations as hard money. Soft money is the result of a loophole in the FECA. National party committees are permitted to raise soft money in unlimited amounts from virtually any source. The national parties can accept corporate and labor union soft money donations as well as PAC and individual contributions beyond the statutory limits for hard money as long as that money is not spent to promote federal candidates.

Although the national parties have been raising and spending soft money since at least 1976,[4] reporting of party soft money proceeds did not begin until the 1991–1992 election cycle as a result of legal action against the FEC. Table 7-3 shows the tremendous growth in party soft money receipts since then. Again, the figures are in constant 1998 dollars to control for the effects of inflation. The parties' national committees (the DNC and the RNC) raise most of the soft money, but their Hill committees raise larger amounts each election cycle (Dwyre 1996). As you can see, there is less of a gap between the Democrats and Republicans in raising soft money than there is in their hard money receipts. This is primarily because the parties can take in thousands or millions of dollars from labor unions, corporations, and wealthy individuals. The labor unions give almost exclusively to the Democrats, and with soft money from the

4. See Corrado (1997, esp. 171–173) for a useful and concise discussion of the rise and use of soft money by the national party committees. Elizabeth Drew (1983, 15) coined the term soft money and discussed its early use.

unions and wealthy individuals the Democrats can rival the Republicans' large individual and corporate contributions.

Regulations governing the raising and spending of soft money have evolved in part as a result of charges by campaign finance reform groups such as Common Cause that soft money allows the parties to violate the contribution and spending limits of the FECA.[5] Even though the regulations do not allow national parties to spend soft money directly on federal candidates, the parties have found a number of other ways to spend these unregulated funds. For example, the national party committees use soft money to raise more soft money, to support state and local candidates directly, or to support state and local parties for party-building activities that do not promote federal candidates (for example, slate cards, yard signs, bumper stickers, and sample ballots distributed by volunteers). Any portion of these activities used to help federal candidates, however, must be paid for with hard money (Federal Election Commission 1996, chaps. 4 and 10). The national parties may also use soft money to support activities that promote the party or its candidates as a class without mentioning specific names (for example, voter registration and get-out-the-vote drives, campaign seminars, and generic media campaigns), to pay for a portion of their own administrative expenses (for example, rent, personnel, and overhead), and for building-fund expenses (that is, costs related to construction or purchase of a party office) (Federal Election Commission 1996, chaps. 4 and 10). Using soft money to help pay for these party expenses and activities has the added benefit of freeing up hard money that can be used for direct contributions to, or coordinated expenditures and independent expenditures on behalf of, federal candidates. Needless to say, parties find soft money quite useful.

The national parties have been able to push the limits of the loose soft money regulations and spend soft money in ways that actually *do* directly influence federal elections. For instance, although the parties cannot contribute soft money directly to federal candidates and cannot use soft money for coordinated or independent expenditures, the national party committees often transfer soft money to state and local party committees as a conduit to direct more resources to federal candidates. For example, in 1996, much of the soft money raised by the national party committees was transferred to state and local parties, because these subnational party committees face fewer federal restrictions on soft money spending. Election laws allow the national party committees to

5. See *Common Cause v. Federal Election Commission,* 692 F. Supp. 1391 (D.D.C. 1987); *Common Cause v. Federal Election Commission,* 692 F. Supp. 1397 (D.D.C. 1988); and Corrado (1997, 174).

Victoria A. Farrar-Myers and Diana Dwyre

make only 35 percent of their total expenditures in the form of soft money, whereas some state parties can spend up to 65 percent of their total in soft money. In 1995–1996 the DNC, DSCC, and DCCC transferred $64.6 million in soft money to Democratic state and local parties, and the RNC, NRSC, and NRCC transferred $50.2 million in soft money to Republican state and local parties (Federal Election Commission 1997, 10–11).

Often a national party committee will transfer soft money to a state or local party and ask that the state or local party, in turn, make hard money contributions to House or Senate candidates. These *money swaps* enable the national parties to get around the hard money contribution and coordinated expenditure limits and therefore to direct more money to their candidates (Dwyre 1996; Herrnson 1998a, 80). One of the most obvious money swaps occurred during the 1991–1992 election cycle, when the NRCC transferred $116,000 in soft money to the Oregon Republican Party after two previous election cycles of no transfers at all. The Oregon Republican Party in turn made $6,000 in hard money contributions to House candidates in Oregon and $110,000 in hard money contributions to House candidates in other states, primarily challengers and open-seat candidates in some of the nation's most competitive races (Dwyre 1996, 417–418). Needless to say, money swaps are a controversial use of soft money that strike some as a violation of the spirit, if not the letter, of the law. Indeed, transfers of soft money to state and local parties and among the various national party committees make soft money expenditures difficult to trace, so that a good deal of campaign finance activity is taking place under the radar.

Another controversial use of party soft money is for the production and broadcast of *issue advocacy advertisements.* These ads encourage citizens to support or oppose public policies, or praise or criticize someone for his or her position on an issue such as the environment, taxes, or abortion. The federal courts have ruled that as long as an issue advocacy ad does not "expressly advocate" the election or defeat of a particular candidate by saying "vote for," "vote against," or some similar phrase, such communications are protected free speech and not campaigning and, therefore, are not subject to the restrictions set out in the FECA and other campaign finance regulations.[6] Thus the parties can use soft money, rather than the more-difficult-to-raise hard money, to pay for issue advocacy ads. An explosion in the use of party issue advocacy ads oc-

6. In the 1976 landmark campaign finance case *Buckley v. Valeo,* the Supreme Court defined *campaign communications* as only those that "expressly advocate the election or defeat of a clearly identified candidate," and *express advocacy* is defined as a communication that uses the so-called magic words such as "vote for" or "vote against" (424 U.S. 1, 80).

curred during the 1996 elections. One estimate is that the Democrats spent about $40 million and the Republicans about $35 million on issue advocacy ads during the 1995–1996 election cycle (Stone 1996). The DNC began running issue advocacy ads intended to boost support for President Clinton a full fourteen months before election day. By the time the Republicans responded with their own soft money–funded issue advocacy ads, they were playing catch-up. The parties' issue advocacy campaigns in 1996 truly unleashed the soft money loophole as a mechanism for negative political advertising.

Many observers argue that issue advocacy ads are indeed campaigning, particularly when they are run during the election season and feature a candidate for office. That is the argument of congressional campaign finance reformers who propose that issue advocacy ads broadcast in the last sixty days before an election that feature the name or likeness of a candidate should be regulated as campaign ads. Such ads would then be subject to the same contribution limits and disclosure requirements as hard money expenditures. Our discussion of campaign finance reform in the next section examines this argument further.

Consider the issue advocacy ad titled "Defend," run by the DNC during the 1995–1996 election cycle:

> *Announcer:* Protect families.
>
> For millions of working families, President Clinton cut taxes.
>
> The Dole/Gingrich budget tried to raise taxes on eight million. The Dole/Gingrich budget would've slashed Medicare $270 billion, cut college scholarships. The President defended our values, protected Medicare. And now a tax cut of $1,500 a year for the first two years of college, most community colleges free. Help adults go back to school. The President's plan protects our values (Beck et al. 1997, 32).

The following is an issue advocacy ad titled "Pledge," run by the RNC in 1996. Both parties' ads were paid for in part with soft money.

> *Clinton:* I will not raise taxes on the middle class.
>
> *Announcer:* We heard this a lot.
>
> *Clinton:* We gotta give middle class tax relief, no matter what else we do.
>
> *Announcer:* Six months later, he gave us the largest tax increase in history. Higher income taxes, income taxes on Social Security benefits, more payroll taxes. Under Clinton, the typical American family now pays over $1,500 more in federal taxes. A big price to pay for his broken promise. Tell Presi-

Victoria A. Farrar-Myers and Diana Dwyre

dent Clinton: You can't afford higher taxes for more wasteful spending (Beck et al. 1997, 54).

Although these ads do not say "vote for" or "vote against" Bob Dole or Bill Clinton, in every other respect they are virtually identical to campaign ads, which must be paid for with regulated hard money that is subject to contribution limits and disclosure requirements. Indeed, negative issue advocacy ads often feature the familiar ominous background music, code words such as "liberal" and "radical," and grainy, unflattering black and white pictures. Positive issue ads use cheery music, code words such as "trust," and family-values pictures while praising the policy stand of an official or party. These are exactly the same techniques used in conventional campaign television ads (Jamieson 1992; West 1997, 4–9), making issue advocacy ads virtually indistinguishable from regulated campaign ads. Preliminary research comparing issue advocacy ads to candidate campaign ads has shown that even the candidates' campaign ads usually do not use express advocacy words such as "vote for" or "vote against," and that the only significant difference between issue advocacy ads and candidate campaign ads is that issue advocacy ads are more negative (Dwyre and Clifford 1999; Herrnson and Dwyre 1998).

Although soft money and issue advocacy ads certainly have contributed to the financial, organizational, and electoral success of the national parties in recent years, their use has come under fire not just from "good government" groups such as Common Cause and the League of Women Voters but also from House members and Senators from both parties, many in the media, and a substantial portion of the electorate. Indeed, candidates from both parties made campaign finance reform a top issue in the 2000 presidential primaries. In the next section we discuss how soft money and issue advocacy ads became the focus of efforts to reform the current campaign finance system and how partisanship plays an important role in the debate over campaign finance reform.

Parties and Campaign Finance Reform

After the campaign finance reforms of the 1970s took hold in the 1980s and the many unintended consequences of these reforms became evident, there were calls to reform the reforms. For example, by requiring that interest groups, corporations, and labor unions form PACs and raise and spend funds according to certain regulations in order to participate in federal elections, the FECA set in motion the exponential growth in the number of PACs. As a result of this and other unintended consequences of the 1970s' reforms, campaign finance reform proposals of the 1980s and much of the 1990s generally focused on two central issues: the rising cost of campaigns and the substantial reliance on PACs as a source of major funding for campaigns and the resulting influence of wealthy and powerful interest groups. Many critics also pointed to the incumbency advantage and the lack of electoral competitiveness in congressional elections as detrimental to our system of representative democracy. Almost all challengers were (and still are) outspent by incumbents, and House incumbents were reelected at rates often well over 90 percent during the 1980s and early 1990s. During this period, Republicans, as the minority party in Congress, often argued that the growing cost of campaigns, as well as the advantages enjoyed by Democratic incumbents (for example, high name recognition, the ability to raise more PAC money because they were the majority party in Congress, favorable district boundaries drawn up by Democratic state legislatures, and the congressional frank[7]), were key explanations for what many analysts believed would be the Republicans' perpetual minority status in the House of Representatives (Connelly and Pitney 1994).

In an effort to address these concerns, the leading campaign finance reform bill in 1987 (S. 2, the Senatorial Election Campaign Act of 1987) called for public financing of congressional campaigns in exchange for voluntary spending limits by congressional candidates, limits on the aggregate amount of PAC money a candidate could raise, and limits on PAC bundling[8] and on independent expenditures. Similar campaign finance reform legislation passed during the 102d Congress (1991–1992), but President Bush vetoed it. The 103d Congress, with Democratic majorities in both chambers of Congress and a new pro-reform Democratic president, came close to passing campaign finance reform, but the reformers could not overcome Republican delaying tactics and filibusters in the Senate.

After 1992 the focus of campaign finance reform efforts began to shift to new issues that were considered more important to address because they represent campaign finance activities that take place outside the reach of the law, namely, soft money and issue advocacy advertising. As Table 7-3 indicates, the parties were raising millions in soft money in huge increments from sources

7. The congressional frank is a Congress member's legal right to send official mail postage free under his or her signature.

8. Bundling involves an intermediate agent, usually a PAC or interest group, collecting checks that are made payable to a specific candidate delivered by that intermediate agent to the candidate.

Victoria A. Farrar-Myers and Diana Dwyre

that were otherwise not permitted to participate in federal elections. Moreover, the parties have to report only the source and amounts of soft money contributions and transfers of soft money to state and local parties. Thus most soft money spending is extremely difficult to track. For example, the money swaps discussed earlier in this chapter are not easily traced. Indeed, one must secure and analyze both FEC data and state-level campaign finance data to find out how a good deal of soft money is spent.

By 1996, limits on PACs and public funding of congressional campaigns were on the backburner as party and outside group soft money spending and issue advocacy communications began to drown out candidates' own efforts to communicate with voters. The 1996 elections were clouded by numerous campaign finance scandals involving soft money and issue advocacy ads, and reformers on Capitol Hill began to push even harder for campaign finance reform. The Democrats were accused of illegal fund-raising on federal property and at a tax-exempt religious venue (the Buddhist temple flap that caught Vice President Gore so off-guard) and of providing favors to contributors, such as overnight stays in the White House Lincoln Bedroom in exchange for large soft money contributions to the Democratic Party. The Republicans were accused of strong-arming PAC managers and large contributors for campaign money and of laundering huge amounts of soft money through outside groups that are not subject to stringent campaign finance regulations.[9] Both parties spent millions in soft money on issue advocacy advertising. Both parties (as well as a number of outside groups) had clearly circumvented the campaign finance laws. The FECA appeared to many observers to be useless. Thus in the wake of intense media attention to the scandals of 1996 and to the inadequacies of the law, congressional reformers optimistically set out to overhaul the campaign finance system in the 105th Congress (1997–1998).

The Partisan Nature of Campaign Finance Reform

Partisanship remains a powerful driving force in the legislative process in Congress (see chap. 9 in this volume). When the role of party in government intersects with the role of party as a campaign organization, as when Congress considers campaign finance reform legislation, partisan divisions become even more pronounced. Although campaign finance reform may not be an issue of great im-

9. See Senate Committee on Governmental Affairs (1998) for a thorough account of the charges each party made against the other.

portance to the general public, it is one of great significance to legislators and congressional parties because the control of Congress is potentially at stake.

So it was in 1998 when the House of Representatives and the Senate considered the Bipartisan Campaign Reform Act, called the Shays-Meehan bill in the House and the McCain-Feingold bill in the Senate after the primary sponsors of the bills. Christopher Shays is a Republican from Connecticut, and Marty Meehan is a Democrat from Massachusetts; John McCain is a Republican from Arizona and was a GOP presidential candidate in 2000, and Russell Feingold is a Democrat from Wisconsin. These bipartisan teams guided their bills through one of the nastiest partisan debates in recent years. The Bipartisan Campaign Reform Act was the most significant attempt to change the nation's campaign finance laws in a number of years. The proposal focused primarily on the issues of soft money and issue advocacy advertising. During this policy debate, party leaders on both sides proclaimed to favor reform legislation but only if it reflected *their* version of reform. The majority of each party's support for one version of reform, and the rejection of the other party's reform proposal, stemmed from one key issue: that the primary goal of both parties is to win elections. Unless that goal is achieved, no other goals, such as enacting the parties' preferred policies, can be realized (Mayhew 1974, 16).

The campaign finance reform debate held great electoral implications for both parties. Republican congressional leaders, concerned about maintaining their majority status in Congress, sought to perpetuate existing rules that seem to favor their party. Thus they were vehemently opposed to the Bipartisan Campaign Reform Act. GOP leaders also tried to pass legislation that would substantially reduce the fund-raising capabilities of labor unions, which overwhelmingly support Democrats. This so-called paycheck protection measure was a clear attempt to remove a perceived Democratic advantage from the campaign finance law, but it was also in retaliation for labor's $35 million issue advocacy campaign against the GOP during the 1996 elections. Similarly the Democrats sought to ban soft money and to bring issue advocacy advertising during the election season under the contribution limits and reporting requirements of the FECA (the major provisions of the Bipartisan Campaign Reform Act) to counter Republican advantages in these areas. Certainly partisan leanings do not explain everything about this issue. Indeed many GOP lawmakers defied their party leaders, most notably Representative Shays and Senator McCain and the fairly large group of Republican legislators who led the bill to victory in the House and gave it majority support in the Senate (but not the sixty votes needed to overcome the Republican filibusters against the Mc-

Cain-Feingold bill).[10] Yet when one considers the positions and tactics used by each party's leaders, it is clear that the electoral implications raised by the proposed reforms were on their minds.

On the issue of campaign finance reform, House Republican leaders found themselves in a rather awkward position. They had ascended to majority status in the House following the 1994 elections, proclaiming themselves to be the party of reform. Indeed, the "Contract with America," the House GOP's manifesto during the 1994 elections, was replete with references to reform—welfare reform, tax reform, tort reform, and congressional reform. Then the new House Speaker Newt Gingrich, in a very public moment in 1995, shook hands with President Clinton and pledged to create an independent commission that would consider campaign finance reform proposals and make policy recommendations to Congress. Moreover, congressional Republicans were extremely critical of President Clinton and the Democratic Party for their alleged campaign finance abuses during the 1996 elections, and GOP leaders in both chambers held formal committee investigations of those charges during the 105th Congress. Of course, these investigations were often merely opportunities to blast the Democrats in front of the television cameras, but Republican leaders appeared hypocritical by calling attention to the loopholes in the campaign finance law through which the Democrats supposedly slipped but not supporting reforms that would eliminate those loopholes.

Despite their rhetoric supporting reform, the GOP leaders did whatever they could to prevent significant campaign finance reform legislation from passing, especially in the House.[11] For example, to stave off growing momentum for consideration of the Shays-Meehan bill in the House, Speaker Gingrich attempted to rush through legislation that included a paycheck protection provision under the guise of campaign finance reform. The Democrats called the antiunion measure the worker gag rule. Gingrich and the Republican leaders were widely criticized for their use of such a hurried process and their attempt to force through the House what many observers in the media and good government interest groups considered "sham" reform legislation. For instance, a

10. Of the 227 House Republicans, 61 (27 percent) voted for final passage of the Shays-Meehan bill in the second session of the 105th Congress. Similarly, 7 of 55 Republican senators (13 percent) supported the McCain-Feingold bill. These Republicans joined an overwhelming majority of Democrats who supported passage of the Bipartisan Campaign Reform Act in both chambers.

11. For a more thorough examination of House and Senate consideration of campaign finance reform during the 105th and 106th Congresses, see Dwyre and Farrar-Myers (2001) and Farrar-Myers and Dwyre (1998).

New York Times editorial characterized the effort as "The Plot to Bury Reform" (1998), and the *Washington Post* charged the GOP with "Hypocrisy on Campaign Funds" (1998). Later in the process, when the House Republican leaders could no longer use the House rules to block or delay the chamber's consideration of the Shays-Meehan bill, they employed what became known as a death-by-amendment strategy. This line of attack was designed to weigh down the Shays-Meehan bill with such unacceptable amendments that reform supporters would not back the bill. In the end, however, the reform coalition behind the Shays-Meehan bill beat back this and other attacks and passed the bill in the House, only to see the bill meet its demise at the hands of a Republican filibuster in the Senate.

Republican leaders tried to couch their opposition to the Shays-Meehan and McCain-Feingold bills in the argument that certain provisions of the bills would violate the First Amendment. They argued that the issue advocacy advertising restrictions were unconstitutional restraints on freedom of speech. Yet, as most observers realized, the Republicans were opposed to the Shays-Meehan and McCain-Feingold bills because these measures would have changed the current rules that give them electoral advantages.[12] Indeed the Republican Party raises more soft money than the Democrats (see Table 7-3). This edge in soft money funds gives the GOP the ability to run more issue advocacy ads and to conduct more of the other activities for which soft money can be used. Moreover, many Republican-supporting interest groups opposed the issue advocacy restrictions in the bill, because these groups also use unrestricted soft money for issue advocacy ads in the final weeks before the election.[13] These advantages helped the Republicans become the majority party in Congress, and they were in no great rush to forsake these electoral tools.

On the other side of the issue, the Democrats in Congress portrayed their support for campaign finance reform as a means to root out corruption and to

12. For instance, a front-page *New York Times* story noted that the "Shays-Meehan measure—and a companion bill in the Senate—have been fiercely opposed by top Republicans, who see it as an effort to cut into their party's advantage in fund-raising" (Mitchell 1998). The *Washington Post* made the same point more directly in an editorial: "The truth is, [the Republicans] like the system; they're better fund-raisers" ("Stretch-Out in the House" 1998).

13. Probably the best example of one of these Republican-leaning groups is the Christian Coalition, which, on the Sunday before election day, distributes millions of "voter guides" in churches throughout the country. The Christian Coalition uses unregulated and unrestricted money to pay for these guides, and the group does not have to report the sources of its funds or its spending to the FEC. Even though the Shays-Meehan and McCain-Feingold bills explicitly carved out an exception for printed voter guides, the Christian Coalition and many other Republican-leaning groups opposed the bills using the same First Amendment arguments that GOP leaders used in Congress.

Victoria A. Farrar-Myers and Diana Dwyre

ensure that everyone was playing by the same rules. They portrayed it as a matter of good public policy. Yet it is clear that banning soft money and restricting issue advocacy ads would help level the playing field between the two parties and take away some of the Republican advantages in the campaign finance system. Indeed the House Democratic leadership devoted many resources to the reform effort. For example, numerous whip counts were conducted on votes for the bill and the many amendments proposed to it, whereby party officers (called whips) round up votes for the party's position from their colleagues. The issue was discussed repeatedly at party caucus and leadership meetings. Party leaders, such as House Minority Leader Richard Gephardt, D-Mo., publicly supported campaign finance reform that banned soft money and regulated issue advocacy ads during elections. President Clinton also spoke out in favor of reform and urged Democrats in Congress to support the Shays-Meehan and McCain-Feingold bills.[14]

Despite this formal party support and overwhelming support from most Democrats, not all Democrats were sure that these bills were in the Democratic Party's best interest. For example, Rep. Martin Frost of Texas, chairman of the DCCC, argued that the bills should be amended to include a nonseverability clause, which would have ensured that if the issue advocacy provision was found to violate First Amendment free speech rights and declared unconstitutional, then the soft money ban would also be nullified. Without such a nonseverability clause, the remaining ban on soft money would disproportionately benefit the Republicans and hurt the Democrats. Interest groups and political parties would be able to run issue advocacy ads but not to give or spend soft money. With its greater level of hard money resources and wealthier allied interest groups, the Republican Party and its supporting groups would be able to far outspend the Democratic Party and its allies, and the Democrats would not be able to make up the difference by raising more soft money. In the end, Frost voted for the Shays-Meehan bill but perhaps only because he knew it would fail in the Senate.

Some members of the Congressional Black Caucus (CBC) also objected to the Shays-Meehan bill at first. They contended that in minority districts, soft money helps pay for vital activities such as voter registration and get-out-the-vote drives. In districts where citizens are less likely to vote, soft money expenditures have effectively increased voter registration and turnout. CBC

14. For example, on May 20, 1998, President Clinton sent personally addressed letters to all House Democrats urging them to vote for the Shays-Meehan bill, and he called for campaign finance reform in his January 1998 State of the Union address.

members were concerned that a ban on soft money would hamper these important efforts in their districts and consequently negatively affect their own campaigns. Eventually most CBC members voted for the Shays-Meehan bill, however. Democratic leaders convinced them that the party's best interests were served by passing the bill without significantly changing its provisions regarding soft money and issue advocacy.

The parties' positions on campaign finance reform illustrate the rational approach each took toward the issue. Each party anticipated the effect the Bipartisan Campaign Reform Act would have on its ability to raise funds and win elections, and each acted accordingly. In effect the bill went to the heart of the parties' remaining strongholds as fund-raisers and governing coalitions. Each party supported the position that would best serve its ability to succeed in these realms. As long as one party perceives a proposed reform as detrimental to achieving these goals, and as long as lawmakers are able to use the filibuster in the Senate to defeat it, such a measure is unlikely to pass. Thus, unless a reform is proposed that changes the system neutrally, some scandal creates enough public demand for reform (as it did after Watergate), or one party elects a filibuster-proof majority in the Senate and controls the House, we are unlikely to see campaign finance reform that addresses both soft money and issue advocacy in the near future.

Conclusion

The national parties have substantially increased their role as campaign funders, and it appears that they will continue to expand their wealth (whether through soft money or some other mechanism) and to direct these resources in ways that help their candidates win elections. Many observers have argued that the national parties have adapted well to the new candidate-centered environment by finding their place as parties "in service" to their candidates (Aldrich 1995, 273; see also Herrnson 1988; Sabato 1988). The national party committees have responded to a campaign system that does not require their presence by making themselves a valuable asset to their candidates. Yet it is important to ask if this new party role is a good development. Do the financially strong parties of the twenty-first century fulfill the expectations we generally have of parties? Do the modern parties, for example, contribute to a healthy representative democracy? We believe the answer is both yes and no.

First, it is with a great sigh of relief that some of us look back at the 1980s and 1990s and find that the parties survived at all. The force of candidate-centered politics and the reforms of the 1970s could have relegated parties to insignificance had the parties themselves not responded with efforts to find a place in the new campaign environment and to revitalize their organizations. Because the parties have developed the ability to raise so much money they can provide valuable assistance to their candidates, who quite rationally prefer to be in the majority than the minority, and the parties help all of their candidates attempt to achieve this goal. Yet this enhanced financial role may come at a price.

Sorauf, perhaps the most insightful observer of political parties and campaign finance, has pointed out some rather negative consequences of the new party role that we believe merit consideration here. First, he counters the assertion that party money is more likely than PAC or individual contributions to enhance the competitiveness of elections. Sorauf points out that not even parties are willing to take a chance on challengers or open-seat candidates who appear early on to have little chance of winning, and "only a source of funds that goes to the candidate regardless of chances of winning will greatly alter the aggregate competitiveness of elections" (Sorauf 1998, 238). Indeed, the incumbency reelection rate has not decreased greatly nor has the number of races that end up being truly competitive increased significantly. Each election cycle, generally fewer than twenty-five House races and far fewer Senate contests end up attracting much attention from PACs, parties, and the media.

Although we agree that the parties have not taken chances on sure losers, we do not expect them to or necessarily think they should. If the national parties are going to play a meaningful role in contemporary candidate-centered campaigns, they must spend their funds wisely and in accordance with their goals of maximizing the number of seats they control. If parties had unlimited resources, we might see their wealth spread more widely among their candidates. Indeed, the wealthier Republican Party helps more of its candidates than the Democratic Party does. Thus as parties continue to raise more and more funds, we may see those resources reach more candidates and even some who may look like a bad bet at first. So, we agree with Sorauf that parties will not push us into a new era of highly competitive federal elections, but we are a bit more optimistic that the parties' growing financial role might help more candidates have a fighting chance.

Sorauf also challenges the conventional wisdom that the parties somehow cleanse the money they receive of the contributors' interests and demands. He contends that this assertion requires too many "leaps of faith . . . [for] it assumes that the policy interest of the original source will not be incorporated into the party program" (Sorauf 1998, 239). We agree with Sorauf that the source of funds does not somehow get forgotten in the process, but we also know that parties often take funds from sources with which they do not agree. For example, the Democratic and Republican Parties and candidates from both parties take contributions from tobacco interests, although both parties certainly do not treat the tobacco industry the same in Congress. Business interests often give to both parties, in part to hedge their bets. And although corporations generally favor the party in power, they are more ideologically comfortable with the Republicans than the Democrats. Finally, both parties also often receive contributions from conflicting interests. Although it is not possible to know if money from one side of an issue will temper a party's responsiveness to the other side of that issue, the parties generally behave in predictable ways on major issues before government. For example, the Democrats are generally perceived as more environmentally friendly than the Republicans, and the Republicans are generally perceived as favoring more defense spending than the Democrats. While parties are surely not cleansing campaign money of its special-interest origins, it does strike us as qualitatively better to have the parties aggregate and redistribute these funds than to have all campaign money go directly to candidates from powerful interest groups.

Finally, Sorauf notes that the parties' new financial role has centralized party activity. The national party committees are now the primary sources of party assistance for congressional candidates. For example, the congressional campaign committees now recruit congressional candidates, a task once performed by the local parties. Moreover, the congressional campaign committees will often assume the spending authority that state parties have in congressional elections by entering into so-called agency agreements with the state parties to spend the state parties' share of coordinated expenditures on behalf of congressional candidates. These developments have weakened the state and local parties and moved the party as organization further away from the grassroots.

As the congressional parties have grown financially independent of the executive party committee (the RNC and the DNC at the national level) because they now have their own well-endowed campaign committees (the DCCC, NRCC, DSCC, and NRSC), the congressional parties in government are now more free to pursue their own policy agendas. Thus instead of working to bind together what the separation of powers has divided, these legislative campaign committees apply the separation of powers outside of government. As Sorauf points out, this importation of the separation of powers into the political party makes "it more difficult for the executive to use the political party to bridge the

Victoria A. Farrar-Myers and Diana Dwyre

gulf between the two branches and unite them behind policy initiatives" (Sorauf 1998, 240). We agree that this is an undesirable consequence of the parties' recent financial growth. Thus as the contemporary party organizations become more financially powerful they will likely also become less able to serve as linkage organizations between the government and citizens and between the different branches and levels of government.

Yet we are not ready to take away the financial power that the parties have gained. The financial role may be the only realistic role that parties can play in today's candidate-centered politics. Unless and until candidates themselves need parties for other reasons—such as to unite candidates, voters, and elected officials to accomplish policy goals—the parties are not likely to depart from their current focus on financing campaigns. Furthermore, if the campaign finance environment changes, the parties' financial influence in campaigns may be weakened. A soft money ban, for example, would significantly decrease the parties' election-related activities. Soft money was created to assist parties in remaining vital organizations in the political process. Thus a soft money ban would curtail activities such as party-sponsored voter registration and get-out-the-vote drives, along with the less desirable activities such as issue advocacy advertising. Yet soft money, given in huge, unlimited amounts from sources not otherwise permitted to participate in federal elections, is not the only way to give parties a chance to thrive. Increasing the hard money contribution limits would bring the parties' activities under the campaign finance laws and into the light of day and perhaps reduce the parties' appetite for unregulated soft money.

8

Party Responsibility and the Future of American Democracy

Gerald M. Pomper

American political parties are changing, the authors of this volume agree. In this chapter I seek perspective on these changes by examining what scholars have called responsible parties. My focus is the classic American work on the subject, a report by five political scientists titled *Toward a More Responsible Two-Party System* (American Political Science Association 1950). Current trends in American politics make that title far more than an intellectual landmark. Both empirically and normatively, it reflects American politics at the beginning of the twenty-first century.

The American Political Science Association (APSA) report was a policy proposal in 1950 by the Committee on Political Parties, an expert group established by the APSA. Severely critical of contemporary politics, it proposed wide-ranging changes to make the parties responsible. It defined party responsibility by two central characteristics: "first, that the parties are able to bring forth programs to which they commit themselves and, second, that the parties possess sufficient internal cohesion to carry out these programs" (American Political Science Association 1950, 1).

Given its age of over fifty years—greater than the working life of virtually every political scientist—the APSA report is remarkable for its continued presence and incitement within the discipline. The APSA Committee's chair, E. E. Schattschneider of Wesleyan University, is remembered as much for this collective work as for his own groundbreaking research on political parties (Schattschneider 1942). The report is still featured in the most recent edition of the leading textbook on political parties (Beck 1997, 353–359); it is the subject of a recent collection of impressive essays (White and Mileur 1992); and it has been cited frequently, by a virtual honor roll of the discipline.[1]

---

1. A computer search located sixty-six articles published in five major journals between 1951 and 1999: *American Political Science Review, American Journal of Political Science, Journal of*

The APSA report not only stimulated scholarly debate but also provoked some emotionally laden denunciations. It was faulted for the quality of its concepts, including alleged contradictory, unsupported, and imprecise arguments. Critics also attempted to prove an empirical case that "it can't happen here," that unique American conditions and institutions barred achievement of the report's recommendations. Finally, even if feasible, these recommendations were assaulted as undesirable, even characterized as threats to the basic character of democracy in the United States.

In this chapter I largely ignore the past controversy. Instead I focus on contemporary realities and consider the values and empirical developments that will shape the future of responsible parties.

Change in the Party System: Did (Some of) It Happen Here?

The empirical case against the APSA report is rooted in the 1950s, not so much temporally but in that decade's celebration of American institutions. The critics asked, "Why are American parties as they are?" (Ranney 1951, 492) and provided an essentialist answer, "The American governmental order has dictated a special type of party system" (Ladd 1987, 359). The Constitution, designed to impede majorities, would inevitably thwart any majorities assembled by responsible parties. The nation's basic political institutions—federalism, separation of the branches, fixed terms, separate and staggered elections— guaranteed that parties could not meet the APSA report's prescriptions of party discipline, cohesion, and centralization.

Empirical arguments are subject to testing, and we now have over fifty years of experience and data to assess the APSA report's analysis and recommendations. If the APSA Committee were pursuing an impossible dream, its expectations should now be clearly falsified. The reality, however, is different.

Among political scientists a common empirical conclusion is to dismiss the practical impact of the APSA report. As Austin Ranney, a prominent and persistent critic, put it after a quarter of a century, "[R]egardless of how enthusiastic college professors might be about the report's prescriptions, party politicians and the man in the street showed no interest whatever, let alone the kind of fervor needed to make possible such sweeping changes" (Ranney 1975, 43–44).

Politics, Political Science Quarterly, and *Public Opinion Quarterly.* See www.jstor.org. The most important articles are Epstein (1980); Joseph (1982); Kirkpatrick (1971); Ladd (1987); Lowi (1985); Pennock (1952); Pomper (1971); Ranney (1951); Sundquist (1988–1989); and Turner (1951).

Ranney supported his argument by detailing the APSA report's recommendations and their limited implementation. After another quarter of a century, we might take another, fuller look. Ranney confined his "boxscore" to proposals on national party organization and nominations (Ranney 1975, 45, referring specifically to pp. 5–10 of the APSA report). He excluded, without explanation, recommendations on elections, voting participation, and party research, as well as individual items dealing with nominations, platforms, congressional parties, and intraparty relationships. A particularly interesting omission is the report's recommendation for direct election in party primaries of delegates to the national conventions. This recommendation was implemented through a Democratic Party commission on which Ranney served, although he later regretted some of its unintended consequences.

Table 8-1 provides a fuller accounting. I include all of the APSA report's recommendations, compare Ranney's status report (1975) with my own for the current analysis (1999), and add, in italics, those proposals he omitted. Through this revised reckoning, coming after passage of more time, I find much greater implementation of the APSA report. Although Ranney saw even partial fulfillment of only 43 percent of the recommendations, by 1999 there was at least some fulfillment of 77 percent of the recommendations. Ranney found that only one recommendation (4 percent) had been adopted by both parties, whereas thirteen recommendations (24 percent) had been fully adopted by 1999.[2]

There is a pattern in the fate of the APSA report's proposals, a pattern of *undirected implementation.* Political change since 1950 has been undirected in two senses. First, there is virtually no evidence that people making political decisions deliberately consulted, much less consciously followed, the report's recommendations. Second, the recommendations for more formally centralized party direction have been those most ignored. The Democratic Party Charter of 1972, detailed by Ranney, has been thrown into the wastebasket of history. Notably absent is any fulfillment of the report's radical recommendations for an authoritative Party Council and for enforceable party discipline against deviant state organizations or legislators. The federal form still remains the basis of party organization.

Nevertheless, there has been a considerable measure of implementation of the APSA report's recommendations. Although the parties' formal federal

---

2. Ranney listed twenty-three recommendations; he rated eleven as receiving "no action" and found movements "opposite" to the APSA report's proposals on two. The 1999 listing contains fifty-three recommendations, with no action on eleven and one opposite movement.

Gerald M. Pomper

structure remains, it is no longer true, as the report's authors complained, "that the national and state party organizations are largely independent of one another, each operating within its own sphere, without appreciable common approach to problems of party policy and strategy" (American Political Science Association 1950, 26). There have been no developments toward disciplining state parties, but there has been marked increase in intraparty loyalty, development of the regional party organizations advocated in the report, far stronger financial ties, and national mandates on selection of national convention delegates.[3]

Other changes have been made in the direction of the report's prescriptions, many occurring since Ranney's evaluation. The national committees now have extensive professional staffs, elaborate research operations, and permanent headquarters. In Congress, seniority is no longer the controlling factor in assignment of members to committees or designation as chairs, leadership powers have grown considerably, a measure of discipline exists on policy issues, and the members are deeply involved in writing the party's platform (although this still occurs only every four years). Party campaign financial resources have increased vastly, as the congressional parties vigorously pursue national majorities (Herrnson 1998a; Kolodny 1998), including some public funding for presidential campaigns. Delegates to the national conventions are now largely chosen in direct primaries, and in the 2000 election we moved considerably toward a national presidential primary—in the form of virtually simultaneous state primaries.

These changes are substantial but cannot be credited to the influence of the APSA report. The changes in electoral laws have been most dramatic. The populations of congressional districts have been largely equalized, owing to the Supreme Court's decision in *Baker v. Carr* and the subsequent reapportionment revolution. Barriers to voting have been lowered considerably, including the "intentional limiting devices," as the report delicately referred to racial discrimination. Yet the diplomatic APSA Committee can hardly receive any accolades for the work done by the civil rights movement—especially since it never even referred to blacks, or even "Negroes." On a more parochial matter, we now have the extensive studies of voting behavior recommended by the APSA report, but the National Election Study (NES) surveys, to my knowledge, have never acknowledged any debt to Schattschneider or his colleagues.

3. Almost a decade after the APSA report, one of its admirers—Stephen K. Bailey (1959)— proposed a similar but shorter list of nine reforms. Of these, seven have been accomplished in some form.

Table 8-1. Status of the Recommendations of the APSA's 1950
Committee on Political Parties

Recommendation	Status	
	1973	*1999*
1. National Conventions		
hold every two years	charter	no
have fewer delegates and alternates	opp	opp
2. National Committees		
convention active in selection of members	Dem	mixed
members reflect party strength of areas represented	Dem	Dem
have larger permanent professional staffs	Rep	both
3. Establish Party Councils of 50 Members, with Power to:		
adopt platforms	charter	no
make recommendations on congressional candidates	no	similar
discipline state, local parties deserting national program	no	no
4. Platforms		
party councils to adopt and interpret platforms	charter	no
considered binding on all party officeholders at all levels	no	no
state party platforms adopted after national platform	no	mixed
adopted every two years	charter	no
members of Congress to participate actively in writing	charter	both
state and local platforms made to conform to national	no	similar
provide platform draft well in advance of convention		both
local party meetings to discuss platform proposals		no
5. Congressional Parties		
consolidate all Senate and House leadership positions into a single effective leadership committee	no	similar
more frequent caucus meetings	no	both
caucus decisions on legislative policy binding members	no	similar
no committee chair by seniority for opponents of party programs	no	similar
replace control of legislative calendar by Rules Committee with control by party leadership	no	similar
party consultation on choice of congressional leaders		no
selection of party leadership at least every two years		both
disapproval of members opposing caucus decisions		similar
committee assignments by party committees, caucus		similar
committee party ratios not dependent on House ratio		both
committee staff for minority as well as majority party		both
amend cloture rule in Senate toward majority cloture		mixed

Gerald M. Pomper

Table 8–1. (continued)

	Status	
Recommendation	*1973*	*1999*

6. Nominations

closed primaries	Dem	Dem
no cross-filing	both	mixed
more preprimary conventions	opp	similar
national presidential primary	no	similar
convention delegates chosen by direct primary votes		both

7. Intraparty Relationships

coordinate national, state, and local organizations		both
regional party organizations		both
regular and frequent local party meetings		no
membership recruitment on the basis of party program		similar
permanent party headquarters		both

8. Elections

stress development of a two-party system in all areas		similar
lengthen term of representative to four years		no
repeal restrictions on national party finance		similar
provide governmental financial assistance to parties		similar
make congressional districts equal in population		similar

9. Barriers to Voting

ease voter registration		similar
ease voting procedures		similar
overcome intentional suffrage limiting devices		similar
extend suffrage to the District of Columbia		similar
adoption of the short ballot		mixed

10. Research on Political Parties

publication of election yearbook by Bureau of the Census		mixed
publish information on party activities and regulations		no
stronger full-time party research activities		both
research on voting trends and voting behavior		both
foundation support of research on political parties		mixed

Source: American Political Science Association, 1950, 5–12.

*Note: both = adopted by both parties; charter = proposed in 1972 Democratic national charter; Dem = adopted by Democrats only; mixed = partial achievement in both parties or government; no = not adopted by either party; opp = movement in the opposite direction by one or both parties; Rep = adopted by Republicans only; similar = political developments in similar direction.

The important question is the present character of American politics, not any credit, or even recognition, due the authors of the APSA report for the partial achievement of its recommendations. That achievement has come not because of abstract agreement with the report's prescriptions but because of trends in American politics, some of them foreseen in the APSA report.

The APSA Committee wanted the parties to be national in scope, more centralized in direction, more democratic in their decisions, more participatory in their activities, and more ideological in their programs. In the face of assertions of the system's inherent stability, the committee hopefully predicted changes that have been made since the 1950s. The APSA report's forecasts included increasing ideological coherence within the parties (p. 21), stronger national party organizations (p. 24), and a decline in sectionalism (p. 34). Today the American political party system partially fits its model, although it is not fully what the committee wanted, or predicted.

Paralleling the committee's hopes and predictions, the ideological range within the parties has narrowed, most fully on the elite level, but also among mass identifiers (Layman and Carsey 1999). The parties now evidence "[h]eightened definition and institutionalization, integration among party units at the national and state/local levels, centralization of influence within national organizations, service provision to partisan candidates, as well as a conscious reinforcement of ideological/issue-oriented bases for participation by party activists" (Bibby 1998a, 143). Two-party competition has spread throughout the nation, eliminating and even reversing the 1950 situation of a solid Democratic South and a Republican Midwest heartland.

In response to the changed competitive and political situation, the parties' self-interests have led them to find better ways to win elections in an intense national competition dominated by money, policy enthusiasts, and mass media. There is more central direction but not central control, more resources funneled through the national party committees, and more voting cohesion in Congress—sometimes accompanied by disciplinary threats or caucus decisions. There is more participation in some critical party decisions—especially the nomination of candidates, but local parties have not become active forums of democratic deliberation.

There has also been an important difference between the two major parties in the character of their remodeling (Crotty 1983). Looking to different concepts of democracy included in the APSA report, Democrats emphasized membership participation, Republicans programmatic unity. Jerome M. Mileur concisely summarizes the trends: "[W]here the Democrats sought to be responsible *to* all

Gerald M. Pomper

of the factions that compose their national party coalition, as enforced internally (by party members) in primaries and caucuses, the Republicans chose to be responsible *for* a philosophy and program of national government, as enforced externally (by the electorate) in general elections" (Mileur 1992, 220).

The parties have indeed moved in the APSA report's direction, but not by dint of deliberate change toward a single form of responsibility. The considerable party changes in the recommended direction can be best explained as serving the electoral interests of candidates and elected officials. They have changed in order to increase their campaign capability. With the revolutions that have occurred in mass communications, and with the aid of legal innovations such as the Federal Election Campaign Act, the parties have become candidate centered, more akin to service agencies than to participatory democracies.

This change is most evident in campaign finance, a subject hardly considered in the APSA report, which urged party help to congressional candidates but described assistance only in terms of nominations and campaign organization, not money. The report obviously could not anticipate the impact of television on contemporary campaigning, leading to weakened local party campaigning. In contemporary practice, party help consists primarily of dollars, so many dollars that party money now accounts for more than one-third of total national election spending.

These trends certainly would not satisfy the APSA report's authors, but they are consistent with the basic character of American political parties, built on the inevitable source of party organization, the "goal-seeking behavior of politicians, channeling and nurturing their ambitions for long and successful political careers, providing access to office and control over its use" (Aldrich 1995, 296). Like their counterparts in other democracies, American political parties have become not movements of passionate activists, but efficient "electoral-professional" vote seekers (Panebianco 1988, ch. 14).

Empirical Realities: What's Happening Now?

These gross trends show the continuing relevance of the APSA report. For the future, American party responsibility will depend on the goodness of fit between the early theory and current realities. In this section I provide data that bear on the APSA Committee's model.

On the theoretical level the APSA report begins with the two essential prescriptive elements of party responsibility: party commitment to programs and party cohesion in implementing programs. Note that the model does not initially require any particular conduct by voters (although Chapter 2 in this volume indicates parallel changes in electoral behavior).

For the parties to be meaningfully responsible, however, and for the system to be democratic, more is needed; the parties must be accountable to the electorate for the content and implementation of their programs. To achieve this accountability the APSA report makes two assertions: "The existence of a national program . . . would prompt those who identify themselves as Republicans or Democrats to think in terms of support of that program, rather than in terms of personalities, patronage and local matters" (American Political Science Association 1950, 69, 90–91). Further, the success of party responsibility would depend on party-switchers, the group of voters "who base their electoral choice upon the political performance of the two parties," and who want "to vote for a program" (American Political Science Association 1950, 69, 90–91). Current data provide appropriate tests of these elements.

Party Commitment to Programs

The parties meet this first prescription, today as in the past. Detailed analyses of party platforms have repeatedly demonstrated that the quadrennial programs of the parties contain considerable proportions of specific policy promises. Further analyses have shown that large proportions of these promises—typically close to 70 percent—are fulfilled in one manner or another (Pomper 1999; Shaw 1996).

The most extensive international study of party platforms confirms the programmatic abilities of American political parties. Based on exhaustive long-term studies of ten advanced democracies, the expert scholars of the Comparative Manifestos Project determined,

> The analyses presented here suggest not only that the Democrats and Republicans are reasonably cohesive internally, when compared with political parties in other systems, but also that their platforms are quite clearly differentiated from each other in an ideologically consistent fashion. . . . [T]hey are equally able to bring into effect their programs in government, despite institutional fragmentation—owing above all to the central position and pivotal forces of the presidency within the federal system (Klingemann, Hofferbert, and Budge 1994, 138).

Their definitive conclusion is pointed: "The United States need not seek 'a more responsible two-party system.' It already has one" (Klingemann, Hofferbert, and Budge 1994, 154).

Gerald M. Pomper

Figure 8-1. Content of Democratic Platforms

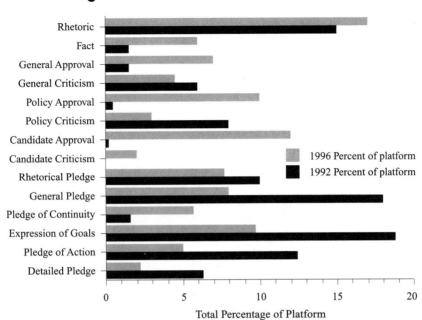

A new analysis, focusing on the 1996 Democratic platform, shows that this element of party responsibility continues to this day.[4] Figure 8-1 depicts the distribution of the 847 sentences (or major clauses) in the two Clinton campaigns. There is plenty of windy rhetoric to bore any reader, and more than enough praise and blame of the candidates to satisfy their acolytes and critics. Yet, and more relevant to party responsibility, there is considerable appraisal of public policy and a large measure of party commitment to future programs.

In 1992 the challenging Democrats devoted nearly 40 percent of their platform to reasonably specific promises (the bottom four categories in Figure 8-1). After the first Clinton term the Democrats put less emphasis on the future and gave more attention to defending their record. Still, despite the uncertainties of Bill Clinton and his administration, nearly one-fourth of the Democratic platform of 1996 consisted of reasonably specific promises.

Despite lack of congressional control and the distractions of Clinton's impeachment, some action was taken in the first two years of the second term on

4. I gratefully acknowledge the work of Andrea Lubin, who conducted the content analysis of platform content and fulfillment.

Figure 8–2. 1996 Platform Fulfillment
(Percent of 190 More Specific Democratic Pledges)

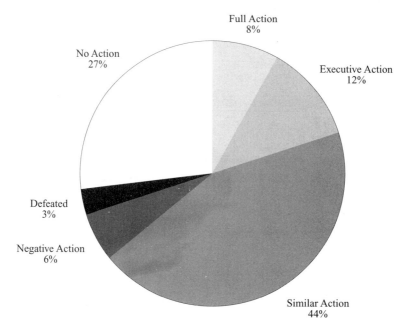

about 70 percent of the party pledges, as seen in Figure 8-2. This measure of achievement was similar to the fulfillment record of previous years. However, the achievements tended to be only partial successes: not full action on platform pledges, but more of the character of executive actions, compromises, and fulfillment of negative pledges.

Party Cohesion

The degree of party cohesion in Congress is now extremely high. Party unity declined steadily for two decades after the 1950s, the time of the APSA report. Since then, it has risen to new heights in both the House and the Senate and among both parties. In the early 1970s the average legislator voted with his or her party on only 60 percent of congressional roll calls. Today the average legislator is loyal on 85 percent of these counts.[5] Partisanship has become so

5. The average party unity scores for 1999 were 86 for House Republicans, 83 for House Democrats, 88 for Senate Republicans, and 89 for Senate Democrats. For the 1999 data and the long-term pattern, see *CQ Weekly,* 57 (December 11, 1999), 2993; and Strahan (1998), 28–29.

Gerald M. Pomper

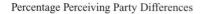

Figure 8-3. Perceptions of Party Differences, 1952–1996

Percentage Perceiving Party Differences

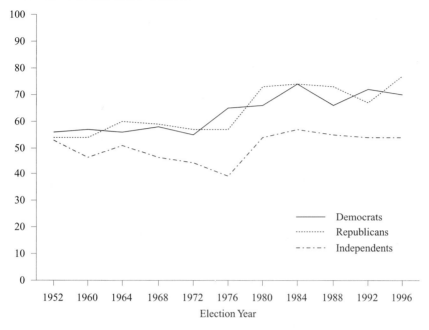

Election Year

Source: American National Election Studies Cumulative File.

strong that the journal *Congressional Quarterly* announced the death of the once-dominant conservative coalition of Republicans and southern Democrats (Gettinger 1999).

Party Identification

The APSA report sought an issue-based partisanship. We know that the bases of partisan preferences have changed, with the direction of partisanship more closely related to particular policy preferences (Miller and Shanks 1996, 178–182). More generally, as seen in Figure 8-3 (also see Layman and Carsey 1999, Figure 5), the proportion of voters who see "important differences in what the Republicans and Democrats stand for" has increased substantially since 1960, and this change in perceptions is evident among all groups: Republicans, Democrats, and independents.[6]

6. The 1952 responses are identical to those in 1960. The question was omitted in 1956.

This changed perception would be expected to alter the foundations of partisanship. In the following statistical analysis of partisanship,[7] we seek to determine the relative importance of traditional party loyalty inherited from parents and party issue positions. A voter may be a Democrat or Republican simply because he or she grew up in a partisan home or, as the APSA Committee preferred, because he or she prefers one party's programs.

The statistical method uses designated characteristics to predict the probability, or likelihood, that persons will consider themselves as *either* Republicans or Democrats. Such characteristics include the political factors we are examining as well as personal features such as sex, age, race, and education. If that probability is 1.0, we can be certain that people with these characteristics will be partisans; if it is 0.0, we can be certain that they will not be partisans. The higher the probability, the better the prediction of partisanship. We use this method (called logistic regression) to analyze partisanship in two periods, the time of the APSA report and the present.[8] (A detailed technical explanation is provided in the appendix to this chapter.)

A significant difference exists between the two periods. Mindless partisanship has diminished considerably over the decades, as the APSA Committee would probably wish. Parental partisanship continues to have a significant impact, but its contribution is now matched by the effect of perceived party differences.

A base group—white male college graduates, aged 35 years old—exemplifies the change, as illustrated in Figure 8-4. In 1952, even with no political cues, the probability of partisanship among these voters is still high (0.61). When cues are provided, that of parental partisanship is far more effective in raising this probability (by 0.13) than the cue of perceived party differences (an increase of 0.06). Acting together, these cues increase the probability of partisanship to 0.80, hardly any improvement in prediction over that provided by parental partisanship alone.

In contrast, in 1992, among the same type of base group, with no political cues, the probability of partisanship is low, at 0.25. Either the parental cue or the party difference cue is equally likely to double this probability, to 0.50. Acting together, they increase the probability of partisanship to 0.74, an increase

7. I gratefully acknowledge the work of Marc D. Weiner, who developed the model, conducted the data analysis, and patiently led me through the methodology. We do not present this model as an explanation of partisanship, only as a prediction of party attachment. In truth the model shows quite low goodness-of-fit, with pseudo R^2s of only .10 for 1952 and .08 for 1992, a finding we will be exploring in other research.

8. We use the NES surveys from 1952 and 1992. The 1992 NES survey was the last one to ask parental partisanship.

Figure 8-4. Sources of Partisanship, 1956,1992

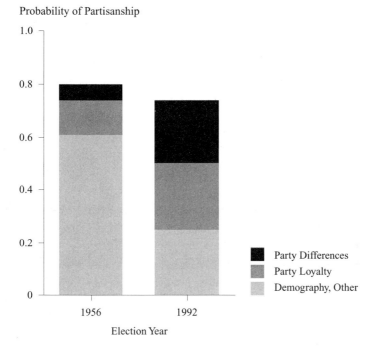

Note: Base group: white, male, age thirty-five, college graduate.

of an additional 0.24 above that provided by either single cue. The results are similar when we examine other demographic groups—women, blacks, different age groups, and different levels of education.

These results do not completely realize the Committee's likely hope—that partisanship would change from an affective consequence of parental socialization to a cognitive appreciation of party differences, but partisanship has clearly become more issue-based. Voters continue to respond to cues about partisanship originating in their early social environment. At the same time they show virtually the same responsiveness to their own calculation of party policies.

Electoral Choice Based on the Parties' Performances

Even at the time of the APSA report, as V. O. Key[9] (1966) would later demonstrate, a considerable proportion of the vote was related to party performance.

9. Although not a member of the APSA Committee, Key's earlier work was cited approvingly. He does not refer to the report in his later book, *The Responsible Electorate,* although it can be read as an extended empirical test of the report's hypotheses.

Table 8-2. Retrospective Judgment in the 1996 Election

Question: "Thinking about the economy in the country as a whole, would you say that over the past year the nation's economy has gotten better, stayed the same, or gotten worse?"

Response	D-D (N = 416)	R-D[a] (N = 119)	D-R[a] (N = 41)	R-R (N = 444)
Gotten better	62%	49%	29%	27%
Same, gotten worse	38%	51%	71%	73%

[a] Includes the few switchers to Perot, excludes switchers from Perot.

The critical group to the APSA Committee were switchers, who would abandon their previous preference if governmental policy proved inadequate. In 1952, disregarding new voters, switchers comprised 18 percent of the electorate. More than forty years later, in 1996, the proportion of switchers was similar, 16 percent. As it turned out, even standpatters, those who maintained their party preference over two elections, appeared to be similarly motivated by performance.

This presumed prerequisite of party responsibility continues to be evident in American politics. The most important performance evaluation in 1952 was the conduct of the Korean War. A majority of those who switched to support of the Republicans that year thought "the U.S. made a mistake in going into the war" (Key 1966, 97), but this unpopular intervention was upheld by those who switched to the Democrats. A similar association existed between opinion and vote among standpatters, those who stayed with the same party (Key 1966, 97).

For a simple temporal comparison, we can examine the most important performance judgment of 1996, the condition of the economy after Clinton's first term. Here, too, as detailed in Table 8-2, switching is closely related to a retrospective evaluation. Among switchers from Clinton, only 29 percent thought the national economy had improved since 1992; among the greater number who switched to him, in contrast, half took this rose-colored view. We can conclude that the APSA Committee's reliance on policy-oriented voting continues in contemporary electoral behavior.

Even as it has become more frequent, performance voting, urged by the APSA Committee, has become less significant in the total political system. The great flaw in the APSA report's logic was its expectation—normal at the time—that a single party would, and should, control all of the national government. This premise can no longer be accepted. We have been living through an

Gerald M. Pomper

extended period of divided government (ironically, beginning in 1955, shortly after the report's publication). The same party has controlled the presidency and both houses of Congress for only eighteen of the past fifty years and for only two years since 1980. This development undermines the report's second major prescription, enhancement of the parties' abilities to carry out their programs.

Although the lack of intraparty cohesion, a major concern of the APSA report, has been eliminated through political events, that very cohesion has had new serious consequences for the character of American politics. When governmental control is divided between these coherent parties, legislative deadlock is more frequent and the resolution of national problems less likely (Binder 1999). The long-term pattern, once seemingly inevitable, of Democratic control of Congress and Republican residence in the White House added partisan conflict to the constitutional conflict of institutions. The pattern was shattered by Clinton's election, only to be replaced by the new partisan deadlock of a Republican Congress and a Democratic president.

Furthermore, policy making generally has become less controlled by elected officials, coming to be determined instead by less politically responsible agencies such as the courts and bureaucracy (Ginsberg and Shefter 1990; also see Chapter 4 in this volume). Certainly the new paradigm has created problems for political science, which lacked a theory to explain the partisan incoherence of divided elections amid divided government (Sundquist 1988–1989).

The overall result is a mixed empirical trend for the directions expected or preferred by the APSA reformers. "Just as the committee proposed, the national party organizations have become more powerful, more centralized, and more democratic. . . . It is largely in subpresidential voting that American politics falls significantly short of the responsible party ideal. . . . The result is what might be called a 'semi-responsible' party system, in which the parties are more ideologically distinct but less clearly accountable for what they actually produce in office" (Mayer 1998, 215).

Party Responsibility in the New Millennium?

After five decades, what lies ahead for American party responsibility? To catch a glimpse of the future we must deal with the conceptual issues fudged in the APSA report, the meaning of party responsibility. This discussion also requires that we consider the ultimate criticism of the original report, the normative objection to majoritarian party government.

The APSA report itself had somewhat of a split personality conceptually.

It wanted "responsible" parties that were both "effective" and "democratic." It wanted a higher degree of party centralization, and also parties that were more broadly participatory and more responsive to their mass memberships. As it tried to meld these concepts, it resorted to ambiguity in the meaning of its central term, arguing for parties that were both responsible to the public and simultaneously responsive to their members.

The controversy over the APSA report stems from these conceptual ambiguities. To be responsible, a person, a party, or a party system must be responsible *to* some entity *for* some behavior. To whom should politicians be responsible—the electoral majority, their party members, officeholders such as a Congressional majority, or unborn generations? For what are they responsible—the development of a policy program, effective government, the national interest, or, perhaps, simply winning elections?

The APSA report essentially evaded these questions. It assumed, somehow, that internal party democracy would lead to party unity on a coherent program: "Responsibility of party leaders to party members promotes the clarification of party policy when it means that the leaders find it necessary to explain the policy to the membership," they asserted confidently (American Political Science Association 1950, 23). But Ranney was properly skeptical that party members would "talk themselves into such a degree of agreement" (Ranney 1951, 490).

By formulating coherent programs, parties become more responsible to their members, but then the parties may be less able to compete for votes more generally, diminishing their responsibility to electoral majorities. Responsibility to the party members may lead a party to take extreme ideological positions that weaken its responsibility to majority opinion, thereby damaging its electoral chances. Indeed, as David G. Lawrence (1996, esp. chap. 5) and William G. Mayer (1996) have shown, intraparty responsibility had this electoral effect on the Democrats in the 1970s and may be similarly harming the Republicans today.

An insistence on policy coherence within parties would make as little electoral sense as an insistence that a baseball team include only right-handed or left-handed hitters, in order to be consistent in the stance presented at the plate. The fans would literally know where the contesting players stood, but the team would be more vulnerable to defeat on the field.

The entire argument, furthermore, rests on a doubtful premise, that elections properly consist only of choices among policy proposals: "[U]nless the parties identify themselves with programs, the public is unable to make an intelligent choice between them. The public can understand the general management of the government only in terms of policies." Otherwise the parties "turn irresponsible because the electoral choice between the parties becomes devoid of meaning" (American Political Science Association 1950, 22).

In regard to policy and voting the APSA report was certainly wrong. Decades of electoral research have demonstrated that voters make choices on grounds beyond policy programs—and that such decision making is rational. Votes are also cast, sensibly, on the basis of both retrospective and prospective evaluations of the parties' records (Fiorina 1981), the competence and values of the candidates (Popkin 1991), and the achievement of consensual goals (Key 1966).

Theodore Lowi brilliantly resolves these problems—conceptually. To eliminate the parties' conflict between policy coherence versus electoral success, and to focus the parties' attentions on policy issues, he argues for a "responsible three-party system" (Lowi and Romance 1998, 3–15), in which no single party could win national or congressional control on its own. Freed from the effort to gain majorities, parties could hold to their policy commitments and remain faithful to their core constituencies. Furthermore, a three-party system would "parliamentarize the presidency" by also making majorities unlikely in the electoral college. Without such majorities, the choice of the president would shift to the House of Representatives, and the constitutional separation of powers would disappear.

Aside from the practical difficulties of willing a third party into existence (both Ross Perot and Lowi himself have tried), a more fundamental problem exists. Parties in this configuration would no longer be responsible in the fundamental sense of being accountable to a democratic majority. Achieving a worthy but individualist meaning of responsibility—rational and serious deliberation—would cost a loss of political responsibility—answerability to the electorate (see Pennock 1952, 802).

To some critics of the APSA report, this is a cost well worth paying. They not only described American institutions as incompatible with the APSA Committee's recommendations but also praised those institutions for the limitations placed on majorities and attacked the APSA report for its majoritarian aims. These critics (for example, Carey 1978; Ladd 1987; Pennock 1952) reflect a neoconservative defense of tradition and an elitist/pluralist and restricted view of democracy (Joseph 1982). Leaders' personal responsibility for good judgment is preferred to their political responsibility through public judgment.

This normative criticism cannot be refuted by empirical data. From James Madison and Alexis de Tocqueville to the present, commentators have worried about the potential instability and despotism of democracy. Indeed the APSA report itself can be read as an effort to strengthen parties as intermediate associations that will prevent dangerous mass movements. In keeping with classic concerns, stronger parties can be promoted as associations that "refine and enlarge the public views, by passing them through the medium of a chosen body of citizens" (Madison 1941, 59) and provide "a necessary guarantee against the tyranny of the majority" (de Tocqueville 1954, Vol. 1, 201–202). Ultimately, however, the APSA report's bias certainly was not conservative in basic political orientation. The APSA Committee favored active government to meet the ills it saw in American society of the time and feared in the future. Its critics were more satisfied with those conditions and with the likely slower pace of change.

The historical perspective of fifty years does not resolve these differences. Perhaps the absence of a fully responsible party system helps to explain America's success in winning the Cold War, building the most prosperous economy in history, and reducing racial and sexual barriers. Or perhaps that very absence helps to explain incoherence in contemporary U.S. foreign policy, magnified class differences, and the persistence of discrimination. Our conclusions are based more on speculation and temperament than on convincing scientific tests.

Attention to history can still be instructive, by reminding us of a final and broader meaning of responsibility, the classic view of Max Weber. In an ethics of responsibility, Weber taught, "[O]ne has to give an account of the foreseeable results" (1946, 120–128), to be responsible for consequences in the future, for the effect of present actions on unborn generations. That concern for the future pervaded the APSA report, but it is barely evident in our contemporary parties.

We have seen the "Contract with America," the Republican congressional program in 1994—a form of responsibility to the electorate based on opinion polls and focus groups but with limited concern for the social consequences of its intended policies. We have seen the impeachment of a president for behavior rooted in his sexual activities on virtually unanimous Republican party-line votes, and the exoneration of a president for lying and possible interference with justice on virtually unanimous Democratic party-line votes. We have seen both parties willing to allow the shutdown of the government in the service of their coherent ideologies. We have seen the rise of bitter partisanship parallel the rise of party-line voting. Are these deeds a fulfillment of party responsibility, or a shirking of broader, social responsibility?

Some alternatives remain available to those who still maintain some com-

Gerald M. Pomper

mitment to American political parties and to the concept of party responsibility. We could see the cause as lost, defeated by the development of a technological, money-driven mass society. We could still optimistically believe, as the APSA Committee apparently hoped, that presenting a good argument will yet gain broad popular support for renewed parties.[10] We could engage in renewed academic advocacy of reforms (Sabato 1988) and even of basic institutional changes—such as concurrent four-year terms for Congress and the president (Hardin 1974); or the selection of additional members of Congress to guarantee a majority for the president's party (Mackenzie 1996, 182–196); or the abolition of the electoral college to further nationalize the parties (Mileur 1992, 228–230).

Or, it may be more useful—and at least safer—to suggest possible directions of change in American politics, rooted in the self-interest of politicians, that will move the system toward a form of party responsibility. It will not be a trip back to the future of the 1950s but may foretell the very short run, the beginning years of the new millennium. This speculative scenario includes these characteristics:

- Seeking power, candidates for president and Congress will cooperate more fully in running parallel, if not joint, campaigns. The advantages of party campaigning will remain important, given the high cost of modern campaigns and the economies of scale available through cooperative efforts. As the parties become more competent campaigners, they will maintain a competitive balance in all national institutions, encouraging efforts to win the trifecta of the presidency, the Senate, and the House of Representatives.

- National party leaders, principally officeholders, will seek to mobilize party loyalists for their campaigns. Mobilization will be necessary because some pallid form of campaign finance reform will inevitably pass but will principally restrict unlimited soft money contributions *to* parties, requiring new forms of party action. Partisan campaigning will still be important, because the Supreme Court or Congress is likely to eliminate present restrictions on party spending or contributions *for* candidates or independent expenditures on behalf *of* these candidates. (See Chapter 7 in this volume for more on campaign finance reform.)

---

10. For twenty-five years I joined many colleagues in this effort through the Committee on Party Renewal. It may be significant that the Committee ended its activities in 1999 and donated its treasury to the APSA commemoration of the original report.

- To achieve such mobilization, parties will be required to offer policy incentives to potential activists, interest groups seeking national government action, and individual donors in a population increasingly composed of issue-oriented college graduates. The parties will seek more members and provide forms of participation in policy making, often only symbolic, such as plebiscites on the party program and mail-in polls of membership opinion (Seyd 1999, 401). They will present reasonably coherent policy programs to win the dollars and endorsements of policy advocates.

The resulting system will be responsible but only in part. Without fuller, meaningful participation within the parties, Carey McWilliams (1992, 201) suggests, partisans will have only shallow policy commitments. They will lack true policy consensus, which can develop only from extensive interaction grounded on discoverable common interests and mutual affection. The nationalized, centralized, campaign-oriented parties emerging today may be responsible for a policy program, but this program will be created by appeals to outside constituencies (contributors and voters), not by the membership. According to Sidney Milkis (1992, 127), we will have "administrative" parties and "entitlement politics," not deliberation and participation.

The ultimate character of America's changing political parties remains uncertain as the twenty-first century begins. Divided government can be expected to occur regularly in an environment of nationally competitive elections. The parties will be centralized, coherent, and cohesive in policy; continental in scope; and at least symbolically participatory. But their attention to continuing social needs is uncertain, their dependence on large contributors is troublesome, and the character of their competition is perilous. As we come to a new era, we might remember an ironic warning about the dangers of reform: "Be careful what you wish for, you may get it." It remains to be seen whether the new party responsibility will foster a revivified ethics of responsibility for the United States.

Methodological Appendix

The analysis of partisanship was based on a logistic regression model. This method is appropriate when the dependent variable includes only two possible values representing, generally, the presence or absence of an attribute of interest, in this case partisanship. Like ordinary least squares (OLS) regression, logistic regression is a generalized linear model; unlike OLS, the interpretation of the per-unit effect of each predictor is complex because the dependent variable is expressed as the logarithmic odds of the dichotomy rather than as a continuous measure. For that reason, we used a fitted values analysis to convert the results to more useful statements of the probability of partisanship for typical groups of respondents.

In terms of goodness-of-fit, the results did not indicate a high degree of explanation: Although the number of cases correctly predicted was 76.3 percent in 1952 (N=1,524) and 65.7 percent in 1992 (N=1,972), the proportional reductions in error values (which indicate how much better the model predicts partisanship above and beyond merely guessing the modal category) were quite low: 0.0110 for 1952 and 0.1175 for 1992. We were frankly puzzled by these results, which do not change under alternative specifications, and are conducting further modeling efforts on the subject.

Coding of the variables was limited by the constraints of NES survey questions. The dependent variable, respondent's partisanship, was coded as a binary variable using responses to the national surveys' perennial question, "Generally speaking, do you think of yourself as a Republican, a Democrat, an independent, or what?" Negative responses included either "independent" or "apolitical," and positive responses included either "Republican" or "Democrat."

The principal political variables were parental partisanship and the perception of party differences. For parental partisanship the effect was deemed absent if the respondent recalled that neither parent was a major party partisan, and present if he or she indicated that at least one parent was a major party partisan. For perception of party differences, the effect was deemed absent if the respondent perceived no differences or minor or not important differences between the parties, and present if he or she indicated perception of important or very important differences between the parties.

Age was coded as an interval measure of exact age anchored to zero so that the minimum voting age was coded 0. In 1952 the minimum age was 21; in 1992 it was 18. Education was measured on an ordinal scale of nine values ranging from none to college degree (1952), or six values from none to post-college education (1992). Sex and race were coded as simple binary values of male/female and white/non-white.

PART THREE

The Parties as Governing Institutions

9

Congressional Parties, Leaders, and Committees: 1900, 2000, and Beyond

Roger H. Davidson

One of the most incisive studies of the U.S. political system was a doctoral dissertation, first published in 1885, in the infant discipline of political science. The Johns Hopkins University graduate student who wrote it, Woodrow Wilson, never bothered to venture to the nation's capital. But his compelling thesis and its flowing prose style have kept the work fresh and relevant to the present day.

Wilson's title, *Congressional Government,* summarizes his view of the workings of the constitutional system: "The actual form of our government," he declared,

> is simply a scheme of congressional supremacy. . . . Congress is the dominant, nay, the irresistible, power of the federal system. . . . The president is the first official of a carefully graded and impartially regulated civil service system . . . and his duties call rather for training than for constructive genius (Wilson 1956, 170).

Wilson's Congress ruled, but it did not lead. Whereas it hoarded power and diligently passed laws on all manner of subjects, Congress had utterly failed in the paramount task of clarifying great public issues and engaging the public in its debates: "the instruction and guidance in political affairs which the people might receive from a body which kept all national concerns suffused in a broad daylight of discussion" (Wilson 1956, 195).

The reason for Congress's failure, Wilson believed, lay in its reliance on standing committees rather than political party caucuses to identify issues and formulate policies. Standing committees had been used by Congress since the early decades of the nineteenth century. In the post–Civil War years they proved ideal arenas for bargaining over the particularized benefits that marked the era described as "the great barbecue"—pensions, government contracts, land deals, patronage, and the like.

Wilson's denunciation of "government by the standing committees of Congress" (Wilson 1956, 82) might seem especially peculiar in light of the robust grassroots strength of nineteenth-century parties. "Outside of Congress," Wilson wrote, "the organization of the national parties is exceedingly well-defined and tangible; . . . but within Congress it is obscure and intangible" (Wilson 1956, 80). Rather than crisp partisanship in floor debates that could illuminate Congress's work, legislation was crafted within the often-inaccessible committee rooms, which Wilson termed the "dim dungeons of silence" (Wilson 1956, 63). Little wonder, then, that the public seemed so disengaged from the bewildering mechanics of lawmaking on Capitol Hill.

Fifteen years later, in 1900, Wilson had a chance to reconsider his work in a new preface for the fifteenth printing. (Uniquely for a dissertation, *Congressional Government* sold well.) By and large, Wilson—by now a professor of politics at Princeton University—thought that his analysis had held up well in the intervening years. But he ended his essay with this observation:

> It may be, too, that the new leadership of the executive, inasmuch as it is likely to last, will have a very far-reaching effect upon our whole method of government. It may give the heads of the executive departments a new influence upon the action of Congress. It may bring about, as a consequence, an integration which will substitute statesmanship for government by mass meeting. It may put this whole volume hopelessly out of date (Wilson 1956, 23).

Seven years later, Wilson had one more chance to reconsider his thesis when he was asked to deliver the Blumenthal Lectures at Columbia University. President of Princeton University and about to become governor of New Jersey, he now saw the president as the single spokesman for the nation:

> He is the only national voice in affairs. Let him once win the admiration and confidence of the country, and no other single force can withstand him. . . . His office is anything he has the sagacity and force to make it. The president is at liberty both in law and conscience, to be as big a man as he can (Wilson 1908, 56–61).

Influenced by momentous changes in American life and politics, Wilson's focus had moved from the Gilded Age's congressional supremacy to a new-century vision of presidential leadership. Whereas his initial remedy for the division and disarray he perceived in the U.S. system was a healthy dose of British-style partisan politics, he eventually found his solution in a reinvigorated presidency that, through its "bully pulpit," could directly engage citizens and sharpen their understanding of public issues and policy alternatives.

Wilson's journey reminds us that the dawn of the twentieth century brought extraordinary upheavals and changes to our political system and its institutions. The 1896 election—in which Republican William McKinley crushed the "boy orator of the Platte," William Jennings Bryan—is regarded as one of the very few "realigning elections," in this case revitalizing the dominant Republican coalition and marginalizing the Democrats in much of the Northeast and Midwest. The popular presidencies of McKinley and Theodore Roosevelt made the White House a source of public and legislative leadership. On Capitol Hill, shifting coalitions set the stage for historic changes in the leadership and organization of both the House and the Senate. The Progressive movement, gathering momentum from reform-oriented states, propelled changes in House leadership and direct election of senators, along with innovations in local and state government, party organizations, and elections and in direct democracy.

The Rise of Congressional Careerism

For most of the nineteenth century Congress was an institution made up of transients. The nation's capital was an unsightly place; its culture was provincial, its summers humid and mosquito ridden. Members stayed in Washington only a few months each year, often spending their time in boardinghouses clustered around Capitol Hill (Young 1966).

Toward the end of the century, however, a new sense of careerism took hold. As late as the 1870s more than half the House members at any given time were freshmen; the mean length of service for members was barely two terms. By the end of the century the proportion of newcomers had fallen to 30 percent, and the average House tenure reached three terms, or six years (Polsby 1968). About the same time, senators' mean terms of service topped six years, or one full term. Despite periodic fluctuations in member turnover, careerism continues to characterize the two chambers (Table 9-1). Today the average senator has served more than two terms, or about sixteen years; the average representative a little more than five terms, or more than ten years.

Rising careerism had a number of causes. For one thing, following the Civil War, the end of Reconstruction in the South, and finally the realignment of 1896, proliferating one-party states and districts brought about repeated reelection of the dominant party's candidates. Militant party organizations dominated entry into elective offices at all levels and tended to select party loyalists to fill safe seats (Kernell 1977). The Republican Party was the party of choice throughout much of the Northeast and Midwest, its durable coalition

Table 9–1. Seniority Before and After 1900

	Congress	
Terms	1st–56th (1789–1900)	57th–106th (1901–2000)
House		
One (up to 2 years)	44.0%	22.8%
Two to six (3–12 years)	53.4%	50.0%
Seven or more (12+ years)	2.6%	27.2%
Average number of terms	2.1	4.8
Senate		
One (up to 2 years)	65.6%	44.9%
Two (7–12 years)	23.4%	22.8%
Three or more (12+ years)	11.0%	32.3%
Average number of terms	1.5	2.2

Source: Adapted from David C. Huckabee. 1995. *Length of Service for Representatives and Senators, 1st–103rd Congresses.* Congressional Research Service Report No. 95-426GOV. Author's calculations for the 104th–106th Congresses.

Note: Figures are derived from the total number of terms claimed by members whether or not those terms have been served out. For example, members in their initial year of service are counted as having one full term, and so on. Thus the figures cannot be equated precisely with years of service.

resting on the tripod of patriotism and loyalty to the Union, western expansion, and friendliness toward business and economic interests. The party's economic platform was not strictly *laissez-faire* but rather a moderately activist program that championed high tariffs for native industries and condoned government spending for corporate benefit and economic growth. After the end of Reconstruction the Democrats had hounded Republicans (and most blacks) from the polls in the South, becoming the party of the white bourgeoisie. Meanwhile, Democratic bosses in the large cities recruited waves of new citizens into elaborate political networks in which votes were traded for jobs, welfare, and community spirit.

Congress's role as the directorate of an enlarged governmental apparatus—epitomized in Wilson's phrase "congressional government"—made federal service ever more attractive and rewarding. Even the capital city reflected the newfound excitement and glamour of the national political scene. Not only career politicians but also wealthy patrons and socialites descended on the city. The *beaux arts* mansions on Massachusetts Avenue and the elaborate summer homes in the Cleveland Park neighborhood bear witness that Washington, D.C., was outgrowing its earlier status as an encampment of transients.

Roger H. Davidson

As members stayed in office for longer periods of time, they insisted on commensurate institutional rewards. Careerism thus led to almost universal adoption of the seniority rule to reward lengthy service. As long as senior members had been scarce, they dominated their chambers and relied more on party loyalty than seniority in naming committees or chairmen. With careerists more numerous, deference had to be paid to longevity in distributing favored committee posts. The 1900 *Congressional Directory* reflected this transition: Members' names were listed in alphabetical order, but their terms of service were also set forth.

The seniority principle triumphed in both chambers at about the same time. In the Senate there was no decisive event; in fact, seniority was largely unchallenged after 1877. In the House an upheaval occurred around 1910. That year's "revolt" occurred in no small part because Republican speaker Joseph G. Cannon of Illinois (1903–1911) passed over senior members for assignments and behaved arbitrarily in other ways. In the wake of this revolt, David Brady relates, "[S]eniority came to be the most important criterion for committee assignments and chairmanships, and committees rather than parties became the major policy actors" (Brady 1991, 8).

Adherence to seniority fostered career patterns within the two houses. New members found themselves on the bottom rung of a career ladder they could ascend only through continued service. The seniority system became virtually inviolable, although chairmen unable or unwilling to serve the interests of a committee and its interest-group clienteles could be, and sometimes were, bypassed. In our own time, seniority barriers have been lowered somewhat: Party and committee reforms of the 1970s multiplied the number of career ladders, and since then both parties have occasionally departed from strict seniority in selecting committee chairs and ranking minority members.

Party Government Comes to Capitol Hill

Political parties of course had no place in the constitutional blueprint, which was deliberately fashioned to divide and dilute factional interests. But factions soon thwarted the framers' intentions by coalescing into more or less stable groups within the House and Senate, and by Andrew Jackson's time, partisanship had spread to the mass electorate.

Parties flourished in the years roughly bounded by the Civil War and World War I. Regional conflicts, along with social and economic upheavals produced by rapid industrialization, nurtured long-standing partisan differences. Indeed these years mark the boundaries of the era of strongest partisanship in the country at large and even on Capitol Hill. Party organizations at all levels were massive and militant by American standards; at the grassroots level they were divided along class, occupational, and regional lines to a degree unimaginable today.

Between the collapse of Reconstruction and the 1890s, however, party control was unsteady in the nation's capital. Divided control or wafer-thin legislative majorities were the order of the day. Between 1874 and 1894, Democrats controlled the House in all but two congresses; Republicans controlled every Senate but one (Summers 1995, Vol. 2, 1006–1007). Only in 1889 did the Republicans regain solid control of Capitol Hill, permitting them to push forward a partisan agenda. Their control remained intact until 1910, when internal dissension and then midterm electoral defeat destroyed their hegemony.

The Rise and Fall of the Strong Speakership

The House was often a chaotic place during the Gilded Age. Centrifugal forces dominated; the two parties battled to stalemate and alternated in power. Legislative outputs were small and insignificant (Summers 1995, Vol. 2, 1006–1007). The House was the object of ridicule; in full public view, small minorities were able to bring the House to a halt by interposing dilatory tactics. In January 1889, Iowa's James B. Weaver led a well-publicized filibuster against a bill organizing the Oklahoma Territory. Newspapers and reformers called for changes in the rules.

The rapid growth in the size of the chamber nonetheless set the stage for the emergence of vigorous central leadership. A series of forceful leaders established precedents that eventually formed the superstructure of party government (Follett 1896). Republican speaker James G. Blaine of Maine (1869–1875), a vivid personality whose followers called him a "plumed knight," exploited the speaker's long-standing power of appointing committees with an eye to legislative priorities. He also revived the party caucus, using it to enforce party discipline. Democratic speaker John G. Carlisle of Kentucky (1883–1889) used the discretionary power of recognition as a weapon. The House rules state that "when two or more members rise at once the Speaker shall name who is first to speak." Carlisle construed the rule expansively, devising a simple query by which he and his successors can avoid recognizing someone who might delay or offer unwanted motions: "For what purpose does the gentleman (or gentlelady) rise?"

Other dilatory tactics fell when Republican Thomas Brackett Reed of Maine (1889–1890, 1895–1899) became speaker at the opening of the 51st

Roger H. Davidson

Congress. A gigantic man, Reed had entered the House in 1876 (taking Blaine's seat) and quickly became a walking compendium of parliamentary knowledge. Intelligent and forthright, he possessed a ready and sometimes acid wit—a quality that may have kept him from the White House. "In half a dozen words [Reed] could annihilate an opponent or, what was worse, make him appear ridiculous," recalled Cannon, at the time a rising House figure who was one of Reed's lieutenants (quoted in Busbey 1927, 168).

The day after he was elected speaker by two votes, Reed blocked adoption of the rules of the preceding House, arranging instead to have them referred to the Rules Committee. Reed chaired this committee and controlled three of its five votes. After ten weeks of deliberation, the new code (written mainly by the speaker) was reported to the floor, debated heatedly for four days, and finally adopted, 161 to 144. The "Reed Rules" completely revised the order of business in the House, outlawing dilatory motions, reducing to one hundred the quorum in Committee of the Whole, authorizing that body to close debate, and permitting every member present in the chamber to be counted in determining whether a quorum was present. This last-mentioned reform quashed the so-called disappearing quorum—the practice, apparently begun by John Quincy Adams during antislavery debates, whereby members on the floor would simply refuse to vote, thus causing the House to lose its quorum for conducting business.

Reed greatly expanded the powers of the speakership. The precedents he established were generally continued by his successors, Charles F. Crisp, D-Ga., and later Cannon. (Crisp developed another weapon of his own by using the Rules Committee to set items on the agenda and determine how each was to be handled.) "If we have broken the precedents of a hundred years," Reed wrote his constituents, "we have set the precedents of another hundred years nobler than the last, wherein the people, with full knowledge that their servants can act, will choose those who will worthily carry out their will" (quoted in Robinson 1930, 233–234). Many, though not all, of Reed's innovations endured; he deserves honor as perhaps the most able parliamentary leader Congress has ever produced.

Joseph G. Cannon, from Danville, Illinois, was an old-fashioned hardshell Republican. A genial, homey man, Cannon was as shrewd as Reed but lacked Reed's glacial manner and rapier-like wit. Even his enemies liked "Uncle Joe." After he became speaker in 1903 he proceeded to exploit the array of powers bequeathed by Reed to further his party's cause. He used the party caucus to bind Republicans to vote with the party. He chaired, and dominated, the Rules Committee; it convened at his pleasure and met in his chambers. Occasionally he was able to report out "special rules" to shape debate or even suspend House rules. Taken individually his powers were little different than Reed's; taken together they bordered on the dictatorial (Jones 1968). His behavior became more erratic, and he moved swiftly to punish those identified as dissidents.

As the years went by, grumbling over Cannon's tactics became increasingly audible. The anti-Cannonites numbered not only the minority Democrats but also a small group of Republican progressives, called insurgents. From reform-minded areas of the upper Midwest, they urged federal action far more aggressive than that condoned by orthodox businessmen who controlled the GOP elsewhere. Reform was in the air: Muckrakers were exposing corruption in politics and industry, and in the White House, Theodore Roosevelt proposed vigorous remedies. Cannon steadfastly refused to deviate from orthodox Republicanism; he opposed such heresies as food and drug laws, income and inheritance taxes, federal intervention in labor disputes, licensing of corporations, and child labor laws.

The anti-Cannon forces began to chip away at Cannon's prerogatives. A unanimous consent calendar was established in 1909 to routinize scheduling of noncontroversial bills. Later that year the Calendar Wednesday device was created, whereby the names of committees are called alphabetically each Wednesday so that committee chairs might call up nonprivileged legislation reported by their committees. This cumbersome procedure, though usually set aside every week, was a potential channel for bypassing the Rules Committee and its powerful head.

Finally, in March 1910, a direct assault was launched on the speaker. A leading insurgent, George W. Norris, R-Neb., rose and obtained recognition for what he claimed was a motion privileged under the Constitution. His resolution, introduced two years earlier but stuck in the Rules Committee, would replace the existing Rules Committee with a larger body on which the speaker could not serve.

Although the timing of Norris's move took everyone by surprise, the basic pact between Democrats and Republican insurgents had been forged some time earlier. The minority Democrats were grasping for leverage, the ability to forge bipartisan alliances that could prevail on the floor. As long as the speaker controlled access to the floor through the Rules Committee, this was impossible. As for the insurgents, they were defying party loyalty, speaking loftily of "fighting a system."

According to a compromise worked out by the anti-Cannon forces, Norris introduced a simplified substitute calling for a ten-person Rules Committee,

Roger H. Davidson

six from the majority party and four from the minority. The speaker would be barred from membership on the committee. The substitute passed by a 191-to-156 vote. The winning coalition included 149 Democrats and 42 Republicans.

The insurgents' victory marked the end of Cannonism. The new rule diluted the speaker's power by removing him from the Rules Committee and depriving him of his power to appoint that committee's members. Appointment of committee members became a party matter. Taken together the changes that followed the 1910 revolt thwarted the development of strong centralized leadership and enlarged the role of the committee chair. Not until the 1970s were the institutional powers of the speakership again aggregated.

The Senate Gains Formal Leaders

The Senate has always had its leaders, even though none were formally elected until the twentieth century. Many were sectional or factional leaders; others headed important committees; still others—like the "great triumvirate" of Henry Clay, John C. Calhoun, and Daniel Webster—possessed singular intellectual or oratorical gifts.

Many senators were local and state party bosses, sent to the nation's capital to gather all forms of government largesse. Thus the Senate was "a great gathering (and bargaining) place of the major party organizations that so dominated late-nineteenth-century politics" (Summers 1995, 1006). Senators treated government offices as their own private patronage. After 1883, however, the Pendleton Act began to build a civil service bureaucracy independent of senatorial control.

The Senate, quipped Speaker Reed, was where good representatives went when they died. A number of senators in fact served apprenticeships in the other body. Republicans John Sherman of Ohio and Finance Chair Nelson W. Aldridge of Rhode Island brought their financial expertise to the Senate; Henry L. Dawes of Massachusetts and William B. Allison of Iowa (who chaired Appropriations from 1881 to 1908), also Republicans, were legislative specialists.

After the mid-1880s, party bodies—the Republican Caucus and Steering Committee—brought a modicum of party and procedural discipline to committee assignments and scheduling. A group of strong-willed senators—among them Republicans Aldrich, Allison, Orville H. Platt of Connecticut, and John C. Spooner of Wisconsin and Democrat Arthur Pue Gorman of Maryland—brought to the Senate a measure of procedural control. Their experience and parliamentary expertise was combined with party discipline to regulate the flow of legislation.

"Party leadership for the first time dominated the chamber's business," as David Rothman put it (Rothman 1966, 5–7). The rise of clearly identifiable party leaders in the Senate, Rothman argued, reflected a "new breed" of senator who valued party unity and "the machinery of [party] organization," especially the party caucus. Soon those senators who chaired their respective party caucuses acquired levers of authority over senatorial affairs. They chaired important party panels, shaped the Senate's schedule, and mobilized votes to back up party positions. From the caucus chairmanships, the position of majority floor leader had informally emerged by 1913. In that year the first formally designated floor leader, John Worth Kern of Indiana, was selected by Democrats—in part to guide the chamber's relations with the activist President Woodrow Wilson.

Twentieth-Century Party Eras in Congress

With the end of Cannonism and turn-of-the-century Republican hegemony, party instability returned to Capitol Hill. Indeed, eras of true legislative harmony—party government in the parliamentary sense of the term—were quite rare in the twentieth century. There have been only three of them: Woodrow Wilson's first administration (1913–1917), Franklin Roosevelt's celebrated New Deal (1933–1936), and the palmiest days of Lyndon Johnson's Great Society (1963–1966). These periods flowed from unique convergences of a forceful chief executive, a popular but unfulfilled policy agenda, and a Congress responsive to presidential leadership. These were periods of frantic lawmaking, which produced landmark legislation and innovative government programs.

I have identified several distinct congressional eras in the post–New Deal period, defined not only by partisan margins but also by internal structure and politics (Davidson 1996). Roosevelt's New Deal soon gave way to a long period of bipartisan conservative dominance, which lasted roughly from the second Roosevelt administration through the mid-1960s. Both parties were split internally between a progressive, internationalist wing and a reactionary wing. Although the progressives tended to dominate presidential selections, the conservatives held sway on Capitol Hill. An oligarchy of senior leaders, often called "the old bulls," wielded the gavels and commanded the votes in the committees and on the floor. Whichever party was in power, congressional leaders overrepresented safe one-party regions (the Democratic rural South and the Republican rural Northeast and Midwest) and reflected the limited legislative agenda of the bipartisan conservative majority that controlled most do-

Roger H. Davidson

mestic policy making. This bipartisan conservative era outlasted several presidents of widely varying goals and skills—from Roosevelt through Kennedy.

The cozy world of the committee barons was eventually overturned by the advent of a liberal activist era (1964–1978). With its huge liberal working majorities in both chambers of Congress, this era spanned the period from Lyndon Johnson through Jimmy Carter. Internally the period saw a series of reforms that pointed Congress in the direction of more open and participatory processes that encouraged legislative innovation and productivity. The power of the committee barons was reined in and redirected both upward to the party leaders and downward to the rank-and-file members—more of whom chaired subcommittees than ever before. Such reforms were propelled by, and in turn helped to facilitate, expansionist policy agendas emanating from the White House. Legislative activity soared, by whatever measure one uses; the processing of freestanding bills and resolutions became the centerpiece of committee and subcommittee work. This legislative outpouring formed a gigantic "bulge in the middle," which David R. Mayhew noticed in his study of lawmaking between 1946 and 1990 (Mayhew 1991, 76). The liberal juggernaut continued during the seemingly conservative presidencies of Richard Nixon and Gerald Ford.

In the 1980s, Congress entered a period of cutback politics. Lagging economic productivity and changing intellectual fashions supported the idea that the federal government should review, refine, and cut back existing programs, rather than design new programs or establish new agencies. Legislative productivity was severely curtailed: Fewer bills were sponsored, huge legislative "megabills" were fashioned, budgetary politics became paramount, and individual legislators engaged in blame avoidance tactics to shield themselves from the adverse effects of curtailing or cutting off government programs or facilities.

During this latter period, congressional party leaders continued to recover power that had been lost after the anti-Cannon revolt. Not only did they benefit belatedly from powers conferred by reform-era innovations of the 1960s and 1970s, they also responded to widespread feelings that they were the only people who could, and should, untangle committee jurisdictional squabbles and orchestrate the legislative schedule.

Party leadership reached a modern high water mark with the Republican takeover of 1995. Speaker Newt Gingrich, R-Ga., conceded to be the architect of the GOP triumph, exerted a range of prerogatives reminiscent of the Cannon era. He chose committee chairs and demanded that their committees send to the floor elements of the GOP "Contract with America" in the first hundred days of the 104th Congress. Leadership-controlled entities—the Rules and

Budget Committees and leadership task forces—often drafted or perfected legislation in competition with the committees. The tenuous equilibrium between committee and party government tilted away from the former and toward the latter. Following the triumphant early months of the Republican regime, the power and credibility of the party leadership (including Gingrich himself) came under fire, and competition between party and committees became the order of the day. In 1998 Gingrich resigned and was replaced by the more conciliatory J. Dennis Hastert, R-Ill.—a sign that party leaders would pay more deference to committee leaders and other centers of power, such as intraparty ideological clusters of members.

Congressional Parties at the Millennium

Ever since the anti-Cannon revolt, party caucuses or committees have assumed responsibility for assigning members to committees and sometimes even for formulating policy. Despite the widely proclaimed death of traditional political parties, partisanship and factionalism are very much alive on Capitol Hill. By dint of party mechanisms, leaders are selected, committee assignments made, and floor debates scheduled. Parties also supply members with voting cues.

Today the parties' formal structure is extensive. Within both chambers, there are policy committees, campaign committees, research committees, elaborate whip systems, and countless task forces. Nearly 400 staff aides are employed by party leaders and perhaps an equal number by assorted party committees (Ornstein, Mann, and Malbin 2000, 129). Party-oriented voting bloc groups (such as the Conservative Democratic Forum or the Republicans' Tuesday Group), so-called class clubs (such as the Republican Freshman Class or the Democratic First Term Class), and social groups complement and reinforce partisan ties.

Party Candidate Recruitment and Campaigning

In their heyday—roughly from the time of Andrew Jackson through the decline of big-city political machines after World War II—party organizations customarily enlisted and sponsored congressional candidates. Then, as local party organizations atrophied, the initiative passed to the would-be candidates themselves: self-starters who pulled their own bandwagons. Today's campaigns are thus called candidate centered: Would-be candidates themselves decide whether, and when, to run, and they are responsible for raising most of the money to fuel their efforts.

Roger H. Davidson

If local party groups are now often amorphous or moribund, the national party entities—including House and Senate caucuses and committees—are visible and organizationally vigorous as never before. Their status represents a reversal of the nineteenth century when, as Woodrow Wilson wrote, the local parties were ubiquitous whereas the national parties remained shadowy (Wilson 1956, 80).

While steering their own careers, therefore, today's candidates often rely on the nationalized networks of party committees and their allied interest groups. At the center of these networks are the Hill's four campaign committees—the National Republican Senatorial Committee, the Democratic Senatorial Campaign Committee, the National Republican Congressional Committee, and the Democratic Congressional Campaign Committee. These committees have become increasingly aggressive in all phases of congressional elections (Hernnson 1988). They seek out and encourage candidates, sometimes even intervening in local contests to ensure their nominations. During the recruiting season—which begins soon after the previous election has been held—party leaders and staff aides crisscross the country in search of political talent. Top prospects can expect calls from presidents, former presidents, governors, high-profile financial backers, and other notables. Another aspect of recruitment is dissuading sitting members from retiring—inasmuch as open seats are riskier than those held by long-time incumbents. Still another function is luring party-switchers to their ranks, often offering to maintain the prospects' committee assignments and accumulated committee seniority.

Despite the prevalence of primary elections, state, district, and even national party entities have leverage in nominations. In nine states, parties have conventions that influence candidates' access to the primary ballot—for example, by conferring preprimary endorsements. In eight other states, party organizations informally influence the process through endorsements or other actions that can boost favored candidates. In 1996, for example, local and national Republican leaders pushed two controversial House freshmen into retirement, coaxed a former member to succeed one of them (with the promise of a committee chairmanship), and worked to quash primary challenges to several incumbents. Three years later, GOP leaders took an erratic and vulnerable colleague aside and warned him to "clean up his act, stay silent, and start raising more money or risk near-certain defeat in the 2000 election" (Bresnahan 1999, 1). In numerous other cases, local or national party leaders work to win nominations for candidates they deem most likely to prevail in the general election. Needless to say, such efforts do not always succeed. Picking winners, moreover, is sure to anger the favored candidates' rivals and their ideological backers.

Once nominated, candidates receive assistance in nearly every phase of their campaigns, from finding financial backers and seasoned campaign professionals to providing briefings and talking points on national issues.

Party Voting

On the House and Senate floors, party affiliation is the strongest single predictor of members' voting behavior, and in recent years it has reached levels nearly as high as a century ago. Of the nearly 2,000 floor votes cast by representatives and senators on articles of impeachment against President Clinton, for example, 92 percent followed partisan battle lines—Republicans favoring impeachment, Democrats resisting it.

In a typical year nearly two-thirds of all floor votes can be called party unity votes (defined by *Congressional Quarterly* as votes in which a majority of voting Republicans oppose a majority of voting Democrats). The current resurgence of party voting recalls the militant parties era of a century ago. At that time more than two-thirds of all roll calls were party unity votes. In several sessions a majority of the votes found 90 percent of one party arrayed against 90 percent of the other—a demanding standard that these days appears only in about one roll call vote in ten (Ornstein, Mann, and Malbin 2000, 194).

It is possible to calculate party unity scores for individual members—the percentage of party unity votes in which each member votes along with his or her party colleagues. According to these scores the average lawmaker now sticks with the party line on at least four out of every five votes. Partisan voting blocs are found also in many committees. As we will see in the next section, the House Judiciary Committee, which both parties have for many years assiduously stacked with party loyalists, is a virtual caricature of today's Capitol Hill partisanship.

Given the presumably individualistic tendencies of today's elected politicians, what can account for the prevalence of party voting in the two chambers? Some people argue that party loyalty is mainly a shorthand term for constituency differences. Partisans vote together, in other words, because they reflect the same kinds of political and demographic areas. Legislators stray from party ranks when they decide their constituents will not benefit from the party's policies. Democratic mavericks these days tend to come from nonminority southern districts, whose voters tend to be to the right of the party's mainstream. Republican dissenters are mostly from New England and the

Northeast corridor, where voters fall to the left of the party's center. Of the ten freshmen Republicans who gave less than 90 percent support to the Republican platform during the first hundred days of 1995, eight were northeasterners. To win in these areas, elected officials have to lean away from their parties' main thrust.

Sorting out the parties' constituency differences also helps explain the upsurge in party loyalty among legislators. Among Democratic representatives, increasing numbers of their southern flank are African Americans. The dwindling number of Democrats from conservative—mostly southern and rural—districts (including the self-named Blue Dog Democrats) try to distance themselves from their leaders. By the same token, Republicans are more uniformly conservative than they used to be. In the South, conservative areas now tend to elect Republicans, not Democrats. Elsewhere many areas once represented by GOP liberals have fallen to the Democrats. The decline of archconservative Democrats and liberal Republicans, especially in the House, underlies much of the ideological cohesion within, and chasm between, today's Capitol Hill parties.

Another source of today's partisanship is institutional: the congressional parties and their activities to promote party loyalty. New-member socialization is dominated by party organizations. Incoming members attend party-sponsored orientations, rely on party bodies for their committee assignments, and often organize into partisan class clubs. When seeking cues for voting, moreover, lawmakers turn to party colleagues to guide their own behavior.

Party leaders repeatedly contact members to solicit views and urge them to support the party. Rep. Mark Souder, R-Ind., described the tactics of then-Speaker Newt Gingrich and his lieutenants during their first year in power:

> They pull us into a room before almost every vote and yell at us. . . . They say, "This is a test of our ability to govern," or "This is a gut check," or "I got you here and you hired me as your coach to get you through, but if you want to change coaches, go ahead" (quoted in Kondracke 1995, 5).

Finally, party leaders exploit each chamber's rules and procedures to encourage favorable outcomes. House procedures sharpen partisanship, inasmuch as a cohesive party majority can normally work its will. By controlling key committees, employing scheduling powers, and using special rules to structure floor debate and voting, majority party leaders can arrange votes they are likely to win and avoid those they are apt to lose. Senate leaders have fewer opportunities to engineer victories because that chamber's rules and procedures distribute power more evenly between the parties and among individual senators. Yet Senate floor leaders can regulate the timing of debates to their advantage and (through their right to be recognized first to speak or offer amendments on the floor) shape the order and content of floor deliberations.

Partisanship is underscored by events of the 1990s. Despite the public's professed antipathy toward partisanship (and toward the two major parties in particular), recent elections have had distinctly partisan results. For example, in the last four congressional elections approximately nine out of every ten Democrats and Republicans voted for House candidates of their own parties. Independent voters split their votes evenly in 1996 and 1998 but tilted toward the Democrats in 1993 and toward the GOP in 1994 (Ladd 1999).

One outgrowth of robust partisanship is the advent of congressional party platforms designed to attract voters and validate the party's bid for power. The House Republicans' manifesto, the "Contract with America," was by no means the earliest such document, but it was shrewdly drafted, aggressively marketed, and then used as the party's working agenda during its first months in power (Bader 1997). Five years later the Clinton impeachment became a pitched battle along party lines, dividing not only lawmakers but also their constituents. With visible party differences and bitter personal battles, Capitol Hill political alignments are rigorous, even with recent tenuous majorities. Current appeals to partisan loyalty would be understood by politicians and voters of a century ago.

Impeachment: The Ultimate Partisan Weapon

The outbreak of the scandal involving President Bill Clinton's relationship with Monica S. Lewinsky raised partisan hostilities to an even higher level. When independent counsel Kenneth W. Starr submitted his report on the affair on September 9, 1998, the House of Representatives began a course of action that led eventually to approval of two articles of impeachment. Two factors raised the likelihood of impeachment by the House: the internal balance of forces between party leaders and committee leaders, and the hardening of partisan divisions on the issue, both inside and outside the chamber.

The most fateful step, as it turned out, was the very first one taken by the House: referral of the matter to the Judiciary Committee. Before the Starr report surfaced, but as it became apparent that the House would be asked to take some action, Speaker Newt Gingrich floated a proposal for a select panel to conduct the investigation. But his trial balloon was quickly punctured by Judiciary Chair Henry J. Hyde, R-Ill., backed by his committee members and other committee chairs. As part of the price for retaining his speakership, Gingrich had early in 1997 made a series of concessions to committee chairs. With a substantially weakened bargaining position, then, the Gingrich proposal had virtually no chance of acceptance. Although select committees had been employed in early impeachment inquiries, the Judiciary Committee had processed most modern cases—including the 1974 inquiry of President Richard Nixon and several subsequent cases. Hyde and his colleagues thus had jurisdictional precedent on their side. Moreover, Hyde himself was a figure accorded respect from both sides of the aisle (grudgingly from Democrats, to be sure). Any deviation in such a high-profile case would be interpreted as a slight to a noted leader as well as a threat to committee prerogatives.

Referring the inflammatory Starr report to the Judiciary Committee was, however, rather like handing matches to a pyromaniac. The committee had long enjoyed a reputation as the most partisan panel on Capitol Hill. The reasons are embedded in the two parties' policy priorities and committee assignment patterns. Republicans staffed the committee with staunch conservatives committed to conservative causes within the committee's jurisdiction: tough crime legislation; minimal gun regulations; and constitutional amendments on subjects such as abortion, school prayer, flag desecration, and balanced budgets. Liberal Democrats gravitated to the committee in the 1960s to fight for civil rights legislation. As the civil rights movement slowed down, it became harder to attract activist Democrats to Judiciary; however, party leaders continued to recruit (and in some instances conscript) liberals in order to quash the very proposals that brought conservatives to the committee.

If the House was partisan, therefore, Judiciary was hyperpartisan. Committee Democrats in the 105th Congress were on average ten points more loyal to their party than the average for all Democrats, according to *Congressional Quarterly*'s party unity scores (Ota 1999). Republicans on the committee were on average more than five points more loyal than their party colleagues as a whole. By the same token, Democrats gave more support to President Clinton, and Republicans less support, than their party colleagues outside the committee, based on *Congressional Quarterly*'s presidential support scores (Hosansky 1999). As a result, Judiciary was virtually a caricature of Sarah A. Binder's portrait of the "vanishing middle" of the ideological spectrum in Congress (Binder 1996). It is no exaggeration to say that there were *no* moderates on the committee, at least as measured by the most commonly cited voting indices. There were, for example, none of the party mavericks—southern Democrats and moderate Republicans, among others—who had so enlivened the Watergate proceedings a quarter of a century earlier.

The partisan rancor manifested itself in ways both blatant and subtle. Chairman Hyde's choice of head counsel for the inquiry, an old friend who claimed to have once been a Democrat, was so rabidly anti-Clinton that he helped the minority Democrats circle the wagons in the president's defense. The decision to release Starr's argumentative report immediately—before members had a chance to read, much less consider, the document—encouraged members to stake out their positions before, rather than after, any deliberation and debate had taken place. The raucous demeanor of committee members, Democrats and Republicans alike, during the televised proceedings merely reinforced the growing conviction of members and the general public that the whole process was tainted by partisanship.

The special House session on impeachment took place in the wake of the 1998 elections. Republican leadership was in visible disarray. Chastened by the loss of five House seats (after a large gain had been expected), Speaker Gingrich had abruptly abdicated and was exerting no leadership on the impeachment vote. His heir-apparent, Appropriations Chair Bob Livingston, R-La., signaled that he wanted the issue resolved before he took over and tried to distance himself from the proceedings. (In the most dramatic moment of the floor debates, he announced his withdrawal from the House because of personal scandal.) Meanwhile, Majority Whip Tom DeLay, R-Tex., arguably the most effective member of the leadership group, was whipping rank-and-file Republicans in support of impeachment. On the other side of the aisle, Minority Leader Richard A. Gephardt, D-Mo., was carefully building support for the president among Democrats. He was aided not only by the Republicans' ill-concealed zeal but also by the continuing public support for keeping the president in office.

In the end the votes on the four articles of impeachment—the last actions taken by the 105th Congress—were mainly along partisan lines. Of the 1,740 votes cast by House members on the four articles—two of which were adopted—a total of 92 percent followed partisan lines. Republicans supported the president's impeachment; Democrats resisted it. It was a partisan exercise in a partisan Congress.

Upon convening in January 1999, the Senate decided to go forward with the trial of President Clinton instead of censuring him. Senate leaders claimed to be following precedent, but in fact the proceedings were choreographed in response to political exigencies, moving toward a conclusion that everyone— most particularly, the chamber's leaders—realized was inevitable. Senators no doubt wished to shield themselves from the raw partisanship of the House's proceedings and to protect their personal and institutional reputations for dignity and probity. But their votes were as partisan as those of their House colleagues. If survey results are to be trusted, the senators failed to alter the public's view of the impeachment as a partisan affair. Citizens had already concluded that the impeachment process was primarily a political vendetta against a president whose moral failings, they reasoned, were not markedly worse than those of many other elected officials. When the proceedings concluded, CBS News asked respondents whether they thought most senators really believed they were doing the right thing, or whether they thought the votes reflected politics and party loyalty. Nearly three-quarters of respondents said most senators followed politics and party interests, whereas only 19 percent said that most senators followed what they thought was right (Kull 1999, 26). Most citizens, in other words, had already made up their minds about the impeachment proceedings, and the Senate's actions did little to change their assessment.

Divided Party Control

The volatile mixture that marked the Gilded Age—intense partisanship coupled with divided party control of government—is all too familiar to late-twentieth-century observers. Divided government has become commonplace in modern times. In almost two-thirds of the congresses elected since the end of World War II, one or both houses were in the hands of the party opposed to the president. So-called divided government marked two stormy years of the Truman presidency; all but two years of Eisenhower's and Clinton's presidencies; and all of Nixon's, Ford's, Reagan's, and Bush's years. And partisan majorities have been slender during the last four congresses controlled by the Republicans (1953–1954 and 1995–2000).

Divided government is the product of the weakening of party identification, the rise of ticket splitting by voters, and the extremely close competition of the two parties nationally. Apparently, presidential candidates are viewed through different lenses than are legislative candidates. During the Reagan-Bush years, voters were inclined to support presidents who promised government cuts and "no new taxes" while electing legislators who stressed constituency service and pledged to preserve cherished federal programs. In the mid-1990s, President Clinton regained popularity, and a second term, by portraying himself as a check against the self-proclaimed Republican revolutionaries on Capitol Hill. Public opinion surveys, moreover, suggest that people prefer having divided party control so that the two branches can keep a watchful eye on one another.

Divided government is widely blamed for policy stalemate and low legislative productivity. But it does not preclude interbranch cooperation or legislative productivity. Despite divided control, legislative productivity was extraordinarily high during the Nixon and Ford presidencies and during Reagan's first year. Some scholars contend that the supposed benefits of unified party control have been exaggerated. Examining legislative productivity levels, I found that they did not correspond very well with presidential administrations, whether party control was united or not (Davidson 1996, 39–41). David R. Mayhew found that unified or divided control made little difference in enactment of important legislation or launching of high-profile congressional investigations of executive-branch misdeeds (Mayhew 1991).

Yet divided control exacts long-term costs in terms of policy stalemate. Congressional party leaders tend to shape legislative proposals and parliamentary maneuvers for their publicity value rather than their likelihood of passage. Uncommon leadership and skillful interbranch bargaining are required to overcome divergent political stakes and resultant inertia. Frustration in achieving their policy goals psychologically wears down presidents, legislators, and their staffs. Policy decisions may be deferred or compromised so severely that the solutions have little impact. Voters find it difficult to hold presidents and lawmakers accountable, as each blames the other for failing to resolve pressing national problems or enact coherent policies. Recent examples include adjustments in Social Security and health care financing—issues that contain broad areas of agreement but that invite partisan position-taking and rhetoric.

Some Millennial Thoughts

At the distance of a hundred years, we are in a position to recall events of the last turn-of-the-century and consider their effects on subsequent politics. Equally—though with far less confidence—we ought to ask ourselves which contemporary developments are most likely to exert equivalent changes in the new century.

At first glance the developments associated with the twentieth century's beginning seem all too familiar. Domestically these developments included a growing and restless population and economic and social policy challenges associated with shifts in what Marxists called the means of production. Internationally the nation explored for the first time its role as an emerging power in the context of globalized trade and warfare. Social and political change was rapid, demanding novel policy responses and institutional changes. Political parties were strong and militant; political combat was fierce, being waged along partisan and ideological lines.

Today's conditions are no less compelling. Population growth is being propelled by new waves of immigrants, geographic mobility, and demographic shifts—the most notable of which is the aging of the population. Economic and social challenges surround the rise of a postindustrial world built on technological advances in information and communication. Globalization has moved beyond the traditional diplomatic and military arenas to embrace nearly every social and cultural detail. People are ideologically divided over proposed solutions to these problems, along lines that roughly parallel the political parties.

Beyond these surface similarities, however, profound differences exist as well. In 1900 the core policy questions were the extent to which the federal government should play an activist part in economic and social arrangements, and the extent of the nation's role in world affairs. By the end of the twentieth century those questions seemed to have been answered affirmatively. Yet real questions remain about the federal government's place. Interventionist solutions that may have seemed necessary to harness an industrial economy often seem clumsy and heavy-handed in dealing with postindustrial problems. Internationally, nation states—though more numerous than ever—are seeing their place challenged by nongovernmental institutions of various types.

What role are political parties likely to play in addressing these issues? Like our counterparts of a hundred years ago, we live in an era of noisy, combative partisanship. But the partisanship of the two eras contrasts radically in character and structure. Party loyalties were deeply ingrained in nineteenth-century political life, mirroring not only ideological beliefs but also social and regional differences. Local party organizations were powerful and extensive, whereas the national parties were just beginning to erect structures. Although the Republican and Democratic Parties organize Congress and dominate its proceedings, the voters profess to dislike both of them. Both parties boast extensive, well-funded national organizations, but in many parts of the country their organizations are weak or nonexistent. Most citizens seem unconcerned about politics. Whereas in 1900 party politics was a form of national entertainment, in 2000 it was a sideshow that struggled for attention in competition with beguiling diversions such as sports, entertainment, hobbies, and the like.

Congress has become, of course, a far more mature institution than it was in 1900. The elements of institutionalization that coalesced in 1900—careerism, division of labor through committees, party organizations and leadership, and routinized procedures—have flourished in recent decades and remain distinctive traits of the House and Senate today. A defect of mature institutions, however, can be their organizational rigidity. Institutions that are too brittle can frustrate policy making, especially in periods of rapid social or political change. The Congress of a hundred years ago succeeded in overcoming many of its earlier defects and in adapting to altered political demands. The evolution was discontinuous, and the details not often pretty. But on the whole the Congress that emerged in the twentieth century was a success story.

Are contemporary changes on Capitol Hill as far-reaching as those of a hundred years ago? Of course no final answer can be given, but impressive changes have taken place in recent years. The Republicans' post-1994 institutional innovations, for example, show that Congress's evolution has by no means run its full course. Continuing changes in Congress's political environment will demand further alterations in the membership, organization, procedures, and policy-making capacities of the House and Senate. As in the past, these alterations will require leadership, ingenuity, and legislative professionalism if Congress is to make its way successfully through the twenty-first century.

10

Can the Parties Govern?

Sarah A. Binder

In 1950, E. E. Schattschneider and the American Political Science Association (APSA) Committee on Political Parties reviewed the condition of the American party system and found it woefully inadequate for the tasks of democratic rule (American Political Science Association 1950). Most worrisome from the committee's perspective was that "either major party, when in power, is ill-equipped to organize its members in the legislative and executive branches into a government held together and guided by the party program" (American Political Science Association 1950, v). The consequences were steep: "The very heartbeat of democracy," the committee warned, was threatened by the state of the political parties. Democracy was contingent on organizing and responding to majorities, and parties were deemed the only viable instrument for doing so.

At the time of the APSA report, unified party control of Congress and the presidency was the norm. In the first half of the twentieth century, twenty-two of twenty-six national elections had produced unified control of government. In other words, even under conditions of unified government, Schattschneider and his contemporaries believed American political parties were too weak to guarantee responsible party government (see Coleman 1999). The combination of ideological divisions within the parties and institutional constraints limited the ability of the major parties to build and enact party agendas once in office, even under unified control. Yet despite these weaknesses, parties were still viewed as the only means of bridging constitutional gaps that limited the production of public policy. Responsible government might not be guaranteed by unified party control, but it was unthinkable without it.

Today innumerable critics of contemporary politics still call for a more responsible and effective government. The predominance of divided government in recent decades (produced by sixteen of the past twenty-three national elec-

---

I thank The Dillon Fund for its generous financial support of this project.

tions) disheartens many such critics, who charge that divided government is frequently the cause of "deadlock, inadequate, and ineffective policies, or no policies at all" (Sundquist 1988–1989). The short period of unified government under the Democrats after the 1992 elections did little to abate criticism of political stalemate in Washington, D.C. "It's back to gridlock, or so it has seemed lately—but of a nasty internecine kind," the *Washington Post* observed as it judged the record of the unified 103d Congress in late 1994 ("The Hollow Branch" 1994).

Such historical and contemporary concerns raise important questions for students of political parties. First, is effective lawmaking more likely under unified than divided party control? If so, how much of a difference is made by unified government? Second, why is unified control rarely a prescription for defeating policy deadlock? Why does gridlock still emerge in periods of unified control? Third, what other institutional or electoral factors might help account for trends in the production of public policy? In this chapter I address these questions, using the experience of the last half of the twentieth century to explore some conventional and alternative notions about Congress and the president's capacity to act on issues of major public import.

The Concept and Measurement of Gridlock

How do we know whether government is deadlocked, productive, or somewhere in between? The most casual observer of Washington can usually tell the difference between a Congress that produces a lot and a Congress that does little. The slim legislative record of the Democratic 102d Congress in 1991–1992—which provoked charges of gridlock by presidential candidates Ross Perot and Bill Clinton—is a prime example of gridlock at its extreme. Efforts to enact lobbying and campaign finance reform; to enact parental leave, banking, and voter registration legislation; and to cut the capital gains tax—to name just a few salient issues during that Congress—all ended in deadlock. Likewise, the most productive Congresses are easily identified; the Great Society Congress under Lyndon Johnson in 1965–1966 is exemplary in this regard. This Congress enacted landmark health care, environment, civil rights, transportation, and education statutes, among many others—a total of twenty-two major laws, a record met only two other times over the past twenty-six Congresses.

Although we can judge gridlock and productivity at their extremes, political scientists lack a metric that would allow us to compare, more or less systematically, changes in the level of gridlock over time. Typically scholars as-

Sarah A. Binder

sess Congress's output, counting the number of important laws enacted each Congress. When output is low, we say that gridlock is high, and vice versa. David Mayhew's well-regarded contribution to these debates, *Divided We Govern,* uses such an approach to evaluate legislative performance between 1947 and 1990 (Mayhew 1991). But measuring output without respect to the agenda of salient issues risks misstating the true level of gridlock. A Congress might produce little legislation because it is gridlocked. Or it might be unproductive because it faces a limited agenda. With little on its legislative plate, surely Congress and the president should not be blamed for producing meager results. We can evaluate the relevance of parties to the production of public policy only if we have some idea of the size of the underlying policy agenda in Washington.

Gridlock is best viewed, then, as the share of salient issues on the nation's agenda left in limbo at the close of each Congress. Just what are the salient issues on the nation's agenda? The editorial page of the *New York Times* (often considered the nation's paper of record) serves admirably as an indicator. Indeed one can reconstruct the policy agenda of American politics in the last half of the twentieth century by identifying the legislative issues of each Congress discussed by the *New York Times* (whether supporting or opposing the issue— to take into account the paper's often-liberal political perspective). Salient issues are those addressed by the *New York Times* at least four times in a single Congress.[1]

This measure provides a sense of the size of the policy agenda over time (Table 10-1). It ranges, as we might expect, from a low point in the 1950s, during the quiescent years of the Eisenhower presidency, through a sharp jump in the 1960s under the activist administrations of Presidents Kennedy and Johnson. The size of the agenda continues to rise steadily in the 1970s and 1980s and begins declining only recently, in the 1990s—likely reflecting the tightening of budgets and the concordant dampening of legislative activism.

How successful were Congress and the president in addressing the most salient of these policy issues? Figure 10-1 shows marked variation in the level of gridlock since 1950. Is Congress particularly gridlocked today? Critics of Congress who claim so are partially right. Gridlock had an upward trend over the period; the level of gridlock was on average twenty-five points higher in the 1990s than it was in the 1940s. Gridlock peaked in the early 1990s, when George Bush faced a Democratic Congress. Fully 65 percent of the twenty-

1. Full explanation of the method used for generating legislative agendas from the *New York Times* appears in Binder (1999, Appendix B).

Table 10–1. Size of the Policy Agenda, 1947–1996

Congress (years)	Number of Issues on Agenda
80 (1947–48)	85
81 (1949–50)	85
82 (1951 52)	72
83 (1953–54)	74
84 (1955–56)	84
85 (1957 58)	89
86 (1959–60)	70
87 (1961–62)	129
88 (1963–64)	102
89 (1965–66)	96
90 (1967–68)	119
91 (1969–70)	144
92 (1971–72)	135
93 (1973–74)	133
94 (1975–76)	138
95 (1977–78)	150
96 (1979–80)	144
97 (1981–82)	127
98 (1983–84)	138
99 (1985–86)	160
100 (1987–88)	140
101 (1989–90)	147
102 (1991–92)	126
103 (1993–94)	94
104 (1995–96)	118

three most salient agenda issues remained unresolved when the 102d Congress drew to a close in 1992. With the arrival of unified government under Bill Clinton and Congressional Democrats after the 1992 elections, gridlock still remained at an historic high, with over half of the sixteen most visible issues left in limbo when the 103d Congress adjourned.

But the level of gridlock does not simply trend upward. After its unprecedented highs in the early 1990s, gridlock dropped fourteen points in the 104th Congress (1995–1996), reflecting election year compromises on reforming welfare, health care, immigration, and telecommunication laws, as well as increasing the minimum wage. Still, no recent Congress has matched the performance of the Great Society, four years of legislative prowess in which Pres-

Sarah A. Binder

Figure 10–1. Level of Policy Gridlock, 1947–1996

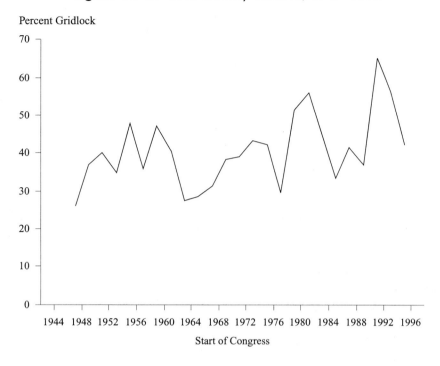

Percent Gridlock

Start of Congress

idents Kennedy and Johnson and their Democratic Congresses stalemated on just roughly a quarter of the policy agenda (gridlocking on fourteen of the fifty most salient issues across those four years).

The Policy Impact of Divided Government

What effect does party control of government have on the policy performance of Congress and the president? Arguments about the effects of divided government typically revolve around the importance of political parties for bridging our separated institutions (Cutler 1988; Kelly 1993; Sundquist 1988–1989). The logic is straightforward: Unified party control of the two branches guarantees an important extra-constitutional link between the legislature and the executive, which ensures common interests and shared purpose. Under unified government, shared electoral and policy motivations of the president and congressional majorities give majority party legislative leaders the incentive and capacity to use their tools and resources to pass legislation. In contrast, under

Can the Parties Govern? **213**

divided government, competing policy views and electoral incentives are said to reinforce institutional rivalries between Congress and the president, which makes it difficult to assemble the coherent policy majorities necessary to forge major legislation (see Fiorina 1996, ch. 6). Both parties seek policy outcomes that enhance their own electoral reputations, but neither side wants the other to reap electoral benefit from achieving its policy agenda.

If the traditional argument about divided government is correct, then stalemate should be higher in periods of split-party control and subside under unified government. This expectation is partially borne out. When control of Congress and the presidency has been divided between the parties, 43 percent of the agenda has ended in gridlock; when unified party control has prevailed, only 38 percent of the agenda has been left undone. Still, given the pointed criticism perennially lodged against divided government, the substantive effect of gridlock—a mere five points—is relatively small.

A comparison of the 102d and 103d Congresses clearly shows the muted effect of unified government. Under divided party control in the 102d Congress, gridlock reached a postwar high of 65 percent: nearly two-thirds of salient policy issues remained in deadlock when Congress adjourned. When the election of Bill Clinton as president in 1992 ushered in unified government for the 103d Congress, expectations were high. Capitol Hill observers anticipated that bills vetoed by President Bush under divided government would be signed into law and that the Democrats would push a heavy agenda of activist policy proposals toward enactment. Expectations were borne out to some extent: Voter registration, parental leave, and gun control reforms were enacted after being vetoed in the 102d Congress. But unified government failed to ensure enactment of the Democrats' more ambitious policy agenda, including economic stimulus measures and health care and campaign reforms. When Congress adjourned in 1994 the overall level of gridlock had subsided to 56 percent but remained well above the average level of deadlock for the postwar period.

What accounts for the muted policy impact of unified government? The experience of the 103d Congress offers a few clues. First, consider the fate of Clinton's proposed package of budget cuts in 1993. The bill passed the House with only Democratic votes. In the Senate, not only Republicans balked; conservative Democrats (including John Breaux of Louisiana and David Boren of Oklahoma) also raised objections. As a result, the Senate eliminated significant tax portions of the package passed by the House. This observation suggests that the constraint of a two-chamber legislature (bicameralism) poses a hurdle for major policy change, even in periods of unified control. Same-party control

Sarah A. Binder

of Congress and the presidency simply cannot guarantee that congressional partisans in both chambers will see eye to eye on salient policy matters.

Second, consider the fate of Clinton's 1993 economic stimulus package. It passed readily with the support of Democrats in the House. In the Senate, a Republican filibuster blocked the president's $16 billion package, resulting in a significantly weakened final bill.[2] Proposals for significant health care reform also ran into filibuster-related problems, as the president's proposal failed to garner sufficient minority party support in the Senate. Because a supermajority is needed to cut off a filibuster and because the majority party rarely has the requisite sixty votes (out of one hundred) from within its party ranks, significant bipartisan support is usually necessary to ensure passage of major legislation. In other words, unified government is not always sufficient for producing significant policy change. Lacking bipartisan support to overcome a filibuster or a presidential veto, significant policy change is unlikely to occur. Thus, although unified government tends to reduce the level of deadlock, it is rarely a cure-all for the passage of major policy change.

Additional Effects of Elections

National elections determine the frequency of divided and unified party control of government. But elections do more than divide control of government. Perhaps the most striking electoral trend in recent years has been the polarization of the two major parties in Congress, which some have called the disappearing political center (Binder 1996). If we think of centrists or moderates as legislators who are closer to the ideological midpoint of the two parties than to their own parties' centers, we can size up the reach of the political center since 1950.[3] By this score, roughly one-third of the members of Congress in the 1960s and 1970s were centrists; today, moderates make up less than 10 percent of the House and Senate combined. Symbolic of the decline of the political center was the death of Sen. John Chafee, R-R.I., in October 1999. President

2. A *filibuster* is said to occur when opponents of a measure refuse to end debate in the Senate. Under the Senate's Rule 22, a three-fifths majority (sixty votes) is required to *invoke cloture* and thus end debate. Lacking a three-fifths majority, it is impossible to cut off debate under Senate rules if any senator or group of senators refuses to end debate. In other words, as long as a coalition can muster forty votes, it can block action in the Senate counter to the wishes of a chamber majority (fifty-one votes). Senators can also threaten to filibuster, meaning they suggest to party leaders that they are likely to filibuster if a particular bill comes to the Senate floor.

3. Ideological placement of legislators and their respective parties is based on Poole and Rosenthal (1997). Here I use their first-dimension W-NOMINATE scores. See extended discussion in Binder (1999).

Clinton lauded Chafee after his death as embodying "the decent center which has carried America from triumph to triumph for over 200 years" (Sullivan 1999). His death left only two moderates in the Senate in 1999, based on their roll call votes for the year.[4]

Many political scientists are now exploring the causes of polarization (for example, Bond and Fleisher 2000). The consequences of polarization must also be considered. In some respects, the prospects for responsible party government should be expected to increase as the two parties each become internally more ideologically cohesive and distant from the other. As the two parties move further apart, their philosophical differences on matters such as the appropriate role and reach of the federal government become more pronounced, giving voters a real choice between party agendas at election time. This, it would seem, was precisely the hope of Schattschneider and the responsible party school, who saw meaningful elections as critical to the stability of democracy.

But a polarized partisan environment might have the opposite effect. Rather than encouraging coherent policy change, party polarization might prevent it. If major policy change is more likely when legislators can forge large, bipartisan coalitions,[5] we might expect the likelihood of gridlock to increase with polarization. The further apart the two parties are, the tougher it is to negotiate compromise, partly because fewer legislators are positioned in the center and partly because others have little incentive to reach into the middle. As Rep. Barney Frank, D-Mass., observed in the fall of 1999, "Right now, the differences between the two parties are so great, it doesn't make sense for us to compromise. We'll show where we stand, and let the people decide" (cited in Grunwald 1999).

The presence of moderate legislators makes bridging party differences easier, because at least a small block of legislators from the two parties share a common centrist electoral constituency. The need to appeal to a similar set of ideological interests at election time would provide an incentive for legislators to try to bridge policy differences between the two parties. When the two parties are clearly polarized, each relying on the support of a different set of con-

4. The remaining moderates were both Republicans: Arlen Specter of Pennsylvania and James Jeffords of Vermont. Other senators of the 106th Congress who in earlier years had scored as moderates based on their ideological scores were Democrat John Breaux of Louisiana, and Olympia Snowe and Susan Collins, both Republicans from Maine.

5. On the connection between the size of coalitions and policy gridlock, see Krehbiel (1998, ch. 4).

Sarah A. Binder

stituencies, the parties start with few policy agreements and face little electoral incentive to compromise.

If ideological moderation encourages policy compromise, we should see a negative relationship between the number of moderates and the level of policy gridlock. The greater the number of centrists, the lower the level of gridlock. In contrast, if ideological moderation makes it harder for the majority party to enact an agenda, moderation and gridlock should go hand in hand. As the number of centrist legislators rises, gridlock should rise as well. For both the House and the Senate, the expectation that moderation reduces gridlock is borne out in the period since World War II, with the relationship stronger for the Senate than the House.[6]

Viewing the effects of elections more broadly, a national election that produces unified government might also yield a Congress with few ideological moderates. This is precisely what occurred with the 1992 elections that installed unified Democratic government in Washington. The elections also returned two political parties with barely any ideological overlap between their members: Moderates made up less than 13 percent of both chambers in the 103d Congress. Not surprisingly, although gridlock subsided slightly between the 102d and 103d Congresses with the arrival of unified government, it did so only marginally. The boost brought by unified control was dampened by the lack of legislative centrists. With such steep ideological differences between the parties, majority Democrats could not attract the necessary bipartisan support to enact major changes in public policy.[7]

In what other ways might elections affect policy making? We might also consider the effect of electoral shocks on the prospects for governance. The most prominent such electoral shocks are those associated with critical elections and realignments, sharp changes in the national electoral landscape that either bring a new dominant majority to power or strengthen the electoral position of the existing majority party. Political scientists usually point to three such major realignments over the course of the nation's electoral history, occurring around the Civil War, during the late 1890s, and during the New Deal of the 1930s (see Burnham 1970; Clubb, Flanigan, and Zingale 1990). Each was accompanied by major changes in public policy (Brady 1988).

6. The correlation between gridlock on salient issues and the percentage of House moderates (80th–104th Congresses) is $-.22$, whereas the correlation between gridlock and Senate moderates is $-.35$.

7. The Republicans' strategy of noncooperation paid royal dividends in the 1994 elections, handing them control of Congress for the first time since 1954.

For the contemporary period, no consensus exists on whether another electoral realignment has occurred (Shafer 1991). But even electoral shocks short of realignment are likely to affect policy stability. The argument was well stated in a *New York Times* editorial in 1948 at the close of the 80th Congress (1947–1948), the first Republican Congress since before the New Deal:

> The Republicans took control of Congress on the basis of an obvious popular revulsion against some of the policies of the Roosevelt-Truman administrations. There was no landslide but there was a perceptible movement of the political terrain. The new legislators certainly had a mandate to liquidate some war measures, to loosen some New Deal controls, to check some New Deal projects and to effect practicable economics ("Eightieth Congress: To Date" 1948).

The effects of such electoral shocks are likely conditioned by the length of time a new congressional majority was in the minority. The longer a new majority has been out of control of Congress, the more dissatisfied it is likely to be with the status quo, and the greater is its incentive to make changes. A new majority also has strong electoral incentive to prove that it can govern, further increasing the likelihood of altering the policy status quo.

The aftermath of the historic 1994 midterm elections that produced unified Republican rule for the first time in forty years illustrates this idea well. The fervor for conservative policy change after forty years as the minority party surely helped maintain the internal cohesiveness of House Republicans in the 104th Congress. Notably, they passed 95 percent of their campaign agenda, the "Contract with America," after taking control of the House.[8] Of course, as discussed later in this chapter, many of those provisions ultimately ended in deadlock, after encountering opposition from the Senate and the president.

The Effect of Institutions

From the very beginning of the American political nation, elites have recognized the impact of institutions on policy outcomes. By institutions I mean the set of constitutional and structural arrangements within which politics takes place. Even before the Constitution had been adopted, Alexander Hamilton warned in the *Federalist Papers* that the institutional arrangements of the Con-

---

8. The fate of the various Contract provisions is chronicled and tallied in Bader (1997).

Sarah A. Binder

tinental Congress were a proven recipe for deadlock. Supermajority requirements, voting by state units, and other internal procedures ensured that the policy views of the Continental Congress would often be frustrated (see Jillson
and Wilson 1994). The idea that institutions can make it difficult to secure the
preferences of a majority has a long history in American politics.

In thinking about the production of public policy today, the critical institutional arrangements are rules and procedures that directly affect the legislative process. Our interest then is in those institutional features that might help
explain why political parties—even highly cohesive ones—often find themselves unable to change public policy. To put it another way, elections are only
as decisive as institutional conditions permit. The case of the Republicans'
"Contract with America" is illustrative here. Although the House passed nearly
all of the provisions of the Contract, less than 40 percent of the Contract was
eventually enacted into law. Of critical importance to understanding the fate of
the Contract—and the fate of agendas more generally—is the impact of bicameralism and supermajority rules in Congress.

The bicameral character of Congress was crafted during the Constitutional
Convention in the late 1780s. Yet, despite the centrality of bicameralism to the
Constitution, students of the policy process often treat Congress as a unicameral actor. Certainly the traditional focus on divided government implicitly suggests that the legislative process can best be explained as the outcome of inter-
actions between the president and a unicameral Congress.[9] But treating
bicameral institutions as if they were unicameral risks overlooking important
differences.

Perhaps most fundamental is the idea that the two legislative chambers
might not hold the same set of preferred policy outcomes. Even when the same
party controls both chambers, elections might distribute policy views unevenly
between the two chambers. Given that only one-third of the Senate is up for reelection at one time, electoral trends that influence House members (all of
whom are up for reelection every two years) might show limited effect on the
Senate. The different constituency bases of House and Senate members also
matter here, as House districts are typically far more homogeneous than the
states from which they are drawn. A House Republican representing a homogeneous conservative district in southwestern Indiana might have little in common with an Indiana senator whose constituency includes more liberal minor-

9. Even scholars diminishing the theoretical importance of divided government often model
the legislative process as a unicameral game (see, for example, Krehbiel 1998).

ity groups from the inner cities of the north. The six-year term of senators might also moderate Senate delegations, given the longer stretch before facing the electorate, compared with House delegations.

Ideological differences between the two chambers are important, because they likely affect the ease with which the two chambers reach policy compromise. If the two chambers are ideologically akin to one another—as "boll weevil" southern House Democrats and the Senate's Republican median were in the early 1980s—bicameral accord should be easier to reach. With the House and Senate quite distant, the prospects for bicameral agreement recede. This was certainly the case during the 104th Congress, when moderate Republicans balked at the excesses of the House Republicans' agenda on regulatory reform, crime issues, property rights, and other issues.

Bicameral differences also provide insight into the limits of a party under unified government to secure its policy goals. President Clinton's health care proposals in 1994 are a prime example of the constraints bicameralism places on unified government. Even though Clinton made health care reform a key priority, significant differences between the House and Senate approaches to health care reform emerged during consideration of the issue, helping to block passage of a reform package during the 103d Congress. Proponents of party government often implicitly ignore bicameral impediments and as a result overstate the policy impact of unified party control. Given the particular institutional context in which parties work, we should not be surprised to find that unified government cannot always guarantee significant change on important public issues.

Supermajority rules in Congress also pose an institutional constraint on political parties and their pursuit of party agendas. Supermajority constraints are particularly important in the Senate, where the filibuster makes simple majorities powerless in the face of a determined minority. "Tit-for-tat" filibustering has compounded the problem, as control of the Senate has passed back and forth between Democrats and Republicans over the past two decades. Republican filibusters stymied much of Clinton's agenda under unified Democratic control in 1993 and 1994. Then, when Republicans regained control of the chamber in 1995, Democrats returned the favor by filibustering conservative initiatives. The effect of the filibuster can be gleaned by comparing a Congress with no filibusters (the 82d, 1951–1952) to one with thirty-five (the 102d, 1991–1992). Some 40 percent of salient issues ended in gridlock in the 82d, compared with 65 percent in the 102d.

Even if a supermajority can be mustered to invoke cloture and kill a filibuster, measures can be significantly watered down by concessions necessary to break the filibuster. Republican opposition to Clinton's economic stimulus plan in 1993 is a key example, with the final product bearing little resemblance to the House-passed measure. The Senate can also be held hostage by a minority of one, as any single senator can place a "hold" on bills or nominations headed to the floor until the senator's (often unrelated) policy or political demands are met. Angered over recess appointments made by Clinton in 1999, for example, Sen. James Inhofe, R-Okla., threatened to block confirmation of all of Clinton's judicial nominations during Clinton's final year in office, placing a blanket hold on all such nominations (numbering thirty-five at the start of 2000) (Preston 2000). By empowering supermajorities in a political system that moves primarily by majority rule, the Senate makes its own contribution to gridlock.

The Effect of Policy Context

Electoral and institutional factors alone are unlikely to account fully for gridlock. Because different types of policies yield different patterns of politics, the question is whether differences in the broader policy context affect the ease with which legislative compromise is reached (Lowi 1964). Budgetary slack and broad national trends are key features of the policy environment that can affect policy stability. Recent studies have not reached a uniform conclusion about the effects of these factors, but some support exists for claims that climates of sunny budgets and a liberal public mood yield more productive seasons of lawmaking.

The logic underpinning the effect of the budget environment is fairly simple. The greater the surplus relative to outlays, the easier it should be to accomplish legislative goals. Once the budget is in surplus, legislative compromise should be easier—because politicians are theoretically no longer caught in a zero-sum game.[10] Whether a coalition seeks higher spending or lower taxes, ample federal coffers can cover the side-payments necessary to forge a successful coalition. The argument rings true at the extremes. The deficit relative to outlays stood at nearly 20 percent during the 102d Congress, when gridlock peaked at over 65 percent. When the surplus relative to outlays reached 20 percent during the 80th Congress, gridlock was a mere 26 percent. Viewed

---

10. Inherited budget rules, however, might alter the strategic context, for instance, imposing statutory caps on discretionary spending or requiring that new spending be offset by budget cuts.

more broadly over the second half of the twentieth century, the relationship generally holds, with sunnier fiscal times generally associated with lower levels of gridlock.

Excess resources by themselves, however, cannot wipe out gridlock, a finding confirmed by Congress's predicament at the end of the twentieth century, despite the emergent budget surplus. When the government turned the corner in 1999 with a series of budget surpluses—the first since 1969—Democrats characteristically responded with a raft of proposals to expand Medicare coverage and other social programs (as well as targeted tax cuts). At the same time, Republicans hoisted up a perennial favorite of across-the-board tax cuts (as well as more limited Medicare expansion) (Babington and Pianin 1999). Despite the budget surplus, little to no progress was made in 1999 on matters of social security reform, Medicare reform, tax cuts, and other issues high on the parties' lists of priorities.

Prevailing national moods are also said to have a significant influence on agendas and policy outcomes (see Coleman 1999; Mayhew 1991, ch. 6). Liberal climates of opinion seem to underlie extended periods of activist government. When such waves of citizen support for change through governmental action ebb, government seems to retrench. Arthur Schlesinger (1986) and Samuel Huntington (1981) have called these periods of *public purpose* or *creedal passion*—times of public engagement that bring an extended phase of legislative accomplishment. Three distinct periods in the twentieth century stand out as exemplary moods: the Progressive era early in the century, the New Deal in the 1930s, and the period from Kennedy through Nixon in the 1960s and early 1970s. In short, moods are ascribed causal importance. A public mood emerges, generates a wave of citizen action, and smoothes the way for a prolonged period of legislative motion—a raft of ideologically coherent legislative accomplishments.

Getting a grasp on the concept of a mood is difficult. A mood, Mayhew has observed, "seems to be one of those phenomena that drive political scientists to despair by being at once important and elusive" (Mayhew 1991, 160). Their boundaries are fuzzy, causes unclear, and effects difficult to peg. They are certainly rooted in mass public opinion and affected by electoral returns, but neither is strictly synonymous with the other. John Kingdon, a scholar of public policy, has perhaps said it best:

> The idea goes by different names—the national mood, the climate in the country, changes in public opinion, or broad social movements. But common to all of these labels is the notion that a rather large number of people out in

Sarah A. Binder

the country are thinking along certain common lines, that this national mood changes from one time to another in discernible ways, and that these changes in mood or climate have important impacts on policy agendas and policy outcomes (Kingdon 1984, 153).

Casting mood in ideological terms, others have suggested that it be interpreted as capturing the general direction of American public opinion—"the public's sense of whether the political 'temperature' is too hot or too cold" (Stimson, MacKuen, and Erikson 1995, 548). Intuitively then, moods represent a prevailing consensus of what is appropriate and necessary for the government to do: shared "global attitudes towards the role of government in society" (Stimson, MacKuen, and Erikson 1995, 544).

It makes sense that surges of liberal opinion would lead to higher levels of legislative output. After all, we think of an era as activist because of its ideological tenor and the sheer volume of legislative motion. The question is whether shared public consensus over the role of government also dampens the chances of gridlock. Is general agreement on the aims of government sufficient to overcome other forces that bolster and protect the status quo from change? Much evidence suggests a tight connection between the public mood and legislative performance; the two generally move in tandem across the postwar period.[11]

Explaining the Trends

Party control of government is thus only one factor that shapes the production of public policy. Broader electoral and institutional forces also influence the record of parties in government. For social scientists investigating general patterns over time, however, a key question remains. Taking each of these forces together, how well do the trends noted here hold up? That is, once subjected to multivariate controls, what can we conclude about the relative impact of electoral and institutional determinants of policy gridlock? How we answer this question ultimately shapes our evaluation of the constraints and opportunities faced by the parties in pursuing major changes in public policy.

A model of policy gridlock appears in Table 10-2.[12] The dependent variable is the level of policy gridlock in each Congress (see Figure 10-1). The sta-

11. Although the correlation between gridlock and the public mood (lagged by one Congress) is only –.11, dropping the 102d Congress (which combined a strong liberal mood and record gridlock) boosts the strength of the correlation to –.32. Support for the hypothesis that a liberal mood boosts productivity appears in Coleman (1999), Mayhew (1991), and Taylor (1998).
12. See Binder (1999) for details on measurement and model estimation.

Table 10–2. Determinants of Policy Gridlock, 1951–1996

Hypothesis	Variable	Coefficient (SE)	Change in x (from, to)	Net change in expected probability of gridlock
Partisan/ Electoral	Divided government	.340* (.142)	(0, 1)	+8%
	Percentage of moderates	−.027* (.013)	(18.47, 33.67)	−10%
	Ideological diversity	6.263* (2.710)	(.47, .55)	+11%
	Time out of majority	−.177** (.049)	(0, 2)	−9%
Institutional	Bicameral distance	2.263** (.818)	(.07, .30)	+13%
	Severity of filibuster threat	.035 (.039)	(0, 7.5)	+6%
Policy	Budget situation	−.006 (.009)	(−19.02, −2.09)	−2%
	Public mood (lagged)	−.034* (.016)	(55.76, 65.20)	−8%
	Constant	−1.509 (1.587)		
	N	22		
	F	4.10**		
	Adjusted R²	.5413		
	Durbin-Watson D	1.921		
	Breusch-Godfrey			
	LM test (lag 1)	.0484		
	LM test (lag 2)	1.7842		
	Portmanteau Q	15.3574		

Note: The entries in each cell in column 1 are weighted least squares logit estimates for grouped data (standard errors in parentheses). Time series model diagnostics based on OLS-generated residuals. * $p < .05$, ** $p < .01$ (one-tailed t-tests). Net change in the expected probability of gridlock is calculated as the independent variables' change between the values in column 2 (i.e., between one standard deviation below and above the mean value for each of the continuous variables and between 0 and 1 for the dichotomous variables). Simulated probabilities are based on the exponential linear probabilities generated by the adjust routine in Stata 6.0 and are calculated assuming the presence of divided government (all other variables are set at their mean values).

tistical importance of the independent variables can be evaluated by the values in column 1. On balance, the model estimates provide strong evidence that electoral factors are critical in explaining trends in gridlock, but it provides only mixed support for the institutional and policy accounts. Most prominently,

Sarah A. Binder

the coefficient for divided government is positive and statistically significant: Divided governments are prone to higher levels of gridlock. Party control does appear to affect the broader ability of the political system to address major public problems. In this sense the party government school that advocates responsible parties is vindicated: Gridlock is more likely when the two major parties split control of Congress.

But interbranch conflict is not the sole factor. Both partisan polarization (as measured by the percentage of moderates) and ideological diversity contribute to policy stalemate. The effect of party polarization is perhaps the most striking. Despite the faith of responsible party advocates in cohesive political parties, the results here suggest that policy change is more likely as the parties become less polarized. Clearly there are limits to the power of political parties to break policy deadlock. Indeed it appears that intense polarization can be counterproductive to fostering policy change. Still, the semblance of a party mandate matters: The longer a new congressional majority has been out of power, the lower is the level of policy gridlock under the new majority.

The substantive effects of these factors can be seen by simulating expected levels of gridlock (column 3), given specified changes in the values of the variables (column 2). Using the past half-century as our guide, we can expect divided control of government to increase the level of gridlock by roughly 8 percent. Given on average twenty-five salient issues on the agenda each Congress, the arrival of unified government should resolve on average only two additional issues. Incremental slips in the share of moderate legislators have similar effects, here increasing deadlock by roughly 10 percent or an additional two or three issues. Such results confirm the sentiments of many members and observers of Congress who claim that partisan polarization limits the legislative capacity of Congress (see Cohen 1996; Grove 1996; Serafini 1995). The "incredibly shrinking middle"—as Sen. John Breaux, D-La., called it (Serafini 1995)—seems to hamper substantially the ability of Congress and the president to reach agreement on the issues before them.

Turning to institutional factors, the bicameral context matters greatly. Even after controlling for the effects of elections on partisan alignments, when ideological differences between the House and the Senate increase, Congress finds it tougher to reach agreement on pressing policy issues, and policy stalemate climbs. Bicameral differences have the greatest substantive impact on the level of gridlock: As the distance between the House and the Senate increases fourfold along the left-to-right spectrum, gridlock increases 13 percent. This observation helps explain why students of Congress might have been overly

Can the Parties Govern?

optimistic about the prospects for governance under unified government in the 103d Congress (Sundquist 1995, 10). Only twice before in the postwar period had the House and Senate been as far apart ideologically as they were in the 103d, and the last occurrence was twenty years previously. Given the high level of bicameral differences (as well as partisan polarization), it is no wonder seasoned observers concluded at the close of the 103d Congress: "The only good news as this mud fight finally winds down is that it's hard to imagine much worse" ("Perhaps the Worst Congress" 1994). Whereas others have highlighted the constraining effects of supermajority rules to account for unified gridlock, bicameral constraints clearly help determine the level of stalemate under unified regimes.[13]

Interestingly the level and severity of filibusters show only marginal effects on policy gridlock.[14] Moderate increases in the severity of the filibuster threat boost gridlock only 6 percent. As it turns out, congresses with filibuster-proof majorities within the ranks of the majority party are also those with the largest political center, making it difficult to disentangle the effects of the two. Still, simulating levels of gridlock across more extreme differences in filibustering activity is instructive. Comparing a Senate in the 1950s that witnessed no filibusters (the 84th Congress, 1955–1956) to a recent Senate that has experienced quite a few (twenty-two, in the 104th Congress), the predicted level of gridlock jumps from 42 percent to 53 percent. Although the impact of supermajority rules is challenged by other sources of variation in the legislative arena, it is premature to reject the hypothesis that Senate supermajority institutions have strong policy and political consequence.

Finally, the policy context conditions the ability of legislators to secure policy change. Improved fiscal discipline only marginally affects the incidence of deadlock; a large fall in the size of the deficit reduces gridlock a mere 2 percent. Much stronger effects are felt by the prevailing public mood. Using James Stimson's (1991, 1999) measure of the liberalness of public opinion, public mood clearly matters in shaping legislative performance. A ten-point

13. On the effects of supermajority rules on unified gridlock, see Brady and Volden (1998), Jones (2001), and Krehbiel (1998).

14. Filibuster threat is measured as an interaction between the number of filibusters each Congress and the ideological distance between the median senator and the "filibuster pivot"—the senator whose ideology places him or her at the sixtieth percentile in the Senate (and thus capable of breaking a filibuster by voting to invoke cloture). Before Rule 22 was reformed in 1975, the relevant filibuster pivot was the sixty-seventh senator. For more explanation of the logic of pivots, see Krehbiel (1998). Substituting Coleman's (1999) alternative measure of the filibuster threat (whether or not the majority party has a cloture-safe majority within its ranks) yields similar results.

Sarah A. Binder

jump in public preference for activist government lowers gridlock by 8 percent. In sum the effects of divided government are challenged by alternative sources of variation in American politics.

The Policy Impact of Resurgent Parties

The passage of time provides over fifty years of perspective on the arguments of Schattschneider and the responsible party school of thought in American politics. As Coleman (1999) has argued, Schattschneider and his colleagues understood well the limitations of party government under the American political system. They recognized that ideological divisions—particularly within the Democratic Party—and institutional and constitutional constraints made it particularly difficult for parties in government to effectively pursue party agendas once in control of government. For Schattschneider, this was worrisome, because political parties were seen as essential instruments for responding to the will of electoral majorities. Weak political parties could be neither doctrinal nor disciplined and thus could not be held responsible by voters at election time.

The contemporary period offers a compelling environment for reconsidering these arguments from over a half-century ago. As scholars and observers of national politics have almost uniformly noted in recent years, the legislative parties in Washington are on the rebound, resurgent after a period of particular weakness in the 1960s and 1970s (Cooper and Young 1997; Rohde 1991; Sinclair 1995). Old divisions within the Democratic Party have largely eroded, and southern Democrats are now looking increasingly like their northern counterparts in terms of their ideology, constituencies, and voting records. Likewise, the Republican Party has lost most of its distinctive northeastern moderate wing, leaving the party far more conservative and southern focused than it has ever been. The question is whether the increased coherence and cohesion of the two major parties has had consequences for the production of public policy.

From Schattschneider's perspective, more disciplined and doctrinal parties should improve lawmakers' capacity to respond to electoral majorities. But as the two parties have polarized and the political center has stretched thin over the recent past, little evidence indicates that legislative performance has improved in lockstep. If anything, the reverse rings more true: The presence of a moderate middle helps pave the way for policy compromise and change. Far from ensuring that voters will be given a meaningful set of choices between competing party programs, the polarization of the parties seems to encourage deadlock and delay. Major change in public policy typically requires bipartisan support, and the current electoral environment makes such cooperation particularly difficult to secure.

These findings suggest the ultimate limits of political parties as policymakers in the American political system. The resurgence of parties at the elite level is unlikely to alter the parties' abilities to shape major change in public law. Despite the recent transformation of the political parties into service organizations for politicians and their emergence as cohesive legislative coalitions, parties still face significant constraints in attempting to alter the policy status quo. Of course, Schattschneider also argued that stronger presidential leadership, bicameral collaboration, and increased mass partisanship was essential for building responsible parties. Absent these additional boosts to the party system, resurgent legislative parties are unlikely to lead to greater government responsiveness to the public's agenda—particularly in an era of divided government. Party polarization on its own seems counterproductive to the goal of building majorities for policy change.

Still, even if the political parties did revitalize beyond the legislative arena, significant institutional and constitutional barriers to party government would remain in place. It may be that Schattschneider and the party government school were right: Parties might be indispensable to organizing and maintaining majorities in a democracy. But inherited institutions will still always limit the possibilities for parties in the American context, particularly as they try to shape and respond to public demand for policy change.

Sarah A. Binder

11

Political Parties and the Future State of the Union

Theodore J. Lowi

Who controls the past controls the future; who controls the present controls the past. —George Orwell, *1984*

The epigraph to my chapter, from Orwell's *1984,* will be a source of optimism, not despair. It is my punchline. Starting with the punchline is a bad way to tell a joke, and some will think my message is a bad joke. But I hope Orwell will hover over us and become meaningful as I tell my story, which I offer as a modest amendment to the established story of American democracy.

Prediction is possible in political science; not only prediction of Democratic votes over Republican votes in a simple electoral outcome but also more complex outcomes. Prediction is possible in any area of politics that has been institutionalized, because the purpose of any institution is to fix the present in order to determine the future. And here is where opportunity presents itself: If we can understand an institution well enough, we have a chance of changing its future. That is what I thought political science was all about: a commitment to the use of critical inquiry in order to perfect democratic institutions through reform.

Lincoln Steffens, the great American social critic, writing home from Russia in 1919, exclaimed, "I have seen the future, and it works." We know now that communism had no future because it never succeeded in institutionalizing itself. Democracy in America, in contrast, is institutionalized, and I can see enough of its present to be convinced that the future is not going to work.

I take inspiration from Martin Luther, as he posted his ninety-five theses as topics of debate in Wittenberg in 1517. I do not have ninety-five theses, but, like Luther, I seek a reformation that is more like a revolution, because reform from within, having failed repeatedly, requires a complete break from our church: the two-party system. Only that way can we reform our democracy.

Luther's main attack was on the sale of indulgences, a well-established, institutionalized practice on which the church depended for a great deal of its revenue. But because it was also fully rationalized as church doctrine, Luther had to confront many of the basic doctrinal assumptions. Luther, the most humble of soldiers in the army of the Catholic Church, was promptly excommunicated. Instead of bringing a few abuses to the attention of his Reverend Father, he brought down upon himself the entire first string of high priests. Two years after he had posted his theses, Luther wrote:

> I hoped the Pope would protect me, for I had so fortified my theses with proofs from the Bible and papal decretals that I was sure he would condemn Tetzel [the archbishop's agent] and bless me. But when I expected a benediction from Rome, there came thunder and lightning instead, and I was treated like a sheep who had roiled the wolf's water. Tetzel went scot-free, and I must submit to be devoured (Luther 1947 [1559], 104).

This is the situation as I see it today in political science, whose high priests and lowly priests scan the literature for doubters who need to be subjected to the preachings of the virtues of our magnificent two-party system and the glories of its services to our civic religion, American democracy. For my sin of opening the black box of multipartism, I have been excommunicated, if by that we mean no longer listened to. Having nothing to lose, I am now changing my tactic. I no longer praise multipartism; I now condemn bipartism.

The Two-Party System: The Charges

I begin with two founding fathers of the two-party religion, Maurice Duverger and V. O. Key. Both embrace the theory that the single-member district electoral method could explain the two-party system, but neither embraced it with enough confidence to let the matter rest there. Duverger was the more forceful of the two, and his statement on the relationship was later elevated to a law, "Duverger's Law."[1] But Duverger went beyond science to assert, without his usual thorough documentation, that "the two-party system seems to correspond to the *nature of things,* that is to say that political choice usually takes the form of a choice between two alternatives" (Duverger 1954, 215, emphasis added). Key echoes all of this, beginning with the concession that "the single-member district theory has not been adequately tested against the evidence" (Key 1964, 209). Key's search for "other influences" led him directly to "patterns of political faith"; he went on to emphasize and define political faith with the assertion

1. Duverger's observation of an empirical pattern was elevated into a "law" by Riker (1982).

that "a pattern of attitudes exists that favors, or at least permits, a political dualism" (Key 1964, 210).

More recently, David Gillespie goes further, reflecting the overwhelming consensus of the American Political Science Association (APSA), with the observation that a "cultural duality [was] probably inherited from the British" (Gillespie 1993, 29). Gillespie contrasts that natural duality with the more scattered political faiths of the French—in the face of France's deep and abiding duality of at least two centuries between church and laity, or clerical versus anticlerical.

Finally, for a genuine mainstream consensus version of a contemporary whose work in this area I generally admire, I draw from a recent essay by Gerald Pomper. Pomper embraces Duverger's Law more unconditionally than Key, but he too seems to recognize it is not enough to clinch the argument. He moves on to chant the two-party catechism and then goes to a well-known quote of Clinton Rossiter: "No America without democracy, no democracy without politics, no politics without parties . . ." (Pomper 1998, vii). But that won't clinch the case because there's no two-party in the quote. He goes then to John Aldrich, whom Pomper commends as "the keenest contemporary scholar of parties" with what Pomper says is a "return" to Rossiter's assertion of forty years earlier. But is it a return? "In America, democracy is unthinkable save in terms of a *two-party system,* because no collection of ambitious politicians has long been able to think of a way to achieve their goals in this democracy save in terms of political parties" (Pomper 1998, vii, citing Aldrich 1995, 296). Note how the two-party system was panhandled into Rossiter's otherwise benign proposition.

The transposition of the Rossiter quote is an example of the insidious influence of political religion. Another example is the foolish, absolutely wrongheaded mainstream belief that the single-member district system holds a constitutional status in the United States. As Steven Rosenstone and associates put it, the single-member district is one of the "constitutional biases" that "discourages the emergence, growth and survival of third parties" (Rosenstone, Behr, and Lazarus 1984, 16).

There is, and should be, a democratic creed. But we cannot allow its particularities to go unquestioned and to be elevated, by repetition, to items for memorization in a catechism. That is ideology at its worst, and it is most unbecoming for a profession built on the ethic of critical inquiry. What will be the future of the APSA if it becomes the Vatican with an office to propagate the faith in the two-party system?

The following is my indictment; it is a bill of particulars, an inventory of items that are known to and accepted by or shrugged off by virtually every educated citizen in America but are devastating when taken together as a "long brief" against the two-party system:

- The 2000 national election cycle will cost $3 billion.
- An increasing proportion of campaign finance is coming from outside congressional and state legislative districts, producing what can only be called indirect representation. Corrupt? Not necessarily. But it creates a dilemma of accountability—democratic accountability to the constituency or fiduciary accountability to donors many miles away.
- Increasing socioeconomic heterogeneity of congressional and state assembly districts destroys virtually all possibility of any kind of representation based on geographic districting. We can no longer maintain our fealty to the principle of geographic representation as espoused by James Madison: "Divide the largest state into ten or twelve districts and it will be found that there will be no peculiar local interests in either which will not be within the knowledge of the representation of the district" (Rossiter 1961, 346–350).
- Even for the few homogenous districts that remain, the value of the votes of any minority—including a minority second party—is reduced toward zero. This is the best answer to those who denounce third parties because a vote for one of them is wasted. The vote may not count, but the voice may— which is more than can be said for the minorities in single-member districts.
- Benign, race-conscious gerrymandered "majority-minority districts" were created as a device to preserve the legitimacy of the two-party system by mandating improved sociological representation. By 1998 the number of minorities in Congress had doubled to fifty-two but without any significant sign of improved substantive or agency representation. Most of the substantive gains went to white conservatives.
- Meanwhile, such benign gerrymandering undermines democratic legitimacy by making "the state" the final arbiter of electoral outcomes and the government the final judge in the circulation of its own leadership. Has this no relevance to the First Amendment?
- The party system marginalizes historically disadvantaged minority groups: As Paul Frymer puts it, "Unlike those in other democratic societies, our party system exacerbates rather than diminishes the marginalized position of a historically disadvantaged minority group. . . . We are . . . one of the few democratic nations where party leaders have an incentive to appeal almost exclusively to the majority group" (Frymer 1999, 7).

Theodore J. Lowi

- Increasing voter apathy and antipathy along with declining voter turnout are surely associated with declining two-party competition. Modest expansions in registration in recent years are attributable not to two-party competition but to efforts outside the party system—such as the Rainbow Coalition—and an anti-two-party movement to adopt the so-called Motor Voter Act in Congress.
- The plebiscitary presidency coupled with "the permanent campaign" is the replacement of the two-party system for purposes of mass support. The presidency has become its own political party, especially in this long era of so-called divided government.
- Divided government is in fact the two-party system converted into a classic duopoly. Divided government for 90 percent of the time since 1980 amounts to a guarantee of market share and therefore a disincentive for electoral competition. Power incrementalism, or "politics by other means," to quote the title of Benjamin Ginsberg and Martin Shefter's 1999 book, is the best statement of the general relationship between the two parties: Competition is okay as long as it is not electoral, which equals Henry Ford's contention that "you can have your Ford in any color, as long as it's black." Major players use exposure by allegations of petty corruption to alter power relations, one individual at a time, without ever trying to win the whole enchilada by bold electioneering.
- The duopoly produces policy incrementalism. Virtually all policy decisions, including nonincremental decisions, are subsumed and masked within the budget and reconciliation process.

The Trial

As the itemized indictment ends, you may be asking, Is the two-party system to blame for all this? I believe as ardently as Martin Luther that the answer is yes. Before I am excommunicated again, however, let's play a mind game for a few minutes.

Suppose that the legal life supports of the two-party system were removed by Supreme Court decisions declaring unconstitutional the key state laws fostering the system. Signs are not good at the moment, but I will demonstrate that this is not beyond the realm of imagination. The most recent case seems at first glance to point the other way. In *California Democratic Party v. Bill Jones, Secretary of State of California,* 120 S.Ct. 2402 (June 26, 2000), Justice Antonin Scalia for a 7-to-2 majority argued that a state law changing California's closed primary system to a blanket primary "violated the First Amendment right of association." He went on to say that the First Amendment protects the freedom to join together to form an association "which presupposes the freedom to identify those who constitute the association and to limit the association to those people." He denied that this violates the spirit of *Smith v. Allright,* 321 U.S. 649 (1944), which held that parties are not private associations when they engage in discriminatory action in violation of the Fifteenth Amendment, but that somehow party exclusion of participation in primaries is protected by the First Amendment. Note that *the majority was willing to intervene against state laws of questionable constitutionality,* even though the holding brings into question three other states with blanket primaries, twenty-one states with open primaries, and eight states with semiclosed primaries. Thus, even though the particular outcome in the blanket primary case seems to reinforce the legal protection of the two established parties, it opens the door for a constitutional attack of much greater threat to two-party system legal protections and at the same time offers great promise for new parties because the opinion indicated that the Court will intervene against states if other cases demonstrate that states have gone too far in those protections. *Timmons v. Twin Cities Area New Party,* 520 U.S. 351 (1997), was a much bigger blow in favor of the two-party system and against new parties because the Court in that case seemed to indicate that it would not intervene against state laws involving political parties, even when, as in *Timmons*, state law prevented the New Party from nominating a candidate already on the Democratic Party's ballot, even though the candidate and the Democratic Party officials were agreeable to the joint nomination. But less than three years later in the blanket primary case, the Court seemed ready to look at the constitutionality of state party laws again and with more critical scrutiny. There is no question that if all of the state laws patently biased in favor of the two-party system and patently biased against new parties were tested, they would not hold up against close constitutional scrutiny.

Merely 10 percent of what Ross Perot spent on his 1992 presidential campaign ($6 million of the $60 million) would be enough to litigate all of those state laws, and in the process American political scientists would have to be drawn in as expert witnesses in their defense. Political scientists would be obliged to testify in defense of all of those laws, including laws ordaining the single-member district system. In fact almost the entire literature of political science is implicated because it argues precisely that the two-party system was maintained (if not literally created) by deliberate discouragement of the formation or persistence of additional parties through devices such as the single-

Theodore J. Lowi

member district. Under oath, political scientists as expert witnesses would also have to give their opinion as to the cost of negating the value of votes for a third party. Many would continue to argue that the cost to third parties is more than compensated for by the benefits provided to our great democracy by our sacred two-party system. But it is quite doubtful that the expert opinions would be unanimous—which would leave some doubt in the minds of some of the justices. That leaves open to doubt the argument that the First Amendment is overridden by a "compelling interest" that each state has to suppress new parties by suppressing the votes for them.

As a collateral matter, these same political scientist witnesses would be forced on cross examination under oath to admit that these state laws also discourage *second* parties as well as third parties, and this is precisely what happened for most of the time between the 1890s and the 1960s, when America had a series of one-party states that gave the appearance of a two-party system only when seen from the national perspective of the U.S. Congress.

Most of the judges on the federal bench, including the justices of the Supreme Court, are virtually certain to perceive some constitutional imperfections in this story of the two-party system and in the doctrine supporting it. As a consequence, this is quite likely to make them less reluctant to consider whether the price paid for legal suppression of new parties and legal suppression of alternatives for voters may be too high. Further, a Court that can on First and Fourteenth Amendment grounds invalidate discriminatory at-large and single-member district laws and on similar grounds invalidate laws restricting political campaign expenditures will surely see that laws discouraging turnout, diluting the value of votes, and severely restricting ballot access deprive millions of citizens of their "freedom of speech . . . or the right of people peaceably to assemble, and to petition the Government for redress of grievances." To convey an impression of how much political favoritism there is in the law, consider the fact that there are more state laws regulating and protecting the institution of political parties than there are state laws dealing with the institution of marriage.[2]

If the Court really embraced the First Amendment and subjected all of the two-party protective laws to strict scrutiny, the single-member district requirement would be one of the first laws to go. And for an extended period of time, elections for legislative representatives would have to be held at-large. In other words, all candidates for state assembly, state senate, and Congress would be

2. This was a hypothesis that I have confirmed tentatively by inspection of the respective laws of Alabama and New York.

elected from the same statewide constituency, and each voter would have the number of votes equal to the number of seats to be filled.

Then comes the test of mainstream political science and its catechism: If the two-party system is part of the nature of things, and if it is a logical consequence of the rational, Anglo-Saxon mentality of dualistic thinking, and if it performs so many functions vital to our democracy, then most cities, counties, and states would continue to have two-party systems. Fine. Then we would have an ideal world—an honest, two-party system resting on real rather than terribly artificial foundations. This would also free political scientists from having to defend an artificial two-party system with distorted political realism, phony functionalism, and strained scientific objectivity. If, however, our present party system is, as I have been arguing for over twenty years, a mere artifact of the bipartisan abuse of the rule of law, then we are likely to get a new party system the minute those biased state and federal laws are wiped out.

The Verdict: Some Possibilities

It is not my intention here to project precisely what that new party system would look like, but here are a few guesses. First, my imagination tells me that the Democratic and Republican Parties would remain the two most important parties. But three- and four-party systems would fairly quickly develop in a number of cities and states as soon as the legal trash was swept away. The direct effect on national politics would come rather slowly, but it would come honestly, through increased voter turnout, expansion of electoral competition, intensification of the policy content of campaigns, and drastic changes for the better in campaign timing and campaign finance. Sociological and agency representation would improve almost immediately. There is of course no guarantee that the presence of non-Democrats and non-Republicans would improve the policy-making process in Congress, but I can confidently predict that the process wouldn't get any worse. How could it?

Let me add that we have had some fairly recent experience with three-party government in Congress. For at least three decades, the Southern Democrats were so distinctive and well organized a force in Congress that *Congressional Quarterly* consistently reported all of its roll call votes with separate tallies for Republican, Democrat, and Southern Democrat. That is fairly good recognition of institutionalization, until a realignment of the Democratic Party severed so much of the South that a distinctive Southern Democratic presence was no longer there to be tallied.

Theodore J. Lowi

An important aspect of at-large election needs to be cleared up here because of some bad experiences with it soon after the Voting Rights Act of 1965 was adopted. In the first big test of the Voting Rights Act, the Supreme Court confronted a Mississippi law that converted a district method of electing county supervisors to an at-large method. The Court invalidated the law as racially discriminatory on the grounds that "the right to vote can be affected by a dilution of voting power as well as by an absolute prohibition. . . . Voters who are members of a racial minority might well be in the majority in one district, but in the decided minority in the county as a whole. This type of change could therefore nullify their ability to elect the candidate of their choice just as would prohibiting some of them from voting." This was the first case to use a minority dilution standard rather than a vote prohibition or vote suppression standard, and it was hailed for recognizing that an electoral system or a voting procedure can be discriminatory (*Allen v. State Board of Elections,* 393 U.S. 544 [1969]; see also Grofman and Davidson 1992, 28–29). But cases like this are patently racially discriminatory and in no way suggest that there is anything inherently discriminatory about at-large elections. Civil rights lawyers have fought conversions of at-large elections in instances in which the intent and almost certain effect were race conscious, involving deliberate efforts at vote dilution; the situation in Allen was a move to the at-large district precisely in order to expand the boundaries of the principality in order to include all-white suburbs knowing that they would genuinely dilute the minority vote, which was contained in a ghetto-like neighborhood at the center of that newly constituted multimember district. No multimember district will dilute the weight of the votes of any minority unless the larger district encompassing the smaller districts is designed to dilute the vote. But if the new, multimember district is the entire state, those boundaries cannot be manipulated. Moreover, if any minority constituted a 15-percent or a 20-percent voting presence in the multimember district, then, by almost any reasonable voting procedure, they would weigh the same amount in the election and therefore in the proportion of legislative representation, instead of weighing zero percent in a winner-take-all district. Or at best, they would constitute a guaranteed majority in a race-consciously designed majority-minority district and zero in all the other districts.

Now we can resume our pursuit of the future. With the end of the single-member district system, everything would take place in an entirely new context or framework. With at-large elections, all members of Congress would have a shared statewide, multimember constituency. Candidates for Congress, including the incumbents, would be thrown together and would face a common problem: Begin with a state large enough to warrant, say, ten congressional seats.

Every voter gets ten votes, and with no law forbidding it, all voters could spend their ten votes as they wished—with all ten going to a single candidate or with the ten votes spread across three or four preferred candidates, or with ten votes spent on ten separate candidates. There are several other ways the law can provide for voting in multimember districts. The one outlined in the scenario here is called "cumulative voting," in which the voters are permitted to concentrate or distribute their multiple vote power. This has the virtue of simplicity, and it is just as effective as more complex voting schemes whenever "a majority is permanent and racially fixed . . . [and when] there are deep racial cleavages . . ." (Guinier 1992, 290 and footnote 13).

What of the nominating process? How would the slates of candidates be constituted? Most states would hurriedly provide for a statewide nominating process in which the first ten Democrats and the first ten Republicans would make the two major slates, but they would certainly be accompanied by other groupings of parties that can meet a minimum standard to appear as a slate on the ballot. The point is that under the conditions then prevailing, the requirements for petitions to get on the slate would have to be equal for all of the contestants rather than having one set of rules for the two major parties and another set for the others. There would be equality of ballot access, literally for the first time in over a hundred years.

What's coming clear from this exploration into the future is that a wide-open, at-large system of elections would most probably produce spontaneously a form of *list voting* for nominations and for elections. Where nominations are concerned, it would work roughly as follows: Assuming parties exist, all those party members seeking the same office would go on that party's list. If more than ten candidates sought the nominations for the ten seats, they or their party leadership would have to determine whether the candidates would be listed according to the support they enjoy, in order of seniority of service, alphabetically, or randomly. In any event, "The list vote . . . obliges the caucuses or local branches of the party to establish amongst themselves a strong system of articulation within the constituency, so that they can agree upon the composition of the lists. . . . [T]he list vote tends towards a system of articulation which goes beyond the local level: it diminishes the influence of men and increases that of ideas, it makes general programmes override parish-pump considerations, and therefore acts in the direction of the national organization of the party" (Duverger 1954, 44–45). European experience reinforced by logic would indicate that list voting in any form would also almost certainly strengthen the internal organizational strength of the two major parties, what-

Theodore J. Lowi

ever it did to encourage new parties. Some states would remain with a two-party system, whereas others would become three- or perhaps four-party systems. But whatever came of the at-large, multimember system of voting, the results would be ethically more honest and functionally superior to the present system of state-sponsored and state-protected two-party systems. We would get a form of genuine proportional representation without an elaborate and complicated statute providing for a formal proportional representation system. And we would get far more diversity in the representation of concentrated minorities without the kinds of legal manipulation in benign gerrymandering that renders almost everybody uncomfortable. One estimate that I find credible and damning is that "a rough rule of thumb holds that the political party that controls both the governor's office and the legislature in a state can redraw district lines so that one of every five districts tilts in its favor" (Ayres 1999, 28). It hurt democratic legitimacy when these unfair redrawings of district lines were strictly between one party and another. It is even more hurtful of democracy when the same gerrymandering power extends to race-conscious manipulation of electoral outcomes. And we don't need that. A proper multimember district would obviate all of that. How long can we continue to hide behind "political realism?"

Let me conclude with a few somewhat more far-reaching predictions. First, every member of Congress would have a broader vision, given the statewide constituency. Second, there would be more honorable, substantive representation, because the average member can know more about the state as a unit than about the district as a unit. Third, with or without party-prepared list voting, the candidates from the same political party (even if there are more than ten candidates on a party's list and only ten can be elected) would be thrown together with a powerful incentive to campaign together. The state party would take on far more meaning as an organization, as an institution, with a policy orientation and a commitment to winning elections. Moreover, the ten elected members would have additional incentive to work as a state delegation—an elected caucus from their state—even if the delegation were composed of members from two, three, or even four different party affiliations.

Finally, at-large representation would literally solve the problem of campaign finance. No new legislation would be needed, and most of the existing legislation could be dispensed with. What we have now is a system too closely akin to a formulation attributed to Norton Long: "An economy of perverse incentives." Under present conditions, all members of Congress and their opposition candidates are forced to rely largely on their own efforts to raise at least the threshold level of financing—enough to warrant sufficient financing from relevant political action committees (PACs), party soft money (unregulated money that is not to be used directly for federal campaigns but can be spent "on the issues"), and money from senior congressional barons, who share in a strategic way the millions of surplus dollars they collect personally and through their own PACs. In contrast, at-large elections, especially when reinforced by list voting, take away the prisoners' dilemma, or should I say the candidates' dilemma. As long as the perverse incentives exist, no law is going to stop the money deluge and the derangement of constituency accountability. Elimination of the single-member district system would put an end to the plutocracy without destroying the parties. Soft money—given to the state party to support the entire party list—can become good money.

Reflection

This imaginary future is not so difficult to consider if we put it in the context of deregulation—because that is a national objective currently embraced by both of the major parties and by a large and growing segment of the political science community. The current effort to save the single-member district system with benign gerrymandering is unwise and counterproductive, contributing to the decline of legitimacy of American politics in general. But how can the critics of those efforts speak so derisively of regulatory excess when they are disregarding more than a hundred years of regulatory excess that created the party system and the representational system they are defending? *Deregulate American politics, and give democracy a chance.* If you stop and think about it, you will have to admit that the democracy American political science has espoused for most of its century of existence is a paternalistic democracy, a state-sponsored democracy. If we are the developed country we claim to be, isn't it time we had a spontaneous rather than a sponsored democracy?

All this could happen, and political science could help make it happen, if we reexamined our story of American democracy and seriously asked if we have been telling it the right way. If we admit that we have made the two-party part of the story a bit too heroic, that admission alone could change the past so much that it would almost inevitably alter the future: We would be removing much of the basis of the Supreme Court's reluctance to apply the strictest scrutiny of the First Amendment to the regulation of democracy. We have the power to change the past, and at least in the business of democracy that gives us a great deal of power over the future. And we can begin this endeavor with encouragement from Mark Twain, who said "Things ain't what they used to be, and pro'bly never were."

Theodore J. Lowi

Conclusion

12

Decline and Resurgence in the American Party System

Jeffrey E. Cohen and Paul Kantor

The chapters of this volume document how political parties have undergone remarkable changes during recent decades. From varied perspectives, our contributors point to powerful crosscurrents of decline and resurgence in the American party system. Beginning in the late 1960s, investigators began to detect evidence of party decline. Party identification in the mass public eroded and voter turnout plummeted. The influence of party leaders, which had been waning since the early 1900s, dwindled even more. By the late 1970s the primary system had completely replaced state party leaders in the nomination of presidential candidates at the national conventions. Complex rules and representation standards eliminated the influence that state party leaders once had over the allocation of seats to delegates at the national conventions. Reforms of the campaign finance system lessened the ties of candidates to their parties, transforming campaigning into candidate-centered contests. Divided government at the national level became the norm, limiting the ability of one party or the other to direct policy making and govern the nation.

Yet there were also signs of party revitalization by the middle to late 1970s. Money poured into national party offices. These national party headquarters became important party-building centers, aiding candidates in the technologies, regulations, and strategies of campaigning. The parties, too, became highly distinct on many issues, where once there was considerable overlap in party positions. Seemingly, the parties now offered voters clear choices in governing philosophy and public policy. Also many voters seemed to be returning to the parties, as levels of party identification began to rise, although not back to levels recorded in the 1950s. And among these late-century partisans, voting loyalty was particularly high. But still, large numbers of voters found third-party candidates attractive, such as Ross Perot, who garnered nearly 19 percent of the vote in 1992. Furthermore, it was common for the major party candidates at all levels of government to run against their parties and "politics as usual." The support for third-party candidates and the antiestablishment campaign behavior of candidates in general are signs of the continued fissure in the party and political systems.

In effect, the parties display signs of decay as well as regeneration at the dawn of the millennium. In some respects they seem to be more resourceful and coherent organizations than they were in the 1970s. At the same time, the public has become disengaged and disaffected from parties, campaigns have become more candidate centered, third-party challenges attract large numbers of voters, and government seems perpetually divided at the national level. What does this mean for a healthy and well-functioning democracy? Most theorists believe that parties are indispensable to democracy (Key 1949; Schattschneider 1942, 1960). With so many observers decrying the current state of American democracy—with its low turnout and an apathetic citizenry cynical toward government and political institutions—one wonders what role the parties play in this matter. Is the ambiguous status of the parties, with elements of both degeneration and regeneration, a symptom of this more general political atmosphere, or is it a cause?

In this chapter we examine why this complex state of decline and resurgence of the political parties arose and consider its significance for the performance of American democracy. We begin by discussing several roles that parties play in a democracy, focusing on how parties help organize politics and how they help link government and citizenry. Then we look at the sources of the trend toward party decline and renewal. Finally, we assess the implications of these changes for our democracy.

Parties in Democratic Theory

Most democratic theories maintain that free and competitive parties are indispensable for a well-functioning democracy. Parties provide a number of important functions that few, if any other, societal institutions provide. Let us focus on two of these functions. First, parties help organize politicians, politics, and government. Second, they help link government and citizenry, stimulate public participation, and provide a vehicle of democratic control and accountability.

Jeffrey E. Cohen and Paul Kantor

Parties and the Organization of Politicians, Politics, and Government

Political parties are the primary society-wide institutions, beside government itself, that help organize the political world. Parties organize politics in at least three senses. First, they organize political elites into identifiable, competitive groups. By attaching a party label to a leader's name, one learns with whom that leader is most likely to work and how amenable that leader is likely to be toward certain groups, causes, and issues. Parties also channel the ambitions of leaders away from their purely personal desires and toward a collective enterprise, the party, with its history, mission, association with issues, and shared fates among its members. In effect, parties as organizations take on a life of their own, part of, but also apart from, the politicians that fill their ranks. This organization of political elites helps steer the political system away from excessive personalization of leadership and the tendency of personal-based leadership to become demagogic. Parties also organize politicians by helping to recruit candidates, and later, when those candidates have assumed offices, parties serve as a pool from which many appointees to office are selected. Thus, not only do parties organize political elites into competitive "teams," but they also organize the members of each team. Perhaps most important, by organizing political leaders under party labels, parties provide a political identity that transcends any individual.

Second, parties organize the issues and political debates of the day. They do this by staking out and developing positions on important issues. The motivations for issue positioning are many. Some derive from ideology or philosophy, as parties look for issues to which they can apply their philosophies. In the 1980s, for example, the Republican Party cast a wide net in applying its conservative, smaller government, promarket vision for the nation, from classic economic issues such as taxation and regulation to social issues such as school reform and prison management. But parties also stake out positions as part of their competitive electoral strategy, seeking issues and positions that are popular with voters. Sometimes this may mean parroting issue positions that the other party has also assumed (Downs 1957), especially when the position is popular among voters. The current support of both parties for the high-tech industry is a good case in point (Alvarez 1999). But parties may also seek positions from which they can criticize the opposition for faulty or failed policies, again in the hope of attracting voters. Parties may even take positions in the absence of any recognition by the opposition, in the hope that the position will resonate with the voters. Yet the forces impelling issue positioning travel even wider, being a response to the demands of internal constituencies, as well as the broader mass public. In this latter sense we can think of parties as representative and responsive institutions.

Issue positioning by parties is important because it creates a public dialogue between the parties, exposing differences and similarities between them while creating a dialogue between the parties and the mass public. Furthermore, by going public in such a way, the parties establish a political context for an issue and frame the terms of debate on that issue, whether it will be a partisan issue or even whether it will be a public issue. The reputation and "brand name" of parties are established in part by taking positions on issues, a process that may or may not entail debate and discourse within parties. In the end, position-taking links issues to parties, gives political meaning to both parties and issues, and involves the public, as the parties attempt to mobilize support behind the party and its issues. Thus party identity is strongly wrapped up in the process of issue positioning; it enables the mass public to make sense of their political world.

Third, parties help organize government. The issues on which parties take positions serve as a guide or blueprint for what the party will do if granted the power to run government, while the partisan organization of politicians determines who will carry out these policies. Organizing government in our Madisonian system of separation of powers, checks and balances, and federalism becomes quite daunting, because the prospects are high that more than one party will occupy critical positions in the government.

Inasmuch as party and policy overlap and there exists a gulf between the policies of the two parties, divided government can impede either party from governing effectively (Binder 1999; Coleman 1999). When divided government exists, but the two parties are not highly distinct in terms of policies, opportunities for cooperation across the two parties improve, as does the likelihood that government will be able to produce policies. But in the current era, where the two parties stand distinct and distant in policy, and where they control different branches of government, the prospects for the production of policy decline. Thus the way that parties organize issues and politicians interacts with the structure of our political system and has major implications for the ability of either party to govern the nation. As we discuss in the next section, divided government also has implications for democratic control and accountability.

Parties, Participation, and Democratic Control
and Accountability

Parties are also important linkage mechanisms between the mass public and the government, enabling the public to hold government accountable. The linkage from public to government via the parties is complex and operates on several levels. First, the parties link people to government by helping them become informed citizens. Parties do this by the way they organize politics. Voters can identify teams of competitive politicians and their issue positions. From this knowledge base, voters can decide whom they like and dislike and with whom they agree and disagree. In this sense, voters participate in government at a most elemental level, by forming opinions and judgments about political objects, issues, and personalities. The great benefit of parties to democracy in this regard is that the partisan organization of the political world helps reduce the costs of learning about politics and, thus, increases the number of people who are likely to participate in the world of public affairs.

Second, parties help to link people to government and political processes by forging political loyalties among people, what we call party identification. Without such political loyalties, the average person would not care much about who ruled or to what end. With such loyalties the average person's concern about who wins and what government does rises. At the most basic level, a person who identifies with one or the other party (like a fan of a sports team) can be made to feel like a winner or a loser depending on the election (or game) outcome. Moreover, not only will a sense of partisan identification establish a psychological link between citizen and party, but a person may begin to identify certain leaders and policies as being beneficial or harmful. That is, self-interested notions may attach to these psychological identifications and in some cases even serve as the roots from which the psychological identification grows. Party identification is likely to persist even after popular leaders have come and gone from the political stage, providing a sense of continuity or history for the average person. Over time such continuity or party history helps reduce the costs of political learning and maintains political participation. In these ways, parties help people feel they are part of the political process, an important linkage between the citizenry and government in democracies.

But parties as linkage bodies have more than just attitudinal and psychological impacts. They have behavioral ones as well. People armed with this attitudinal and psychological base are more likely to participate in politics, across a wide array of forms, from expressing opinions, to supporting candidates and causes, to contributing money, to voting. Parties help establish and maintain a participatory society, one of the defining aspects of democracy.

Parties may also actively mobilize the population to political participation. Participation grows not only out of the personal, psychological, and self-interest motivations of the average person; parties as organizations also pull people into the political process.

Competitive parties have incentives to seek the support of all people who have the vote. At times this has meant that at least one of the parties has sought to expand the franchise to those excluded from it in the search for more voter support. As historical practice, this has often meant that the poor, racial minorities, and others have been brought into the franchise.

Even when all adult populations are eligible to vote, parties may actively pull people to the polls, increasing turnout and voter participation, to secure more votes for their candidates for office. Parties may stimulate turnout by rewarding some voters with patronage, by providing transportation to the polls and instruction on filling out ballots, by imposing social pressures to participate, and through other devices. These mobilizing efforts often increase the likelihood that those who have been the least likely to vote in the past will vote. Thus, in at least these three senses, parties help the fabrication of a participatory society, linking citizens and their government.

Parties also help connect government to citizenry by providing a method of implementing democratic control and accountability. This democratic function derives from the need of the party for votes, which makes parties to some degree responsive to the citizenry. To attain the reins of government, parties require the votes of the electorate. Because the electorate can turn incumbents out of office come the next election, those in office have a strong incentive to provide services to those who voted for them and to new voters whom they are trying to attract. These services might include access to jobs, as was the case for the patronage-based parties of the late nineteenth and early twentieth centuries. Services may also include public policies that materially benefit electoral supporters; other services may be more symbolic, speaking to less materialistic needs in the electorate. This may be no more, for example, than making a group feel politically included, that it is meaningful. In any event, if the electorate deems the job of those in government to be inferior to what could be had by replacing them, a means of democratic control and accountability is constructed.

Inasmuch as those in government are not a permanent elite, but must seek reelection with every new election cycle, the voting public possesses an enor-

Jeffrey E. Cohen and Paul Kantor

mous power to determine who rules. Insofar as parties are critical to the electoral success of candidates for office and provide a means of coordinating those in office, parties become vehicles for the expression of the electorate's demands of government and for ensuring those demands become public policy. In other words, parties help the public hold government accountable for its actions and policies, motivating those in government to produce policies that the public prefers.

Assessing the Place of Parties in the Current Political System

In theory, parties provide several important functions to democracy, including helping to organize the political world, promoting citizen participation and democratic activity, and providing a means to ensure that government is democratically accountable. But how well have the parties of the last quarter of the twentieth century been performing these functions?

The Current Parties and the Organization of the Political World

With regard to the organization of politicians and issues, in one sense the current parties are doing a better job than a generation ago, but in another sense they are doing a worse job. By associating leaders with well-defined and distinguishable labels, the Democratic and Republicans Parties are better at organizing politicians than was previously the case. Whereas the parties once were home to a divergence of political opinions and views, which often erupted into intense intraparty bickering, now the two parties are more homogeneous in their internal composition. William Crotty's contribution to this book, on delegates to the national party conventions (Chapter 6), demonstrates the ideological and policy differences of these activists of the two parties. Similarly, Gerald M. Pomper's contribution (Chapter 8) also finds distinct policy differences between the two parties, a point echoed in Roger H. Davidson's chapter on the parties in Congress (Chapter 9). Jon R. Bond and Richard Fleisher suggest in Chapter 3 that the same policy distancing has also been occurring at the mass public level.

Thus, at all levels, from the mass base to the election activist to the incumbents in office, we see important differences in the policy and ideological positions of the members of the two competing parties. Further, within each party the membership at each level holds fairly similar policy beliefs. In this sense the parties are not only coherent in political beliefs, being either liberal or conservative, but also organizationally coherent in that each level adheres to this uniformly liberal or conservative belief structure.

Consequently the days of liberal Republicans and conservative Democrats are now virtually over. They have been replaced by a Republican Party made up of decidedly conservative leaders, whereas the Democratic Party is now the home of liberals. Even moderates seem absent from the ranks of the elected and the appointed of the two major parties. Thus the labels Democrat and Republican have more meaning than they once did from an issue perspective. Voting for one party will definitely garner different policies than will voting for the other. As we discuss later in this chapter, there is a price to pay for this party distinctiveness in terms of government accountability.

Just as the party label might be more meaningful in organizing politicians and their supporters around a set of policy orientations, the parties do less in the way of recruiting candidates for office than in the past. Candidates now self-select instead of being recruited by party leaders, as L. Sandy Maisel points out in Chapter 5. Today candidates tend to run their own campaigns, although many receive support from the parties in the form of training, issue position research, advice on finance and compliance with federal campaign finance regulations, and even soft money (money spent on their behalf by other organizations such as the political parties), as Victoria Farrar-Myers and Diana Dwyre report in Chapter 7. On balance, candidate recruitment and political careers are driven more by the candidates themselves, with less input from party leaders than once existed.

Despite the policy consistency of each party, Maisel's point about recruitment efforts (or their lack) and Farrar-Myers and Dwyre's point about campaign and party finance reveal the new style of parties that emerged from the malaise of the 1970s. As John H. Aldrich so aptly puts it, each party acts "'in service' to its ambitious politicians but not 'in control' of them as the mass party sought to be" (Aldrich 1995, 273).

One of the ironies of the modern age is that as the two parties have become more distinct in terms of policy, the voters have not rewarded either with complete control of government but have frequently forced them to share through control of one or the other branch of government. At the same time, the two parties are further apart on many pressing issues of the day, giving rise to governmental gridlock, or the inability to produce policy, as Sarah A. Binder argues in Chapter 10. Some analysts feel that this situation has led to voters' exasperation with the acrimony and lack of results from government (see Hib-

Jeffrey E. Cohen and Paul Kantor

bing and Theis-Morse [1995] for evidence on negative public attitudes toward Congress). Thus, although parties today seem better able to organize politicians around policy than in the past, they seem less able to organize government because of divided government, the norm for most of the past thirty years.

The Current Parties and Democratic Linkages

In some respects, party-related democratic linkages have improved, but in other respects they have not. We see both aspects with regard to citizen participation. On the level of helping the public develop and express political opinions, the policy and ideological coherence of the parties may be a plus. It may be easier now for citizens to see party differences and identify the political leanings of politicians, as Bond and Fleisher demonstrate in Chapter 3. Moreover, such party coherence on a national level may have been instrumental for the realignment of political loyalties in the South, such that southern politics now resembles politics in the rest of the nation. As a result, the South has become more politically integrated into the nation.

Yet increasing party coherence has had less impact on party identification, according to David G. Lawrence (Chapter 2). True, party identification has been on the upswing since about 1980; however, its revival has not fully recovered from the losses suffered in the 1970s. Some observers even contend that much of this recovery simply is a function of the association between party identification and the aging process. Because the U.S. population is aging, party identification has been increasing (Miller and Shanks 1996). In a similar vein, James E. Campbell demonstrates in Chapter 1 that election contests are still mostly party affairs, despite the candidate centeredness of political careers and, supposedly, campaigns. Voters who are undecided at the outset of the presidential campaign usually go home to their parties as the election campaign progresses.

In another sense, party has recovered in the mass public. Lawrence shows in Chapter 2 that citizens with a sense of party identification are more loyal in their voting behavior to their parties than at any time since the 1950s, the period for which we have survey data. Both party identification and party impact on the vote have recovered much ground lost in the 1970s. Party identification has not recovered fully, but party impact on the vote has, even if it has not surpassed the levels of the 1950s.

Although increased party coherence may be stimulating party loyalty among many in the mass public, a large segment of the populace, perhaps as much as one-third, seems to be put off by this *policy extremism* of the major parties. Those in the middle, the moderates, may feel less comfortable with the modern parties than the more heterogeneous variety of party that existed a generation or two ago. Their discontent has produced a foundation for third-party attacks, like the Ross Perot candidacies of 1992 and 1996, and the Reform Party that grew out of Perot's presidential candidacies. This discontent has also provided the foundation for insurgency inside the parties, such as from the John McCain candidacy for the Republican nomination in 2000. What is historically odd about third-party outbreaks in the late twentieth century is their moderate character. Most third-party movements historically have been found on the political extremes of the right and left, not the center (Rosenstone, Behr, and Lazarus 1996). Theodore J. Lowi's point in Chapter 11, that the two-party system does not seem to serve our democracy well, is reflected in these patterns of centrist discontent, third-party challenges, and intraparty insurgency.

That the two major parties are situated to the right and left, and that there are so many discontented citizens in the center, makes the existence of such centrist third parties and intraparty insurgency understandable. But such centrist discontent is also probably a reaction to the inability of the two major parties to forge compromises in the policy-making process, a point we address later in this chapter.

With regard to active political participation, the parties seem to serve the public less well than in previous eras, except for the impact of party on the vote, as we discussed earlier. Turnout has been on the decline since its modern high in 1960, and upswings in turnout, such as in the 1992 election, seem more a function of third parties than the two major parties. The decline in turnout is partly the result of the parties as organizations not pulling people into the electorate like they once used to (Rosenstone and Hansen 1993). Campaigning is less personal, focusing on media advertisements. And the party machines, which once provided transportation and voting instructions, as well as other inducements and help, no longer exist. Citizens are left on their own in the voting process. Not surprisingly the greatest losses in turnout are among those who could least well afford to pay the price of participation, for example, the poor and the less educated, those who benefited the most from the mobilization efforts of the old party machines (Rosenstone and Hansen 1993).

But as Matthew Crenson and Benjamin Ginsberg argue in Chapter 4, we can also explain this participatory disengagement as a result of changes in the political culture, especially regarding notions of citizenship. People now view themselves as customers of government who receive individual benefits, not as citizens who belong to collectives such as classes or parties. As a result, voting

Jeffrey E. Cohen and Paul Kantor

has become less relevant as a form of political expression or as a way of securing government benefits. Again, citizens are left on their own.

As a means of popular control of government, the parties, because of the high incidence of divided government, do not offer the degree of control or accountability that might be possible under unified control. Arguably, divided government is not completely the making of the parties. One could easily argue that those in power would prefer unified control. But when the parties are so clearly conservative (the Republicans) and liberal (the Democrats), and seem so uncompromising in their public philosophies, the public may purposefully chose divided government as a means to check the policy extremism that each party offers. The lack of trust of voters toward either party might account for the high incidence of divided government, another implication of the discontent of the center mentioned earlier.

By dividing government, the public also reduces its ability to hold those in government accountable. For example, the party controlling Congress could point an accusing finger to the opposition party controlling the executive, and vice versa. Even in the face of policy gridlock, in which government is unable to produce policies to address issues the public wants dealt with, divided government enables each party to avoid responsibility by shifting it onto the party in control of the other branch of government.

At the same time that each party can point an accusing finger, neither has an incentive to compromise, a point that Davidson and Binder reveal in Chapters 9 and 10, respectively. Here lies a great paradox. The parties are better able to corral their members in government, in part because of their coherent but distant policy positions. Yet this seems to undermine their ability to govern and to be held accountable for what they do in government. The result: divided government, a point that Pomper makes in Chapter 8.

In summing up, we see strong crosscurrents in our party system. In some respects the parties are better servants of democracy than they were thirty or forty years ago, but in other ways they do not do as able a job in promoting and fostering democratic processes. Why have the parties strengthened in some ways but weakened in other ways (or at least not rebounded from the decline of the mid-1960s to mid-1970s)?

Why These Crosscurrents?

Looking back over the essays in this book, we see hints of four possible reasons why the parties evidence aspects of resurgence and decline. They are

(1) the change to a postindustrial society, (2) changes in citizen participation, (3) the role of organized money in politics, and (4) the strategies of candidates for office to control an increasingly uncertain political environment.

Postindustrial Society and Collective Mass Mobilization

The decline of collective political participation is not limited to the exercise of the franchise or to citizens in the United States. Turnout has declined across the advanced western democracies, including Great Britain (Dalton 1996), Germany (Kaase and Klingemann 1994), and Norway (Narud and Valen 1996), as has party identification in the United States, Canada, and Great Britain (Clarke and Stewart 1998). Participation in other collective action organizations, such as labor unions, has declined even more precipitously than voting, and it has done so across the western world (Johnson 1991; Putnam 1993, 1995; Troy 1986). There are many sources of the decline in unions, such as changing economic structures and job bases, government attacks on labor in the United States, and public disenchantment with labor (for a review, see Cohen 2000, 130–135). But it may not be an accident that labor is in a state of decline across the advanced democracies; many other forms of mass, collective action organizations, such as parties, also are in decline.

Underlying this state of decline may be a change in the structure of the economy, from industrial to postindustrial, which affects the political and social culture of societies (Ingelhart 1990). Rather simply, parties and unions are organizations of industrial society. With the rise of postindustrial society, their social roles and functions have ebbed, as people of postindustrial society invest less of their time, energy, loyalty, and resources in such arcane organizations.

The organization of industrial societies revolved mostly around social class and economic divisions, although national, linguistic, religious, ethnic, racial, and regional cleavages sometimes also played a role. Where social class and economic fault lines assumed great prominence, political parties and labor unions spoke to these divisions. Typically the parties offered programs designed to attract supporters seeking collective benefits based on these economic divisions. The American political system resonated with this kind of politics for decades during the twentieth century. Despite deviations and considerable overlap that muted divisions, Democrats generally sought the support of the middle, working, and lower classes, whereas Republicans sought support of the middle to upper classes. In industrial society the individual could easily place himself or herself into the grand scheme of things, identifying readily with class and party, which reinforced each other. In fact, in many

Jeffrey E. Cohen and Paul Kantor

countries in Europe, many parties of the left grew out of the labor union movement, such as the Labour Party in Great Britain.

In postindustrial society, however, the traditional social divisions have weakened. First, the rise of knowledge workers does not fit easily into broad class or other collective categorizations because of the sense of professionalism shared by these workers. Career advancement is based more on individual effort, merit, and the like, rooted in professional norms and identifications. In industrial society, unionized employees rise and fall together. Also closely tied to the professionalization of the worker in the postindustrial economy has been the loosening of ties between worker and employer. Neither is as loyal to the other as they once were. Corporations now easily downsize managers and white collar workers, a growing share of their workforce, in the name of efficiency, and these employees will easily jump ship to a new employer for personal reasons such as pay, promotion, and job duties.

Because of these weaker ties, organizations that pursue the interests of classes of people, especially large economic classes, speak less loudly. Professional workers are not highly likely to identify with an economic class, a party, or other people, even of similar background, occupation, and the like. Individual competition has grown among workers of the new postindustrial economy, replacing to a large extent the class and other collective sorts of competition of the industrial age.

Of course, one should not exaggerate how much postindustrialism has changed American society. Substantial social and economic inequality persists, and racial divisions add to political tensions. Nevertheless, in many ways the social cleavages associated with industrialism have become muted. To the extent that this has happened, the rise of postindustrial society answers at least half of our question, why parties are less able to mobilize as many people as they once could. Yet postindustrial theory helps little in understanding the roots of greater coherence, organization, and resources that parties now claim.

Government and Demobilization

The United States in the 1960s and 1970s witnessed a two-pronged participation revolution. The first prong of that revolution involved the expansion of the franchise to minorities, the transient, and the young. The second prong involved the movement of citizen efforts and resources away from parties and to interest groups. Thus, although turnout and electoral-related activities may have declined, membership in and financial contributions to interest groups surged.

The rise of the interest group sector of the political system has several important implications for government. First, government now faces a larger array of demands on it for government policies and services. Second, advocates of interest groups are not likely to compromise their demands on government, making the job of social conflict management much more difficult for government. Third, coalitions that form among interest groups are specific to each issue that arises, rarely spanning across issue areas. Thus a different set of allies and antagonists form for each issue. In all, this interest group trend has made the political environment more complex for government to deal with. When government is not able to manage such a demand environment, it is said to be in "overload" (Huntington 1981).

One way to deal with demand overload is to find a way to either insulate government from demands or reduce the number of demands made on government. One can insulate government from demands by decreasing the access of claimants to government. One can also reduce the number of demands made on government by altering the political legitimacy of demands. Both approaches were taken in the United States beginning in the 1970s and they continue today.

Changes in the public philosophy and the conception of citizenship have reduced the number of demands on government. We can think of the public philosophy as the broad outlines of what is legitimate for government to do and how government should relate to its citizenry. The dominant public philosophy in the United States has undergone transformations over time. Initially that philosophy stressed limited government and personal responsibility and individualism. Thus government tended to be small and rarely regulated or interfered in domestic matters, at least compared with the stronger states of Western and Central Europe. In the 1930s, owing to the Great Depression, this public philosophy changed to allow a greater role in government management and regulation of the economy. With the 1960s came another transformation in the public philosophy. People began to take for granted a whole host of rights or entitlements. Further, government was viewed as being responsible for stopping harm before it could occur, the notion of positive government (Beer 1978).

By the late 1970s the idea of smaller government began to be incorporated into a new public philosophy. Although first espoused by the Reagan administration, even Democrats soon began to declare that view, with Bill Clinton going so far as proclaiming that the "era of big government is over." Government would no longer be responsible for every problem that surfaced.

At the same time, the nature of citizenship, which defines the relationship between citizens and government, also changed, as Crenson and Ginsberg argue in Chapter 4. Citizens are apt to be regarded as customers or clients who receive government services and benefits. Such redefinition has implications for citizen participation. First, it defines citizens as individuals, not as part of collective movements or issues. Second, it places citizens in a passive position vis-à-vis government. The result is lower levels of citizen participation, especially through collective and active mechanisms such as voting.

Government can also reduce demand pressures on it by decreasing access. Ironically this has been accomplished at the same time that the franchise has been expanded and every political leader espouses the view that participation should be enhanced and voting rates increased. Despite the legal expansion of voting rights, government has done little to actively encourage increased participation. Even the touted "Motor Voter Act," which enables one to register as a voter while filling out forms at motor vehicle offices, leaves the vote decision up to the individual. Registration, what some consider a large barrier to voting, is still in place.

Thus, although government has not actually closed doors, it has done little substantively to encourage broad-scale participation. By keeping voting a voluntary act, and by not replacing the organizations, such as the old party machines, that pulled people into the voting booth and educated them about their vote decisions, government and political leaders have effectively reduced the volume of demands placed on it. In other words, although interest group demands have heated up, electoral demands have been cooled off.

Like the postindustrial theory presented earlier in this section, this theory, with its emphasis on the nexus between government and participation, helps account for the drop in participation and aspects of party decline, but it does not account for the rise and reinvigoration of the parties.

The Role of Organized Money

Money has always had an important part to play in democratic politics. Early in the nation's history, incumbents in office channeled government contracts to printers. These contracts supported the business side of operations, enabling these printers to publish political tracts and pamphlets in support of parties, factions, and candidates.

Although such contracts no longer exist, money has become even more apparent because of the large expense of campaigning, which now relies heavily on television and involves hiring expert talent to run election campaigns. Parties, too, use such resources, partly to build their organizations and develop campaign and policy strategies and partly to channel resources to candidates for office. Moreover, the use of soft money, that is, party spending during election cycles, implicitly if not explicitly in support of candidates for office, enables parties and candidates to skirt the federal campaign contribution and expenditure regulations and limitations. Thus, by accumulating money resources, parties have been able to build their organizational apparatus, becoming year-round bodies that supply policy and campaign expertise. In this way, money has helped rebuild the parties.

Still, this influx of money in the political system is a double-edged sword, fueling public discontent with the political finance system. For instance, a *Los Angeles Times* poll in November 1999 found that 78 percent of respondents thought "the campaign finance system [should] be changed to reduce the role of big money that is spent by political parties on behalf of the candidates," citing this as an important or one of the most important changes that could be made. According to an NBC News/*Wall Street Journal* poll taken in March 1997, 54 percent of respondents thought that soft money should be prohibited, even though the question included the phrase, "[S]ome say that [prohibiting soft money] would violate the First Amendment right to free speech"; 37 percent of respondents thought soft money should be allowed. Both polls indicate the public has strong disaffection for the amount and role of money in our current political and party systems.

Why is the public so incensed about money in politics? This complaint has several sources. One such source resides with the origin of the money, which comes disproportionately from the wealthy and from corporations. Many people also are alarmed about the vast sums of money being funneled into the parties and into candidate campaigns. Another point is that the public feels that such sums are used to buy influence with politicians. Thus the political system is steered away from the concerns of the average citizen and toward the concerns of big corporations and the wealthy. The electoral arena, once meant to be the place where the common person's voice would be loud and clear and forceful, has been tilted, much like the rest of the political system, to those who have money. The electoral arena, consequently, looks no different from any other political venue.

This view of the political order has many consequences. Citizens are disquieted about politics. It is also harder to mobilize voters to support candidates who are viewed as a part of the system. And many citizens are ripe for mobilization by third parties, extremists, and others promising reform or change in the way that politics operates. Thus money has a dual effect. It has helped rebuild the party organizations, as Farrar-Myers and Dwyre document in Chap-

Jeffrey E. Cohen and Paul Kantor

ter 7, but it also has led to public discontent, straining the ties between people and the parties.

The Strategies of Politicians: The Search for Certainty in a Volatile World

Another way to answer the question of the simultaneous decline and resurgence of the parties is to look at the behavior and strategies of elected politicians. First, we begin with the assumption that many, if not most, elected politicians want a career. To establish such a career requires the accumulation and maintenance of campaign resources and voter support. Although short-term strategies such as raising money and seeking issues are used to secure these two requisites, career building requires attracting campaign resources and voter support over the long run. In other words, a career requires predictability, and the future is more predictable the more that career-oriented politicians are able to control sources of unpredictability and uncertainty.

From this perspective the career-minded politician must establish and maintain reliable sources of campaign resources and voter support. Doing the former, in our current political world, is much easier than doing the latter, in part because voters overall have become more and more volatile and thus unpredictable, in terms of vote choice. One solution to this problem is to demobilize less predictable voters. This not only makes the electorate more predictable but also increases the predictability and acquisition of campaign resources.

This way of looking at politics has become more compelling in recent decades, as uncertainty with regard to the behavior of voters has been on the rise. There are at least two major sources of voter unpredictability or volatility: population changes and the increase in political independence among voters.

There has been a rapid influx of new or potential voters into the population in recent years. Some of this influx comes from the massive migration into the United States, which in magnitude and diversity is unlike anything seen since the late 1800s and early 1900s. Similarly, a massive intranational migration of people has occurred, with great population movements from the Northeast and Midwest to the South and West. It may be impossible to predict the future political loyalty of new immigrants to the country, and the internal migration patterns may mean that people bring their political attitudes, affiliations, and behaviors to new locales, upsetting the patterns established there. For example, what are the political consequences of New Yorkers and Californians moving to Texas?

The rise of political independence adds another layer of unpredictability to the political environment of elected politicians. Partisan, ideological, and programmatic appeals have less sway with independents than with partisans. Candidates and the politics and issues of the moment mobilize independents into politics, not long-standing political loyalties and traditions. Moreover, national movements are more potent on the average than local ones in pulling independents into the voting booth. Thus district-based elected officials may be greatly affected by these national and short-term political tides and movements.

The upshot is that it is difficult for politicians at any level to predict moderately into the future what the composition of the electorate will look like. Will new immigrants become politically active? Who will they support? Will native Americans from other regions migrate to their locality? How will the political loyalties of these voters mix with and possibly alter the existing local political alignment? What will be the mood of the independent voters? Will they be angry at incumbents or extremists as opposed to moderates? How will the operation of government and fluctuations in the business cycle affect the mood and the political activation of migrants, both foreign and native, in the district?

Such concerns have always been present in U.S. society, dynamic and changeable as it is. But the *magnitude* of these forces on the political landscape is greater than ever before because of the size and rapidity of population shifts and the large number of voters who are up for grabs. They present an increase in the degree of uncertainty and unpredictability faced by modern elected officials.

The acquisition of campaign resources, in contrast, is less problematic. In fact, a system of mutually reinforcing networks among campaign activists and financial contributors has developed, such that getting one helps get the other. Moreover, what is available to politicians of one party is not available to politicians of the other party. In other words, there are identifiable sets of campaign activists and financial contributors for each party, and both sets of campaign resources, within each party, are reasonably identifiable and stable in contribution level and programmatic motivation and orientation.

Thus we find within the ranks of the activist strata of society people who involve themselves in political campaign activities over successive elections. These people tend also to be identifiably liberal for the Democrats and conservative for the Republicans. Moreover, even when there is circulation over time in the individuals who give their time and support to electoral campaigns, the ideological–party pairings remain stable. Republicans running for office count on there being pools of committed conservative activists upon which to draw. Democrats have loyal liberals to draw upon.

Jeffrey E. Cohen and Paul Kantor

Financing campaigns also has the same basic structure. Business political action committees (PACs) give the most money, which usually goes to Republicans, although some industries reliably give to Democrats. Of non-business PACs, the remaining generally give consistently to either Democrats or Republicans. Few PACs give to candidates of both parties, and when they do, their contributions tend to be lopsided in favor of one party over the other. Furthermore, PACs tend not to change partisan sides from one election to the next, something that adds to stability across election cycles.

Last, and most significant, the policy positions of financial contributors, PACs or otherwise, and the positions of campaign activists, are in basic harmony. Although PACs may take fewer stands than campaign activists, when both articulate a position on the same issue, the positions tend to be the same or very close. In a nutshell, both will be conservative in the Republican case, and the policy bias will be decidedly liberal in the Democratic case. Consistency and stability characterize the structure of campaign resources to candidates of both parties. This is a stable environment, and given that almost all electoral nominations must be won in primaries, these sources have grown in consequence and importance to politicians over the years.

Thus building and maintaining an electoral career requires that politicians tap into these highly structured and predictable campaign resources, but doing so may be costly to voters. In particular, the fact that Americans on average prefer the moderate policy course runs counter to the candidate's search for campaign resources, which tends to push the candidate to either the conservative or the liberal pole. At the same time, a candidate may alienate voters not only by perhaps taking issue positions that are too liberal or conservative but also by being identified with these campaign supporters, be they rich PACs or extremist party activists. However, alienating voters will not be so high a price to pay if the alienated do not come out to vote.

The theory being proposed here is that candidates for office will not encourage, and may even actively discourage, unpredictable elements of the electorate from exercising their voting rights. Instead their aim is to recast the electorate so that it resembles the candidates' campaign resource base. Thus candidates will attempt to mobilize only conservative Republicans or liberal Democrats in the electorate and to ignore other voters. Whenever the politician is uncertain about the ideological or partisan leanings of a group or a voter, the effective strategy is to demobilize (or more benignly, not mobilize). The strategy of demobilization or nonmobilization helps a candidate control his or her political environment, as the electorate mirrors the coalition of campaign supporters and contributors.

Demobilization may be a misnomer. Rather the candidate conducts a two-pronged campaign, one to mobilize the like-minded, and another to demobilize those who are not committed, like-minded voters. How are candidates able to conduct such a segmented strategy? Several campaigning techniques are open to candidates. One that has found wide application is attack or negative campaigning. There is considerable debate among political scientists and others about the effectiveness and consequences of negative campaigning. Among many in the world of campaign consulting, the technique is thought to be highly effective (see Lau et al. [1999] for a wide-ranging review of the studies on negative campaigning). An early study by Stephen Ansolabehere and Shanto Iyengar (1995) found that negative campaigning increased cynicism in the mass public and reduced turnout. More recent work has refined the finding of this study. Negative campaigning does not have such effects on all voters, but it seems to affect moderates and independents the most (Kahn and Kenney 1999). This observation is consistent with the argument being offered here. The least predictable elements of the electorate, the elements that candidates least want to see mobilized to vote, are the ones most likely to drop out and fail to vote if confronted by negative campaigns. Thus the high degree of negative advertising in campaigns noted in recent years may be one consequence of candidates searching for greater certainty and less unpredictability in their political environments.

These career-enhancing techniques may not even be conscious on the part of candidates. They may be something stumbled onto that proved successful in the past and then became a habit after being associated with reelection victories. As campaign consultants and advisors circulate from candidate to candidate, they export with them the electoral solutions discovered in earlier campaigns to their new campaign settings and experiences. These techniques become, in effect, the folklore of campaigning.

Conclusion

The political party system has undergone remarkable change over the past several decades. As we have documented in this book, there are indications of both party decline and party revitalization. In this chapter we have tried to assess why these crosscurrents exist, pointing to four possible explanations: the rise of postindustrial society, the nexus between government and participation, the role of money in politics, and the strategies of candidates for office.

Jeffrey E. Cohen and Paul Kantor

In reviewing the four theories presented here, two of them, the postindustrial transformation and the nexus between government and participation, seem best suited in accounting for aspects of party decline. The other two, the role of money and the strategies of candidates, help explain party decline as well as party resurgence. Because party decline and party renewal are complex, multifaceted phenomena, each of the proposed theories is useful in explaining part of the puzzle of the current state of the parties. The relevance of all four theories suggests that the crosscurrents of change that are affecting the party system are deeply rooted and are bound up with forces that influence the whole character of the American political order. Understanding these developments is essential for anticipating the future of democracy in the United States and the role that the political parties will play in enhancing or frustrating democracy.

References

Abramson, Paul R., and John H. Aldrich. 1982. "The Decline of Electoral Participation in America." *American Political Science Review* 76 (June): 502–521.

Abramson, Paul R., John H. Aldrich, and David W. Rohde. 1999. *Change and Continuity in the 1996 and 1998 Elections.* Washington, D.C.: CQ Press.

Aldrich, John H. 1995. *Why Parties? The Origins and Transformations of Party Politics in America.* Chicago: University of Chicago Press.

Alvarez, Lizette. 1999. "A High-Tech Industry, Long Shy of Politics, Is Now Belle of Ball." *New York Times,* December 26, A1.

American National Election Studies, 1948–1997. 1998. CD-ROM.

American Political Science Association, Committee on Political Parties. 1950. "Toward a More Responsible Two-Party System." *American Political Science Review* 44 (Supplement).

Anderson, Benedict. 1983. *Imagined Communities: Reflections on the Origin and Spread of Nationalism.* London: Verso.

Ansolabehere, Stephen, Roy Behr, and Shanto Iyengar. 1993. *The Media Game: American Politics in the Television Age.* New York: Macmillan.

Ansolabehere, Stephen, and Shanto Iyengar. 1995. *Going Negative: How Political Advertisements Shrink and Polarize the Electorate.* New York: Free Press.

Ayres, Drummond, Jr. 1999. "Political Briefing." *New York Times,* October 24, 28.

Babington, Charles, and Eric Pianin. 1999. "Clinton and Congress Agree on Budget Goals." *Washington Post,* July 13, A1.

Bader, John B. 1997. *Taking the Initiative: Leadership Agendas in Congress and the "Contract with America."* Washington, D.C.: Georgetown University Press.

Bailey, Stephen K. 1959. *The Condition of Our National Political Parties.* New York: Fund for the Republic.

Baker, Peter. 1996. "A Motor Voter Apparently Didn't Drive Up Turnout." *Washington Post,* November 6, B7.

Bartels, Larry M. 2000. "Partisanship and Voting Behavior, 1952–1996." *American Journal of Political Science* 44 (January): 35–50.

Beck, Deborah, Paul Taylor, Jeffrey Stanger, and Douglas Rivlin. 1997. *Issue Advocacy Advertising During the 1996 Campaign.* Philadelphia: Annenberg Public Policy Center.

Beck, Paul Allen. 1984. "The Dealignment Era in America." In *Electoral Change in Advanced Industrial Democracies,* ed. Russell J. Dalton, Scott C. Flanagan, and Paul Allen Beck. Princeton: Princeton University Press.

Beck, Paul Allen. 1997. *Party Politics in America,* 8th ed. New York: Addison-Wesley.

Beer, Samuel H. 1978. "In Search of a New Public Philosophy." In *The New American Political System,* ed. Anthony King. Washington, D.C.: American Enterprise Institute.

Bellah, Robert N., Richard Madsen, William M. Sullivan, Ann Swidler, and Steven M. Tipton. 1985. *Habits of the Heart: Individualism and Commitment in American Life.* Berkeley: University of California Press.

Berelson, Bernard R., Paul F. Lazarsfeld, and William N. McPhee. 1954. *Voting.* Chicago: University of Chicago Press.

Berry, Jeffrey M. 1993. "Citizen Groups and the Changing Nature of Interest Group Politics in America." *The Annals of the American Academy of Political and Social Science* 528 (July): 30–41.

Bibby, John F. 1998a. "Party Organizations, 1946–1996." In *Partisan Approaches to Postwar American Politics,* ed. Byron Shafer. New York: Chatham House.

Bibby, John F. 1998b. "State Party Organizations: Coping and Adapting to Candidate-Centered Politics and Nationalization." In *The Parties Respond: Changes in American Parties and Campaigns,* 3d ed. Ed. L. Sandy Maisel. Boulder, Colo.: Westview Press.

Biersack, Robert, and Melanie Haskell. 1999. "Spitting on the Umpire: Political Parties, the Federal Election Campaign Act, and the 1996 Campaigns." In *Financing the 1996 Elections,* ed. John C. Green. Armonk, N.Y.: Sharpe.

Binder, Sarah A. 1996. "The Disappearing Political Center." *The Brookings Review* 14 (fall): 36–39.

Binder, Sarah A. 1999. "The Dynamics of Legislative Gridlock, 1947–96." *American Political Science Review* 93 (September): 519–533.

Blyth, Dale A., Rebecca Saito, and Tom Berkas. 1997. "A Quantitative Study of the Impact of Service Learning Programs." In *Service-Learning: Applications from the Research,* ed. Alan S. Waterman. Mahwah, N.J.: Lawrence Erlbaum.

Bond, Jon R., and Richard Fleisher. 2000. *Polarized Politics: Congress and the President in a Partisan Era.* Washington, D.C.: CQ Press.

Brady, David W. 1988. *Critical Elections and Congressional Policy Making.* Stanford: Stanford University Press.

Brady, David. 1991. "After the Big Bang House Battles Focused on Committee Issues." *Public Affairs Report* 32 (March): 8.

Brady, David W., and Craig Volden. 1998. *Revolving Gridlock.* Boulder, Colo.: Westview Press.

Bresnahan, John. 1999. "Cook Lectured by GOP Leaders." *Roll Call,* September 23, 1, 29.

Broder, David. 1971. *The Party's Over.* New York: Harper & Row.

Brody, Richard A. 1991. *Assessing the President: The Media, Elite Opinion and Public Support.* Stanford: Stanford University Press.

Brokaw, Tom. 1998. *The Greatest Generation.* New York: Random House.

Brubaker, Rogers. 1992. *Citizenship and Nationhood in France and Germany.* Cambridge: Harvard University Press.

Burnham, Walter Dean. 1970. *Critical Elections and the Mainsprings of American Politics.* New York: Norton.

Burnham, Walter Dean. 1975. "Insulation and Responsiveness in Congressional Elections." *Political Science Quarterly* 90 (fall): 411–435.

Bryce, James. 1909. *The American Commonwealth* (Vol. 2). New York: Macmillan.

Busbey, L. White. 1927. *Uncle Joe Cannon: The Story of a Pioneer American.* New York: Holt.

Campbell, Angus. 1972. "Change in the American Electorate." In *The Human Meaning of Social Change,* ed. Angus Campbell and Philip E. Converse. New York: Russell Sage Foundation.

Campbell, Angus, Philip E. Converse, Warren E. Miller, and Donald E. Stokes. 1960. *The American Voter.* New York: Wiley.

Campbell, Angus, Gerald Gurin, and Warren Miller. 1954. *The Voter Decides.* Evanston, Ill.: Row, Peterson, and Company.

Campbell, James E. 1997. *The Presidential Pulse of Congressional Elections,* 2d ed. Lexington: The University Press of Kentucky.

Campbell, James E. 2000a. *The American Campaign: U.S. Presidential Campaigns and the National Vote.* College Station: Texas A&M University Press.

Campbell, James E. 2000b. "The Science of Forecasting Presidential Elections." In *Before the Vote: Forecasting American National Elections,* ed. James E. Campbell and James C. Garand. Thousand Oaks, Calif.: Sage.

Canon, David. 2000. "A Pox on Both Your Parties." In *The Enduring Debate,* ed. David Canon et al. New York: Norton.

Carey, George W. 1978. "Separation of Powers and the Madisonian Model." *American Political Science Review* 72 (March): 151–164.

Carmines, Edward G., and Geoffrey C. Layman. 1997. "Issue Evolution in Postwar American Politics: Old Certainties and Fresh Tensions." In *Present Discontents: American Politics in the Very Late Twentieth Century,* ed. Byron E. Shafer. Chatham, N.J.: Chatham House.

Carmines, Edward G., and James A. Stimson. 1989. *Issue Evolution: Race and the Transformation of American Politics.* Princeton: Princeton University Press.

Cass, Ronald. 1986. "Models of Administrative Action." *Virginia Law Review* 72 (March): 363–398.

Ceasar, James W. 1979. *Presidential Selection: Theory and Development.* Princeton: Princeton University Press.

Ceasar, James W. 1982. *Reforming the Reforms.* Cambridge, Mass.: Ballinger.

Chambers, William N., and Philip C. Davis. 1978. "Party, Competition, and Mass Participation, 1824–1852." In *The History of American Electoral Behavior,* ed. Joel Silbey, Allan G. Bogue, and William H. Flanigan. Princeton: Princeton University Press.

Chesterton, G. K. 1922. *What I Saw in America.* New York: Dodd, Mead.

Clarke, Harold D., and Marianne C. Stewart. 1998. "The Decline of Parties in the Minds of Citizens." *Annual Review of Political Science* 1: 357–378.

Cloward, Richard, and Frances Piven. 1971. *Regulating the Poor: The Functions of Public Welfare.* New York: Pantheon.

Clubb, Jerome, William Flanigan, and Nancy Zingale. 1990. *Partisan Realignment,* 2d ed. Boulder, Colo.: Westview Press.

Cohen, Jeffrey E. 2000. *Politics and Economic Policy in the United States,* 2d ed. Boston: Houghton-Mifflin.

Cohen, William S. 1996. "Why I Am Leaving." *Washington Post,* January 21, C7.

Coleman, John J. 1996. *Party Decline in America: Policy, Politics, and the Fiscal State.* Princeton: Princeton University Press.

Coleman, John J. 1999. "Unified Government, Divided Government, and Party Responsiveness." *American Political Science Review* 93 (December): 821–836.

Conlan, Timothy. 1998. *From New Federalism to Devolution: Twenty-Five Years of Intergovernmental Reform.* Washington, D.C.: Brookings Institution Press.

Connelly, William, and John Pitney. 1994. *Congress' Permanent Minority? Republicans in the U.S. House.* Lanham, Md.: Rowman & Littlefield.

Converse, Philip E., and Gregory B. Markus. 1979. "Plus ca Change . . . The New CPS Election Study Panel." *American Political Science Review* 73 (March): 32–49.

Cooper, Joseph, and Garry Young. 1997. "Partisanship, Bipartisanship, and Crosspartisanship in Congress Since the New Deal." In *Congress Reconsidered,* 6th ed. Ed. Lawrence C. Dodd and Bruce I. Oppenheimer. Washington, D.C.: CQ Press.

Corrado, Anthony. 1997. "Party Soft Money." In *Campaign Finance Reform: A Sourcebook,* ed. Anthony J. Corrado, Thomas E. Mann, Daniel R. Ortiz, Trevor Potter, and Frank J. Sorauf. Washington, D.C.: Brookings Institution Press.

Corrado, Anthony J., Thomas E. Mann, Daniel R. Ortiz, Trevor Potter, and Frank J. Sorauf, eds. 1997. *Campaign Finance Reform: A Sourcebook.* Washington, D.C.: Brookings Institution Press.

Craig, Stephen C. 1996. "Change and the American Electorate." In *Broken Contract: Changing Relationships Between Americans & Their Government,* ed. Stephen C. Craig. Boulder, Colo.: Westview Press.

Crenson, Matthew A. 1974. "Organizational Factors in Citizen Participation." *Journal of Politics* 36 (May): 356–378.

Crenson, Matthew, and Francis Rourke. 1987. "American Bureaucracy Since World War II." In *The New American State: Bureaucracies and Policies Since World War II,* ed. Louis Galambos. Baltimore: Johns Hopkins University Press.

Crotty, William. 1978. *Decision for the Democrats.* Baltimore: Johns Hopkins University Press.

Crotty, William. 1980. "The Philosophies of Party Reform." In *Party Renewal in America,* ed. Gerald M. Pomper. New York: Praeger.

Crotty, William. 1983. *Party Reform.* New York: Longman.

Crotty, William. 1984. *American Political Parties in Decline.* Boston: Little, Brown.

Crotty, William, and John S. Jackson III. 1985. *Presidential Primaries and Nominations.* Washington, D.C.: CQ Press.

Crotty, William, John S. Jackson III, and Melissa Miller. 1999. "Political Activists over Time: Working Elites in the Party System." In *Comparative Political Parties and Party Elites,* ed. Birol Yesilada. Ann Arbor: University of Michigan Press.

Crowley, Elizabeth. 1999. "More Young People Turn Away from Politics and Concentrate Instead on Community Service." *Wall Street Journal,* July 16, A28.

Cutler, Lloyd. 1988. "Some Reflections About Divided Government." *Presidential Studies Quarterly* 17 (summer): 485–492.

Dalton, Russell J. 1996. *Citizen Politics: Public Opinion and Political Parties in Advanced Industrial Democracies,* 2d ed. Chatham, N.J.: Chatham House.

Davidson, Chandler. 1992. "The Voting Rights Act: A Brief History." In *Controversies in Minority Voting—The Voting Rights Act in Perspective,* ed. Bernard Groffman and Chandler Davidson. Washington, D.C.: Brookings Institution Press.

Davidson, Roger H. 1996. "The Presidency and Congressional Time." In *Rivals for Power: Presidential-Congressional Relations,* ed. James A. Thurber. Washington, D.C.: CQ Press.

de Tocqueville, Alexis. 1954 [originally published 1835]. *Democracy in America,* ed. Phillips Bradley. 2 vols. New York: Vintage Books.

de Tocqueville, Alexis. 1960. *Democracy in America,* trans. Henry Reeve. 2 vols. New York: Vintage Books.

Dewar, Helen. 1993. "Motor Voter Agreement Is Reached." *Washington Post,* April 28, A6.

Didion, Joan. 1999. "Uncovered Washington." *The New York Review of Books,* June 24, 72–80.

Dionne, E. J., Jr. 1991. *Why Americans Hate Politics.* New York: Simon & Shuster.

Dionne, E. J., Jr. 1996. *They Only Look Dead: Why Progressives Will Dominate the Next Political Era.* New York: Touchstone.

Dodd, Lawrence C. 1995. "The New American Politics: Reflections on the Early 1990s." In *The New American Politics: Reflections on Political Change and the Clinton Administration,* ed. Bryan D. Jones. Boulder, Colo.: Westview Press.

Downs, Anthony. 1957. *An Economic Theory of Democracy.* New York: Harper.

"Eightieth Congress: To Date." 1948. *New York Times,* June 20, 8E.

Drew, Elizabeth. 1983. *Politics and Money: The New Road to Corruption.* New York: Macmillan.

Drew, Elizabeth. 1999. *The Corruption of American Politics: What Went Wrong and Why.* New York: Birch Lane.

Duverger, Maurice. 1954. *Political Parties: Their Organization and Activity in the Modern State,* trans. Barbara and Robert North. New York: Wiley.

Duverger, Maurice. 1963. *Political Parties: Their Organization and Activity in the Modern State,* 2d ed. Trans. Barbara and Robert North. New York: Wiley.

Dwyre, Diana. 1994. "Party Strategy and Political Reality: The Distribution of Congressional Campaign Committee Resources." In *The State of the Parties,* ed. Daniel M. Shea and John C. Green. Lanham, Md.: Rowman & Littlefield.

Dwyre, Diana. 1996. "Spinning Straw Into Gold: Soft Money and U.S. House Elections." *Legislative Studies Quarterly* 21 (August): 409–424.

Dwyre, Diana, and Ellie Clifford. 1999. "Who Controls the Dialogue of Democracy? Campaign Communications in 1998." Paper presented at the annual meeting of the Western Political Science Association, Seattle.

Dwyre, Diana, and Victoria Farrar-Myers. 2001. *Legislative Labyrinth: Congress and Campaign Finance Reform.* Washington, D.C.: CQ Press.

Edwards, George C., III, with Alec M. Gallup. 1990. *Presidential Approval: A Sourcebook.* Baltimore: Johns Hopkins University Press.

Eliasoph, Nina. 1998. *Avoiding Politics: How Americans Produce Apathy in Everyday Life.* New York: Cambridge University Press.

Epstein, Leon. 1980. "What Happened to the British Party Model?" *American Political Science Review* 74 (March): 9–22.

Erie, Steven P. 1985. *Rainbow's End: Irish-Americans and the Dilemmas of Urban Machine Politics, 1840–1985.* Berkeley: University of California Press.

Erikson, Robert S., and Christopher Wlezien. 1998. "The Timeline of Political Campaigns." Paper presented at the annual meeting of the American Political Science Association.

Everson, Daniel H. 1980. *American Political Parties.* New York: New Viewpoints.

Farlie, Henry. 1978. *The Parties: Republicans and Democrats in This Century.* New York: St. Martin's.

Farrar-Myers, Victoria, and Diana Dwyre. 1998. "Campaign Finance Reform in the 105th Congress: A Behind-the-Scenes Look at Bipartisan Maneuvering." *American Review of Politics* 19 (winter): 345–360.

Federal Election Commission. 1996. *Campaign Guide for Political Party Committees.* August.

Federal Election Commission. 1997. "FEC Reports Major Increase in Party Activity for 1995–96." News Release, March 9.

Federal Election Commission. 1999. "Political Party Fundraising Continues to Climb." News Release, January 26.

Federal Election Commission. 2000. "FEC Announces 2000 Presidential Spending Limits." News Release, March 1.

Feld, Melissa. 1999. "Campaign Finance Laws and Practices." MA thesis, Department of Political Science, Johns Hopkins University.

Finkel, Steven E. 1993. "Reexamining the 'Minimal Effects' Model in Recent Presidential Campaigns." *Journal of Politics* 55 (February): 1–21.

Fiorina, Morris P. 1981. *Retrospective Voting in American National Elections.* New Haven: Yale University Press.

Fiorina, Morris. 1996. *Divided Government,* 2d ed. Boston: Allyn & Bacon.

Fleisher, Richard. 1993. "Explaining the Change in Roll-Call Voting Behavior of Southern Democrats." *Journal of Politics* 55 (May): 327–341.

Fleisher, Richard, and Jon R. Bond. 1996. "The President in a More Partisan Legislative Arena." *Political Research Quarterly* 49 (December): 729–748.

Follett, Mary Parker. 1896. *The Speaker of the House of Representatives.* New York: Longmans, Green.

Fox, Edward Whiting. 1991. *The Emergence of the Modern European World: From the Seventeenth to the Twentieth Century.* Cambridge, Mass.: Blackwell.

Frendeis, John P., James Gibson, and Laura Vertz. 1990. "The Electoral Relevance of Local Party Organization." *American Political Science Review* 84 (March): 225–236.

Funk, Carolyn L. 1999. "Bringing the Candidate into Models of Candidate Evaluation." *Journal of Politics* 61 (August): 700–720.

Frymer, Paul. 1999. *Uneasy Alliances—Race and Party Competition in America.* Princeton: Princeton University Press.

Gelman, Andrew, and Gary King. 1993. "Why Are American Presidential Election Campaign Polls So Variable When Votes Are So Predictable?" *British Journal of Political Science* 23 (October): 409–451.

Gettinger, Stephen. 1999. "R.I.P. to a Conservative Force." *CQ Weekly,* January 9, 82–83.

Gillespie, David. 1993. *Politics at the Periphery—Third Parties in Two-Party America.* Columbia: University of South Carolina Press.

Ginsberg, Benjamin, and Martin Shefter. 1990. *Politics by Other Means.* New York: Basic Books.

Ginsberg, Benjamin, and Martin Shefter. 1999. *Politics by Other Means,* 2d ed. New York: Norton.

Glendon, Mary Ann. 1991. *Rights Talk: The Impoverishment of Political Discourse.* New York: Free Press.

Godwin, Kenneth R. 1988. *One Billion Dollars of Influence: The Direct Marketing of Politics.* Chatham, N.J.: Chatham House.

Gopoian, J. David, and Sissie Hadjiharalambous. 1994. "Late-Deciding Voters in Presidential Elections." *Political Behavior* 16 (March): 55–78.

Gore, Al. 1993. *From Red Tape to Results, Creating a Government That Works Better and Costs Less: Report of the National Performance Review.* Washington, D.C.: U.S. Department of Commerce, National Technical Information Service.

Greve, Michael S. 1987. "Why 'Defunding the Left' Failed." *The Public Interest* 89 (fall): 93–99.

Grofman, Bernard, and Chandler Davidson, eds. 1992. *Controversies in Minority Voting—The Voting Rights Act in Perspective.* Washington, D.C.: Brookings Institution Press.

Grove, Lloyd. 1996. "The So-Long Senators." *Washington Post,* January 26, F1.

Grunwald, Michael. 1999. "Gephardt's Tireless Quest: Put Democrats Atop House." *Washington Post,* July 12, A1.

Guinier, Lani. "Voting Rights and Democratic Theory: Where Do We Go From Here?" In *Controversies in Minority Voting—The Voting Rights Act in Perspective,* ed. Bernard Groffman and Chandler Davidson. Washington, D.C.: Brookings Institution Press.

Hardin, Charles. 1974. *Presidential Power and Accountability: Toward a New Constitution.* Chicago: University of Chicago Press.

Hartz, Louis. 1955. *The Liberal Tradition in America: An Interpretation of American Political Thought Since the Revolution.* New York: Harcourt, Brace.

Herrnson, Paul S. 1988. *Party Campaigning in the 1980s.* Cambridge: Harvard University Press.

Herrnson, Paul S. 1998a. *Congressional Elections: Campaigning at Home and in Washington,* 2d ed. Washington, D.C.: CQ Press.

Herrnson, Paul S. 1998b. "National Party Organizations at the Century's End." In *The Parties Respond: Changes in American Parties and Campaigns,* 3d ed. Ed. L. Sandy Maisel. Boulder, Colo.: Westview Press.

Herrnson, Paul S. 2000. *Congressional Elections: Campaigning at Home and in Washington,* 3d ed. Washington, D.C.: CQ Press.

Herrnson, Paul. S., and Diana Dwyre. 1998. "Party Issue Advocacy in Congressional Election Campaigns." In *The State of the Parties: The Changing Role of Contemporary American Parties,* 3d ed. Ed. John C. Green and Daniel M. Shea. Lanham, Md.: Rowman & Littlefield.

Hibbing, John, and Elizabeth Theiss-Morse. 1995. *Congress as Public Enemy: Public Attitudes Toward American Political Institutions.* New York: Cambridge University Press.

Hill, Kevin A. 1995. "Does the Creation of Majority Black Districts Aid Republicans? An Analysis of the 1992 Congressional Elections in Eight Southern States." *Journal of Politics* 57 (May): 384–401.

Hintze, Otto. 1975. "Military Organization and State Organization." In *The Historical Essays of Otto Hintze,* ed. Felix Gilbert. New York: Oxford University Press.

Holbrook, Thomas M. 1996. *Do Campaigns Matter?* Thousand Oaks, Calif.: Sage.

"The Hollow Branch." 1994. *Washington Post,* August 26, A24.

Hosansky, David. 1999. "Clinton's Biggest Prize Was a Frustrated GOP." *CQ Weekly,* January 9, 75–77, 86–91.

Huntington, Samuel P. 1981. *American Politics: The Promise of Disharmony.* Cambridge, Mass.: Belknap.

"Hypocrisy on Campaign Funds" [editorial]. 1998. *Washington Post,* April 1, A18.

Inglehart, Ronald. 1990. *Culture Shift in Advanced Industrial Society.* Princeton: Princeton University Press.

Jackson, John S., III. 1992. "The Party-as-Organization: Party Elites and Party Reforms in Presidential Nominations and Conventions." In *Challenges to Party Government,* ed. John Kenneth White and Jerome M. Mileur. Carbondale: University of Southern Illinois Press.

Jackson, John S., III, Barbara L. Brown, and David Bositis. 1982. "Herbert McClosky and Friends Revisited." *American Politics Quarterly* 10 (April): 158–180.

Jackson, John S., III, Jesse C. Brown, and Barbara L. Brown. 1978. "Representation and Political Values." *American Politics Quarterly* 6 (April): 187–212.

Jacobson, Gary C. 2000. "Party Polarization in National Politics: The Electoral Connection." In *Polarized Politics: Congress and the President in a Partisan Era,* ed. Jon R. Bond and Richard Fleisher. Washington, D.C.: CQ Press.

Jacoby, William. "Liberal-Conservative Thinking in the American Electorate." *Research in Micropolitics,* in press.

Jamieson, Kathleen Hall. 1992. *Dirty Politics: Deception, Distraction and Democracy.* New York: Oxford University Press.

Jensen, Richard. 1971. *The Winning of the Midwest.* Chicago: University of Chicago Press.

Jewell, Malcolm E., and Sarah McCally Morehouse. 2001. *Political Parties and Elections in the American States,* 4th ed. Washington, D.C.: CQ Press.

Jewell, Malcolm E., and David M. Olson. 1988. *Political Parties and Elections in the American States,* 3d ed. Chicago: Dorsey.

Jillson, Calvin, and Rick K. Wilson. 1994. *Congressional Dynamics: Structure, Coordination, and Choice in the First American Congress, 1774–1789.* Stanford: Stanford University Press.

Johnson, Paul Edward. 1991. "Organized Labor in an Era of Blue-Collar Decline." In *Interest Group Politics,* 3d ed. Ed. Allan J. Cigler and Burdett A. Loomis. Washington, D.C.: CQ Press.

Jones, Charles O. 1968. "Joseph G. Cannon and Howard W. Smith: An Essay on the Limits of Leadership in the House of Representatives." *Journal of Politics* 30 (August): 617–646.

Jones, David R. 2001. "Party Polarization and Legislative Gridlock." *Political Research Quarterly* 54 (March): in press.

Joseph, Lawrence. 1982. "Neoconservatism in Contemporary Political Science." *Journal of Politics* 44 (November): 955–982.

Kaase, Max, and Hans Dieter Klingemann. 1994. "Electoral Research in the Federal Republic of Germany." *European Journal of Political Research* 25 (April): 343–366.

Kahn, Kim Fridkin, and Patrick J. Kenney. 1999. "Do Negative Campaigns Mobilize or Suppress Turnout? Clarifying the Relationship Between Negativity and Participation." *American Political Science Review* 93 (December): 877–890.

Kayden, Xandra, and Eddie Mahe, Jr. 1985. *The Party Goes On.* New York: Basic Books.

Keith, Bruce E., David B. Magleby, Candice J. Nelson, Elizabeth Orr, Mark C. Westlye, and Raymond E. Wolfinger. 1992. *The Myth of the Independent Voter.* Berkeley: University of California Press.

Kelley, Stanley, Jr., and Thad W. Mirer. 1974. "The Simple Act of Voting." *American Political Science Review* 68 (June): 572–591.

Kelly, Sean Q. 1993. "Divided We Govern? A Reassessment." *Polity* 25 (spring): 475–484.

Kerbel, Matthew Robert. 1998. *Remote and Controlled: Media Politics in a Cynical Age,* 2d ed. Boulder, Colo.: Westview Press.

Kernell, Samuel. 1977. "Toward Understanding the Nineteenth Century Congressional Career Patterns: Ambition, Competition, and Rotation." *American Journal of Political Science* 21 (November): 669–693.

Kerstein, Robert J., and Dennis R. Judd. 1980. "Achieving Less Influence with More Democracy: The Permanent Influence of the War on Poverty." *Social Science Quarterly* 61 (March): 208–220.

Key, V. O. 1942. *Politics, Parties and Pressure Groups.* New York: Crowell.

Key, V. O. 1949. *Southern Politics in State and Nation.* New York: Knopf.

Key, V. O. 1964. *Politics, Parties and Pressure Groups,* 5th ed. New York: Crowell.

Key, V. O. 1966. *The Responsible Electorate.* Cambridge: Harvard University Press.

Kingdon, John. 1984. *Agendas, Alternatives, and Public Policies.* Boston: Little, Brown.

Kirkpatrick, Evron M. 1971. "'Toward a More Responsible Two-Party System': Political Science, Policy Science, or Pseudo-Science?" *American Political Science Review* 65 (December): 965–990.

Kirkpatrick, Jeane. 1976. *The New Presidential Elite: Men and Women in National Politics.* New York: Russell Sage Foundation and the Twentieth Century Fund.

Kleppner, Paul. 1982. *Who Voted? The Dynamics of Electoral Turnout, 1870–1980.* New York: Praeger.

Klingemann, Hans-Dieter, Richard I. Hofferbert, and Ian Budge. 1994. *Parties, Policies, and Democracy.* Boulder, Colo.: Westview Press.

Kolodny, Robin. 1998. *Pursuing Majorities: Congressional Campaign Committees in American Politics.* Norman: University of Oklahoma Press.

Kondracke, Morton. 1995. "Who's Running the House? GOP Freshmen or Newt?" *Roll Call,* December 18, 5.

Koshner, Andrew J. 1998. *Solving the Puzzle of Interest Group Litigation.* Westport, Conn.: Greenwood Press.

Kousser, Morgan J. 1974. *The Shaping of Southern Politics: Suffrage Restriction and the Establishment of the One-Party South, 1890–1910.* New Haven: Yale University Press.

Krehbiel, Keith. 1998. *Pivotal Politics.* Chicago: University of Chicago Press.

Kull, Steven. 1999. *Expecting More Say: The American Public on Its Role in Government Decisionmaking.* Washington, D.C.: Center on Policy Attitudes.

Kymlicka, Will, and Wayne Norman. 1994. "The Return of the Citizen: A Survey of Recent Work on Citizenship Theory." *Ethics* 104 (January): 352–381.

Ladd, Everett C. 1982. *Where Have All the Voters Gone? The Fracturing of America's Political Parties,* 2d ed. New York: Norton.

Ladd, Everett C. 1987. "Party Reform and the Public Interest." *Political Science Quarterly* 102 (autumn): 355–369.

Ladd, Everett C., ed. 1999. *America at the Polls 1998.* Storrs, Conn.: Roper Center, University of Connecticut.

Ladd, Everett C., Jr. 1985. "On Mandates, Realignments, and the 1984 Presidential Election." *Political Science Quarterly* 100 (spring): 1–26.

Ladd, Everett C., Jr., with Charles D. Hadley. 1978. *Transformations of the American Party System,* 2d ed. New York: Norton.

Lasch, Christopher. 1995. *The Revolt of the Elites.* New York: Norton.

Lau, Richard R., Lee Sigleman, Caroline Heldman, and Paul Babbitt. 1999. "The Effects of Negative Political Advertisements: A Meta-analytic Assessment." *American Political Science Review* 93 (December): 851–876.

Lawrence, David G. 1996. *The Collapse of the Democratic Presidential Majority: Realignment, Dealignment, and Electoral Change from Franklin Roosevelt to Bill Clinton.* Boulder, Colo.: Westview Press.

Lawrence, David G. 1999. "On the Resurgence of Party Identification in the 1990s." Paper presented at the Fordham University Forum on American Politics, Political Parties and the Future of American Politics: An Assessment at the Millennium, November 5.

Layman, Geoffrey C., and Thomas M. Carsey. 1999. "Ideological Realignment in Contemporary American Politics." Paper presented at the annual meeting of the American Political Science Association.

Lazarsfeld, Paul F., Bernard Berelson, and Hazel Gaudet. 1944. *The People's Choice.* New York: Duell, Sloan & Pearce.

Lipset, Seymour Martin. 1996. *American Exceptionalism: A Double-Edged Sword.* New York: Norton.

Lowi, Theodore. 1964. "American Business, Public Policy, Case Studies and Political Theory." *World Politics* 16 (July): 689–690.

Lowi, Theodore. 1969. *The End of Liberalism: Ideology, Policy, and the Crisis of Public Authority.* New York: Norton.

Lowi, Theodore J. 1985. "Presidential Power: Restoring the Balance." *Political Science Quarterly* 100 (summer): 185–213.

Lowi, Theodore J., and Joseph Romance. 1998. *A Republic of Parties?* Lanham, Md.: Rowman & Littlefield.

Luther, Martin. 1947. "The Leipsic Debate (July, 1559)." In *Pageant of Europe, Sources and Selections from Renaissance to the Present Day,* ed. Raymond P. Stearn. New York: Harcourt Brace.

Mackenzie, G. Calvin. 1996. *The Irony of Reform.* Boulder, Colo.: Westview Press.

Madison, James. 1941 [originally published 1787]. *The Federalist #10.* New York: Modern Library.

Maisel, L. Sandy, ed. 1998. *The Parties Respond: Changes in American Parties and Elections,* 3d ed. Boulder, Colo.: Westview Press.

Maisel, L. Sandy. 1999. *Parties and Elections in America: The Electoral Process,* 3d ed. Lanham, Md.: Rowman & Littlefield.

Maisel, L. Sandy, and John F. Bibby. 2000. "Election Laws and Party Rules: Contributions to a Stronger Party Role?" Paper presented at the annual meeting of the American Political Science Association, Washington, D.C.

Maisel, L. Sandy, and Walter J. Stone. 1997. "Determinants of Candidate Emergence in U.S. House Elections: An Exploratory Study." *Legislative Studies Quarterly* 22 (February): 79–96.

Mayer, William G. 1996. *The Divided Democrats.* Boulder, Colo.: Westview Press.

Mayer, William G. 1998. "Mass Partisanship, 1946–1996." In *Partisan Approaches to Postwar American Politics,* ed. Byron E. Shafer. New York: Chatham House.

Mayhew, David R. 1974. *Congress: The Electoral Connection.* New Haven: Yale University Press.

Mayhew, David R. 1991. *Divided We Govern: Party Control, Lawmaking, and Investigating, 1946–1990.* New Haven: Yale University Press.

McClosky, Herbert, Paul J. Hoffman, and Rosemary O'Hara. 1960. "Issue Conflict and Consensus Among Party Leaders and Followers." *American Political Science Review* 54 (June): 406–427.

McGerr, Michael. 1986. *The Decline of Popular Politics: The American North, 1865–1928.* New York: Oxford University Press.

McWilliams, Carey. 1992. "Tocqueville and Responsible Parties." In *Challenges to Party Government,* ed. John Kenneth White and Jerome M. Mileur. Carbondale: University of Southern Illinois Press.

Mead, Lawrence. 1986. *Beyond Entitlement: The Social Obligations of Citizenship.* New York: Free Press.

Meining, D. W. 1993. *Continental America, 1800–1867,* Vol. 2 of *The Shaping of America: A Geographic Perspective on 500 Years of History.* New Haven: Yale University Press.

Melnick, R. Shep. 1983. *Regulation and the Courts: The Case of the Clean Air Act.* Washington, D.C.: Brookings Institution Press.

Milbank, Dana. 1999. "Virtual Politics: Candidates' Consultants Create the Customized Campaign." *New Republic,* July 5, 22–27.

Mileur, Jerome M. 1992. "Prospects for Party Government." In *Challenges to Party*

Government, ed. John Kenneth White and Jerome M. Mileur. Carbondale: University of Southern Illinois Press.

Milkis, Sidney. 1992. "Programmatic Liberalism and Party Politics." In *Challenges to Party Government,* ed. John Kenneth White and Jerome M. Mileur. Carbondale: University of Southern Illinois Press.

Miller, Warren E. 1988. *Without Consent: Mass-Elite Linkages in Presidential Politics.* Lexington: The University Press of Kentucky.

Miller, Warren E., and M. Kent Jennings. 1986. *Parties in Transition: A Longitudinal Study of Party Elites and Party Supporters.* New York: Russell Sage Foundation.

Miller, Warren E., and J. Merrill Shanks. 1996. *The New American Voter.* Cambridge: Harvard University Press.

Mitchell, Alison. 1998. "Some House Democrats Balancing Doubts and Party Loyalty in Fund-Raising Debate." *New York Times,* June 8, A14.

Mitchell, Stewart, ed. 1931. *Winthrop Papers,* 5 vols. Boston: Massachusetts Historical Society.

Morehouse, Sarah McCally. 1998. *The Governor as Party Leader.* Ann Arbor: University of Michigan Press.

Morgenthau, Hans. 1964. *The Purpose of American Politics.* New York: Vintage Books.

Mutch, Robert E. 1988. *Campaigns, Congress, and Courts: The Making of Federal Campaign Financing Laws.* New York: Praeger.

Myrdal, Gunnar. 1944. *An American Dilemma: The Negro Problem and American Democracy.* New York: Harper.

Narud, Hanne Marthe, and Henry Valen. 1996. "Decline of Electoral Turnout: the Case of Norway." *European Journal of Political Research* 29 (March): 235–256.

Nelson, Lars-Erik. 1999. "Undemocratic Vistas." *The New York Review of Books,* August 12, 9–12.

Nie, Norman H., Jane Junn, and Kenneth Stehlik-Barry. 1996. *Education and Democratic Citizenship in America.* Chicago: University of Chicago Press.

Nie, Norman H., Sidney Verba, and John R. Petrocik. 1979. *The Changing American Voter,* enlarged edition. Cambridge: Harvard University Press.

Norberg, Kathryn. 1994. "The French Fiscal Crisis of 1788." In *Fiscal Crises, Liberty, and Representative Government, 1450–1789,* ed. Phillip T. Hoffman and Kathryn Norberg. Stanford: Stanford University Press.

Nye, Joseph S., Philip D. Zelikow, and David C. King, eds. 1997. *Why People Don't Trust Government.* Cambridge: Harvard University Press.

O'Brien, Ruth. 1997. "Taking the Conservative State Seriously: Statebuilding and Restrictive Labor Practices in Postwar America." *Journal of Labor Studies* 21 (winter): 33–63.

Ornstein, Norman J., Thomas E. Mann, and Michael J. Malbin. 2000. *Vital Statistics on Congress, 1999–2000.* Washington, D.C.: AEI Press.

Ostrogorski, Moisei. 1902. *Democracy and the Organization of Political Parties.* New York: Macmillan.

Ota, Alan K. 1999. "Partisan Voting on the Rise." *CQ Weekly,* January 9, 79–83, 92–95.

Page, Benjamin I., and Robert Y. Shapiro. 1992. *The Rational Public: Fifty Years of Trends in Americans' Policy Preferences.* Chicago: University of Chicago Press.

Panebianco, Angelo. 1988. *Political Parties: Organization and Power.* Cambridge: Cambridge University Press.

Pennock, J. Roland. 1952. "Responsiveness, Responsibility, and Majority Rule." *American Political Science Review* 46 (September): 790–807.

"Perhaps the Worst Congress." 1994. *Washington Post,* October 7, A24.

"The Plot to Bury Reform" [editorial]. 1998. *New York Times,* March 30, A16.

Polsby, Nelson W. 1968. "The Institutionalization of the House of Representatives." *American Political Science Review* 62 (March): 144–168.

Polsby, Nelson W. 1983. *Consequences of Party Reform.* New York: Oxford University Press.

Polsby, Nelson, and Aaron Wildavasky. 1996. *Presidential Elections: Strategies of American Electoral Politics,* 9th ed. New York: Scribner's.

Pomper, Gerald M. 1971. "Toward a More Responsible Two-Party System? What, Again?" *Journal of Politics* 33 (November): 916–940.

Pomper, Gerald M., ed. 1980. *Party Renewal in America.* New York: Praeger.

Pomper, Gerald M. 1998. "The Place of American Political Parties." In *A Republic of Parties? Debating the Two-Party System,* ed. Theodore Lowi and Joseph Romance. Lanham, Md.: Rowman & Littlefield.

Pomper, Gerald M. 1999. "Parliamentary Government in the United States?" In *The State of the Parties,* 3d ed. Ed. John C. Green and Daniel M. Shea. Lanham, Md.: Rowman & Littlefield.

Poole, Keith T., and Howard Rosenthal. 1997. *Congress: A Political-Economic History of Roll Call Voting.* New York: Oxford University Press.

Popkin, Samuel L. 1991. *The Reasoning Voter.* Chicago: University of Chicago Press.

Preston, Mark. 2000. "Inhofe Will Block All Clinton Judicial Nominations." *Roll Call,* January 10.

Putnam, Robert D. 1993. *Making Democracy Work: Civic Traditions in Modern Italy.* Princeton: Princeton University Press.

Putnam, Robert D. 1995. "Bowling Alone." *Journal of Democracy* 6 (January): 66–78.

Putnam, Robert D. 1996. "The Strange Disappearance of Civic America." *The American Prospect* 24 (winter): 34–45.

Ranney, Austin. 1951. "Toward a More Responsible Two-Party System: A Commentary." *American Political Science Review* 45 (June): 488–499.

Ranney, Austin. 1956. *The Doctrine of Responsible Party Government.* Urbana: University of Illinois Press.

Ranney, Austin. 1975. *Curing the Mischiefs of Faction.* Berkeley: University of California Press.

Riesenberg, Peter. 1992. *Citizenship in the Western Tradition: Plato to Rousseau.* Chapel Hill: University of North Carolina Press.

Riker, William. 1982. "The Two-Party System and Duverger's Law: An Essay on the History of Political Science." *American Political Science Review* 76 (December): 753–766.

Robinson, William A. 1930. *Thomas B. Reed: Parliamentarian.* New York: Dodd, Mead.

Rohde, David. 1991. *Parties and Leaders in the Postreform House.* Chicago: University of Chicago Press.

Rosenstone, Steven J., and John Mark Hansen. 1993. *Mobilization, Participation, and Democracy in America.* New York: Macmillan.

Rosenstone, Steven J., Roy L. Behr, and Edward H. Lazarus. 1984. *Third Parties in America: Citizen Response to Major Party Failure.* Princeton: Princeton University Press.

Rosenstone, Steven J., Roy L. Behr, and Edward H. Lazarus. 1996. *Third Parties in America: Citizen Response to Major Party Failure,* 2d ed. Princeton: Princeton University Press.

Rossiter, Clinton, ed. 1961. "Federalist 56." In *The Federalist Papers, Hamilton, Madison and Jay.* New York: New American Library—Mentor Books.

Rothman, David J. 1966. *Politics and Power: The United States Senate, 1869-1901.* Cambridge: Harvard University Press.

Sabato, Larry J. 1988. *The Party's Just Begun.* Glencoe, Ill.: Scott, Foresman.

Sacks, David Harris. 1994. "The Paradox of Taxation: Fiscal Crises, Parliament, and the Liberty of England." In *Fiscal Crises, Liberty and Representative Government, 1450–1789,* ed. Philip T. Hoffman and Kathryn Norberg. Stanford: Stanford University Press.

Sayer, Derek. 1992. "A Notable Administration: English State Formation and the Rise of Capitalism." *American Journal of Sociology* 97 (March): 1382–1415.

Schattschneider, E. E. 1942. *Party Government.* New York: Holt, Rinehart, and Winston.

Schattschneider, E. E. 1948. *The Struggle for Party Government.* College Park: University of Maryland Press.

Schattschneider, E. E. 1960. *The Semisovereign People.* New York: Holt, Rinehart, and Winston.

Schier, Steven E. 1999. "The End of Mobilization: Contemporary Party, Interest Group and Campaign Strategies." Paper presented at meeting of the Midwest Political Science Association, Chicago, April 15–17.

Schier, Steven E. 2000. *By Invitation Only: The Rise of Exclusive Politics in the United States.* Pittsburgh: University of Pittsburgh Press.

Schlesinger, Arthur M., Jr. 1986. *The Cycles of American History.* Boston: Houghton Mifflin.

Schudson, Michael. 1998. *The Good Citizen: A History of American Civic Life.* New York: Free Press.

Senate Committee on Governmental Affairs. 1998. "Investigation of Illegal or Improper Activities in Connection with 1996 Federal Election Campaigns" (Vols. 1–6). Washington, D.C.: U.S. Government Printing Office.

Serafini, Marilyn. 1995. "Mr. In-Between." *National Journal,* December 16, 3080–3084.

Seyd, Patrick. 1999. "New Parties/New Politics?" *Party Politics* 5 (June): 383–405.

Shafer, Byron E. 1983. *Quiet Revolution: The Struggle for the Democratic Party and the Shaping of Party Reform.* New York: Russell Sage Foundation.

Shafer, Byron E., ed. 1991. *The End of Realignment? Interpreting American Electoral Eras.* Madison: University of Wisconsin Press.

Shaw, Carolyn. 1996. "Has President Clinton Fulfilled His Campaign Promises?" Paper presented at American Political Science Association.

Shefter, Martin. 1994. *Political Parties and the State: The American Political Experience.* Princeton: Princeton University Press.

Shogan, Robert. 1998. "Politicians Embrace Status Quo as Nonvoter Numbers Grow." *Los Angeles Times,* May 4, A5.

Silbey, Joel H. 1991. *The American Political Nation, 1838–1893.* Stanford: Stanford University Press.

Silbey, Joel H. 1998. "From 'Essential to the Existence of Our Institutions' to 'Rapacious Enemies of Honest and Responsible Government': The Rise and Fall of American Political Parties, 1790–2000." In *The Parties Respond: Changes in American Parties and Campaigns,* 3d ed. Ed. L. Sandy Maisel. Boulder, Colo.: Westview Press.

Sinclair, Barbara. 1995. *Legislators, Leaders, and Lawmakers.* Baltimore: Johns Hopkins University Press.

Skocpol, Theda. 1999. "Associations Without Members." *The American Prospect* 45 (July/August): 66–72.

Sorauf, Frank J. 1998. "Political Parties and the New World Order of Campaign Finance." In *The Parties Respond: Changes in American Parties and Campaigns,* 3d ed. Ed. L. Sandy Maisel. Boulder, Colo.: Westview Press.

Stanley, Harold W., and Richard G. Niemi. 2000. *Vital Statistics on American Politics 1999–2000.* Washington, D.C.: CQ Press.

Sterett, Susan. 1992. "Legality in Administration in Britain and the United States: Toward an Institutional Explanation." *Comparative Political Studies* 25 (July): 210–211.

Stimson, James. 1991. *Public Opinion in America: Moods, Cycles, and Swings.* Boulder, Colo.: Westview Press.

Stimson, James. 1999. "Public Policy Mood, 1952–1996: Annual Data File" (accessed April 21,1999).

Stimson, James A., Michael B. MacKuen, and Robert S. Erikson. 1995. "Dynamic Representation." *American Political Science Review* 89 (September): 543–565.

Stone, Peter H. 1996. "The Green Wave." *National Journal,* November 9, 2411.

Stone, Walter J., Ronald B. Rapoport, and Alan I. Abramowitz. 1994. "Party Polarization: The Reagan Revolution and Beyond." In *The Parties Respond: Changes in American Parties and Campaigns,* 2d ed. Ed. L. Sandy Maisel. Boulder, Colo.: Westview Press.

Stone, Walter J., and L. Sandy Maisel. 1999. "The Not-So-Simple Calculus of Winning: Potential House Candidates' Nomination and General Election Chances." Paper presented at the annual meeting of the American Political Science Association, Atlanta.

Stone, Walter J., L. Sandy Maisel, and Cherie Maestas. 1998. "Candidate Emergence in U. S. House Elections." Paper presented at the annual meeting of the American Political Science Association, Boston.

Strahan, Randall W. 1998. "Partisan Officeholders, 1946–1996." In *Partisan Approaches to Postwar American Politics,* ed. Byron E. Shafer. New York: Chatham House.

"Stretch-Out in the House" [editorial]. 1998. *Washington Post,* June 21, C6.

Sullivan, Paul. 1999. "R.I. Senator Dead at 77." *Boston Herald,* October 26, 2.

Summers, Mark W. 1995. "History of Congress: The Age of the Machine." In *Encyclopedia of the United States Congress* (Vol. 2), ed. Donald C. Bacon, Roger H. Davidson, and Morton Keller. New York: Simon & Schuster.

Summers, Mark W. 1994. *The Press Gang: Newspapers and Politics, 1863–1878.* Chapel Hill: University of North Carolina Press.

Sundquist, James L. 1988–1989. "Needed: A Political Theory for the New Era of Coalition Government in the United States." *Political Science Quarterly* 103 (winter 1988–winter 1989): 613–635.

Sundquist, James L., ed. 1995. *Back to Gridlock? Governance in the Clinton Years.* Washington, D.C.: Brookings Institution Press.

Taylor, Andrew J. 1998. "Explaining Government Productivity." *American Politics Quarterly* 26 (October): 439–458.

Thucydides. 1960. *The History of the Peloponnesian War,* trans. Sir Richard Livingstone. New York: Oxford University Press.

Tilly, Charles. 1992. *Coercion, Capital, and European States.* Cambridge, Mass.: Blackwell.

Tolchin, Susan J. 1996. *The Angry American: How Voter Rage is Changing the Nation.* Boulder, Colo.: Westview Press.

Troy, Leo. 1986. "The Rise and Fall of American Trade Unions: The Labor Movement from FDR to RR." In *Unions in Transition: Entering the Second Century,* ed. Seymour Martin Lipset. San Francisco: ICS Press.

Turner, Julius. 1951. "Responsible Parties: A Dissent from the Floor." *American Political Science Review* 45 (March): 143–152.

U. S. Bureau of the Census. 1998. *Statistical Abstract of the United States.* Washington, D.C.: U.S. Government Printing Office.

Verba, Sidney, Kay Lehman Schlozman, and Henry E. Brady. 1995. *Voice and Equality: Civic Voluntarism in American Politics.* Cambridge: Harvard University Press.

Wang, Jianjung, Betty Greathouse, and Veronica Falcinella. 1998. "An Empirical Assessment of Self-Esteem Enhancement in a High School Challenge Service-Learning Program." *Education* 119 (fall): 99–106.

Ware, Alan. 1988. *The Breakdown of Democratic Party Organization, 1940–1980.* New York: Oxford University Press.

Wattenberg, Martin P. 1984. *The Decline of American Political Parties.* Cambridge: Harvard University Press.

Wattenberg, Martin P. 1990. *The Decline of American Political Parties, 1952–1988.* Cambridge: Harvard University Press.

Wattenberg, Martin P. 1991. *The Rise of Candidate-Centered Politics: Presidential Elections in the 1980s.* Cambridge: Harvard University Press.

Wattenberg, Martin P. 1994. *The Decline of American Political Parties, 1952–1992.* Cambridge: Harvard University Press.

Wattenberg, Martin P. 1996. *The Decline of American Political Parties, 1952–1994.* Cambridge: Harvard University Press.

Wattenberg, Martin P. 1998. *The Decline of American Political Parties, 1952–1996.* Cambridge: Harvard University Press.

Weber, Max. 1946 [originally published 1919]. "Politics as a Vocation." In *From Max Weber,* ed. H. H. Gerth and C. Wright Mills. New York: Oxford University Press.

West, Darrell M. 1993. *Air Wars: Television Advertising in Election Campaigns, 1952–1992.* Washington, D.C.: CQ Press.

West, Darrell M. 1997. *Air Wars: Television Advertising in Election Campaigns, 1952–1996,* 2d ed. Washington, D.C.: CQ Press.

White, John K., and Jerome M. Mileur, eds. 1992. *Challenges to Party Government.* Carbondale: Southern Illinois University Press.

Wilson, James Q. 1994. "Reinventing Public Administration." *PS* 27 (December): 667–673.

Wilson, Woodrow. 1908. *Constitutional Government in the United States.* New York: Columbia University Press.

Wilson, Woodrow. 1956. *Congressional Government: A Study in American Politics.* New York: Meridian Books.

Wright, Gerald C. 1994. "The Meaning of 'Party' in Congressional Roll Call Voting." Presented at the annual meeting of the Midwest Political Science Association.

Young, James Sterling. 1966. *The Washington Community: 1800–1828.* New York: Columbia University Press.

Index

AARP. *See* American Association of Retired Persons

Abramson, Paul R., 34

ACTION, 79

Activists and activism
avoidance of politics, 80–81
campaign activists, 260
community activism, 99
ideology, 131
issue-orientation, 83
role of, 109, 111

Adams, John Quincy, 193

Administrative Procedure Act (1946), 95, 99

African Americans. *See* Racial and minority issues

Agencies, federal, 96

Aldrich, John H., 34, 57, 75, 104, 140, 231, 250

Aldrich, Nelson W., 195

Allen v. State Board of Elections (1969), 237

Allison, William B., 195

American Association of Retired Persons (AARP), 97

American National Election Studies, 31

American Political Parties in Decline (Crotty), 138

American Political Science Association (APSA)
100th anniversary, 103
report of 1950, 103, 106–107, 122–125, 127, 138, 162–182, 209

American Voter, The (Campbell), 1, 11, 30, 31, 32, 33, 39, 41n6, 53

Americorps, 79, 81

Anderson, John, 34, 42, 43n11, 45–46, 47

Ansolabehere, Stephen, 61, 262

APSA. *See* American Political Science Association

Aristotle, 91, 94

Baca, Joe, 116

Bailey, Stephen K., 165n3

Baker v. Carr (1962), 165

Binder, Sarah A., 6, 7, 203, 250, 253

Bipartisan Campaign Reform Act (1998), 154, 155n10, 158

Bipartism, 230–240

Blaine, James G., 192

Blue Dog Democrats, 201

Bond, Jon R., 4, 7, 249, 251

Boren, David, 214

Brady, David, 191

Breaux, John, 214, 216n4, 225

Brock, William, 141

Broder, David, 138

Brokaw, Tom, 89

Brown, George, 116

Brown, Marta, 116

Bryan, William Jennings, 189

Bryce, Lord, 104, 105

Buckley v. Valeo (1976), 149n6

Budget issues, 133, 214, 221–222, 226

Bush, George H. W.
campaign finance reform, 152
candidacy of, 25
elections of 1988, 1992, 128–129
Motor Voter Act (1992), 89
presidential performance evaluation, 66
"thousand points of light," 81
vetoes, 152, 214
votes received, 44n13

Bush (George H. W.) administration, 205, 211–212

Business issues, 160, 255, 261

Calendar Wednesday, 194

Calhoun, John C., 195

California, 116, 233–234

California Democratic Party v. Bill Jones, Secretary of State of California (2000), 233–234

Campaign committees. *See* National party organizations

Campaigns. *See also* Candidates; Elections; Fund-raising and finance; Voters; Voting
advertising, 85, 145
candidate centered, 14–15, 16, 18–19, 55–56, 107, 136, 140, 198, 243
issues of, 25, 149–151
militarist style of, 84
mobilization in, 78
negative campaigning, 61–62, 85, 262
"permanent," 233
political parties in, 107, 108, 110, 120, 138–161, 165, 169
reforms, 110–111, 151, 181
role of organized money, 257–259

Campbell, James E., 3, 4, 7, 11, 30, 251

Canada, 254

Candidate Emergence Project/Study (1997), 112–115, 120–121

Candidates. *See also* Campaigns; Elections and electoral process; Fund-raising and finance; Voters; Voting
campaign organizations, 139, 160
candidate-centered campaigns, 14–15, 16, 18–19, 55–56, 107, 136, 140, 198, 243, 251
congressional, 112–115

Index

public opinion of, 258
reforms, 151–158, 181, 243
regulations, 143–151
Republican Party, 141–143, 145, 149, 150, 153–158
role of organized money, 257–259
sources of funds, 159–160, 232, 261
spending, 85
state and local parties, 149, 160
tables, 142, 144, 147
trends, 78–79

Gephardt, Richard, 117, 157, 204
Germany, 254
Gerrymandering, 232
Gibson, James, 112
Gillespie, David, 231
Gingrich, Newt
    campaign finance reform, 155
    Democratic Party and, 75
    impeachment of Clinton, Bill, 202–203, 204
    political action committee (GOPAC), 117
    Speakership of, 197–198, 201
Ginsberg, Benjamin, 4, 5, 7, 83, 84, 233, 252, 256
Giuliani, Rudolph, 116
Glendon, Mary Ann, 97
Globalization, 207
Goldwater, Barry, 18
GOP (Grand Old Party). *See* Republican Party
GOPAC, 117. *See also* Political action committees
Gore, Albert, 82, 153
Gorman, Arthur Pue, 195
Government
    accountability of, 247–249, 253
    activist, 222
    antipoverty measures, 98
    bureaucracy, 81–82
    citizens and the public, 93–95, 97–98, 223, 250, 256–257
    competition in, 119
    demand overload, 256
    elections and, 215
    gridlock, 210–213, 214, 216, 217, 220, 221–222, 223–227, 250, 253
    interest groups and, 256
    policy impacts, 213–215
    political parties and, 111–118, 176–177, 209–228, 234–235, 246, 252–253
    problems in governing, 136–137, 209–228, 246, 256
    role of, 63, 106, 256–257
    separation of powers, 246
    tables, 213, 224
    unified, 209, 213, 215, 217
    voter view of, 136
    Wilson, Woodrow and, 187
Government—divided
    causes of, 3, 205–206
    classic duopoly of, 233

continued role, 31, 86, 176–177, 182
    effects of, 209–210, 213–215, 243, 246, 253
    gridlock in, 224–227
    political dealignment, 2, 4, 53–54
    public attitudes and, 250–251
    state, 119
Gramm, Phil, 28n14
Grand Old Party (GOP). *See* Republican Party
Great Britain, 88, 90, 254
Greatest Generation, The (Brokaw), 89
Great Society, 99, 196, 210, 212–213
Gridlock. *See* Government
Gun control, 116
Guzman, Rob, 116

Hamilton, Alexander, 218–219
Hartz, Louis, 93
Hastert, J. Dennis, 198
Healthcare reforms, 215, 220
Herrnson, Paul S., 138, 139, 141
Hintze, Otto, 90
Hoffman, Paul J., 126
House of Representatives. *See* Congress
Humphrey, Hubert, 36, 42, 128
Huntington, Samuel, 93, 222
Hyde, Henry J., 202, 203, 204

Ideology, 64–65, 127, 178, 215–216, 220, 223, 260. *See also* Conservatives and conservatism; Liberals and liberalism
Immigration, 106, 207, 259–260
Impeachment, 86, 87, 88, 171, 180, 200, 202–205
Independent voters, 30, 32, 202, 260
Industrial and postindustrial society, 254–255
Inholfe, James, 221
Institutions, 218–221, 225–226
Interest groups, 95, 96–98, 109, 152, 160, 255–257
Issue positioning, 245–246
Issues. *See* Political issues
Iyengar, Shanto, 61, 262

Jacksonians, 87, 88
Jackson, John S., III, 126, 127, 129
Jeffersonians, 87, 88
Jefferson, Thomas, 86, 93
Jeffords, James, 216n4
Jennings, M. Kent, 126
Jesuit Volunteer Corps, 80
Jewell, Malcolm, 118
Johnson, Lyndon B., 18, 196, 212–213
Johnson (Lyndon B.) administration, 210, 211

Kantor, Paul, 7, 8
Kayden, Xandra, 138
Keith, Bruce E., 15
Kennedy, John F., 81, 212–213
Kennedy (John F.) administration, 211
Kern, John Worth, 196
Key, V. O., 86, 87, 175, 230

Political issues *(continued)*
  neoclassical theory of political participation, 86
  party identification, 11–12, 25–26, 104
  party responsibility, 2, 176, 180–182
  personal democracy and party politics, 78–99
  polarization, 62–65, 73–74, 75–76
  policy formulation, 127
  political machines, 83, 106
  political parties and, 245–246
  political realignment, 2, 217–218
  rights and, 97
  tables, 64, 69, 71, 130, 131
  two-party system, 230–240
  vote choice and, 40–46, 48–52
Political parties. *See also* Democratic Party;
    Partisanship; National party organizations; Republican Party; *Toward a More
    Responsible Two-Party System*
  ability to govern, 209–228
  abuses of, 105–107
  activists and, 83
  bipartism, 230–240
  campaigns, 110, 138–161, 252
  candidate and issue orientation, 46, 48–52, 251
  coalitions, 57
  collapse of New Deal party system, 30, 53–54
  competition, 168
  conventions, 118, 126, 165
  cross pressures and, 40–46
  dealignment, 2, 4, 53–54, 55–56, 61, 67, 68, 70–71, 73
  democratic linkages and, 251–253
  differences between, 27n13, 166–167, 168–169, 170, 173–174, 249–250, 261
  generational cohort effects, 71, 251
  historical background, 78, 83, 104–105, 108–109, 124, 189–198, 206–208
  institutionalization of party organizations, 139–140
  legal issues, 233–234
  minority issues, 232
  moderation and, 216–217
  multipartism, 230, 252
  personal democracy and, 78–99
  platforms, 166, 170–172, 178–179
  polarization, 55–77, 216, 225, 227
  policy issues, 122–137, 146
  reforms, 85–86, 95, 106–107, 117, 118, 120, 123–125, 127, 158, 162–183
  responsibility of, 2, 162–183, 252–253
  resurgence of party identification, 30–54, 228
  role of, 103–105, 108, 111, 119–121, 122, 136, 139, 161, 179–180, 199–200, 244–249
  state and local parties, 149, 160, 165, 198, 199
  subcultures, 27–28, 82–83
  three-party system, 179
  voter choice and, 33–39, 175–177
  voter mobilization, 82–83, 85–89
Political parties—decline and resurgence
  cross pressure and, 47–48
  current political system, 249–253
  democratic theory and, 244–249
  effects of, 110
  historical background, 107, 108, 158–159, 243–244
  institutionalized national parties, 139–140
  partisanship, 57
  policy-making elites, 7, 55
  problems of today's politics, 111–121
  Progressive era reforms, 106
  reasons for, 253–263
  strong identifiers, 51–52
  voter identification, 24, 52–54
Political parties—evaluations
  1950s, 123–124
  candidates and parties, 59–62
  historical background, 106–107, 126–127, 209
  performance of, 134–137
  place of parties in political system, 249–253
  policy coherence, 128–134
Political parties—identifiers
  Democratic Party, 40
  distribution of, 57, 62–64, 65, 67
  elite and mass identifiers, 128, 129
  ideology, 131
  parties and, 135, 173–175
  polarization and, 58, 59, 60–61, 62–63
Political parties—tables and figures
  APSA recommendations, 166–167
  budgetary resolutions, 133
  contact by party committees, 112, 113
  cross pressures, 41, 44, 47, 48
  differences between parties, 173
  evaluation, 62, 72
  funds and fund-raising, 142
  party identification, 32, 36, 49, 51
  party identifiers, 68
  party unity scores, 135
  platforms, 171, 172
  polarization, 60, 64, 77
  policies, 132
  presidential approval, 66
  president's programs, 134
Politicians
  historical background, 83
  political parties and, 104–105, 245, 250
  responsibility of, 2, 178, 181
  strategies and careers, 259–262
Polls, public opinion
  campaign finance system, 258
  effects of, 85
  impeachment of Clinton, Bill, 205
  interest groups and, 97
  national mood, 222–223
  national polls, 145
  political parties and, 115
Polsby, Nelson, 138
Pomper, Gerald, 6, 7, 231, 249, 253